Necropolitics

PENNSYLVANIA STUDIES IN HUMAN RIGHTS

Bert B. Lockwood, Jr., Series Editor

A complete list of books in the series is available from the publisher.

NECROPOLITICS

Mass Graves and Exhumations in the Age of Human Rights

Edited by

Francisco Ferrándiz *and*
Antonius C. G. M. Robben

Foreword by
Richard Ashby Wilson

PENN

UNIVERSITY OF PENNSYLVANIA PRESS

PHILADELPHIA

Published by
University of Pennsylvania Press
Philadelphia, Pennsylvania 19104–4112
www.upenn.edu/pennpress

Printed in the United States of America on acid-free paper
10 9 8 7 6 5 4 3 2 1

Library of Congress Cataloging-in-Publication Data
Necropolitics (2015)
Necropolitics : mass graves and exhumations in the age of human rights / edited by Francisco Ferrándiz and Antonius C.G.M. Robben; foreword by Richard Ashby Wilson. — First edition.
    pages cm. — (Pennsylvania studies in human rights)
Includes bibliographical references and index.
ISBN 978-0-8122-4720-6 (alk. paper)
1. Repatriation of war dead—Case studies. 2. War victims—Identification—Case studies. 3. Exhumation—Case studies. 4. Mass burials—Case studies. 5. Forensic anthropology—Case studies. I. Ferrándiz, Francisco, editor. II. Robben, Antonius C. G. M., editor. III. Wilson, Richard, writer of added text. IV. Title. V. Series: Pennsylvania studies in human rights.
JZ6405.N43 2015
355.02'8—dc23
                                                                2015004444

Contents

Foreword

Richard Ashby Wilson

In May 1988, I drank coffee in the sweltering heat with Father José Parra Novo, a Spanish priest nicknamed "Papito," in the imposing Catholic church compound in Cahabón, a regional town center in the department of Alta Verapaz in highland Guatemala. I fumbled to explain my fieldwork research, which sought to understand how villagers reconstructed their lives and communities after three decades of armed conflict. "Ah," Papito said immediately, "Then you must go to Pinares." Why, what happened there?" I asked. He replied, "You'll find out soon enough." Arriving in Pinares, I encountered a small, sleepy rural Maya-Q'eqchi' village surrounded by cacao plantations. At first, I found nothing out of the ordinary. Farmers tended their small plots of corn, beans, and cacao, women washed clothes in the river, youth played football on a meticulously groomed field, and the whole community attended the small village chapel perched on a hillside.

Only after three days did my hosts begin to open up, and recount how, in August 1982, the Guatemalan army arrived from the military base in Cobán. With local men from the "Civil Patrol" leading them house to house, the soldiers rounded up twenty-one male villagers who were accused of being communist agitators for agrarian reform. The soldiers marched the men to the edge of the village, shot them, and threw their corpses into a pit in the ground. This was no "clandestine grave." Everyone in the village knew exactly where it was located—even the children motioned in the direction of the pit when asked where the men were *mukmu*, Q'eqchi' for "buried," or "hidden." The bodies lay where they had been tossed, untouched and unrecovered. Their relatives were too terrorized to exhume them, and life went on in the village, as abnormal.

Eight years later, in 1996, I traveled again to Cahabón with staff from

(REMHI) (Recuperation of Historical Memory Project), the Catholic Church's truth commission project. Families streamed into the town from the surrounding villages to tell their stories to the REMHI statement takers. The mere presence of Q'eqchi'-speaking REMHI personnel opened a space for highland indigenous peoples to testify about the past. Once public secrets were articulated outside the community, families in Pinares rapidly turned to pursuing avenues of legal remedy. The massacre was, for the first time, formally denounced at the Congressional Human Rights Office and the Office of the Public Prosecutor. Villagers contacted the United Nations Mission in Guatemala (MINUGUA), which helicoptered a forensic team to the village in May 1996 to begin exhumations. Under constant threat from armed local perpetrators, the forensic team worked day and night for eight days. They removed the bodily remains to the capital for further investigation, before returning them for a proper burial in the community. This story was repeated across the country, as seventeen mass graves were exhumed in 1996 by forensic anthropologists working in conjunction with the UN Mission, and many dozens more followed in subsequent years. Once they got under way, the forensic teams worked relatively rapidly, but criminal accountability for the perpetrators took longer, and it is a painful truism that the wheels of justice, especially in Guatemala, turn agonizingly slowly. Twenty-five years after my first trip to Pinares, evidence from exhumations across the Guatemalan highlands became central to the prosecution case in the criminal trial of military dictator Efraín Ríos Montt, whose military junta brought unprecedented violence and terror to rural Guatemala in 1982–1983.

As this excellent and timely volume shows in detailed case studies from around the world, regimes that massacre a civilian population as part of a widespread and systematic policy of terror create social disorder and disruption. Their methods generate physical and social entropy, with regard to both the bodies of victims and the body politic. As several contributors observe, exhumations and DNA testing reassemble bodies and reattach names, and thereby are part of a wider collective process of memorializing the dead, reordering the social world, and reclaiming territory from military occupation. Exhumations are a social process that reconfigures time, space, and identity, and they can be understood historically and subjectively, with attention to the symbolism and meaning of the constituent acts. At the same time, the social dimensions of exhumations encounter other forms of knowledge and authority, including forensic science and the law, each with its own methods of creating and evaluating evidence. Both law and science, despite their universalizing ambitions, necessarily construct a partial account of the past. The approaches in each of the fields represented and analyzed in this book—photographic art, ethnography, history, forensic anthropology, and criminal law—are motivated by distinct principles and based on divergent epistemologies. Understanding how they interact and inform and influence one another, and ultimately shape our comprehension of "who did what to whom" and what it has meant, is a formidable challenge. This volume rises to that challenge and opens up new avenues of global comparison, investigation and comprehension.

As if the task of understanding the past were not daunting in itself, the chapters in this collection provide fascinating accounts of the political and legal struggles surrounding exhumations, and these often include popular mobilizations that are both intensely local and globally connected. I know of no other volume that addresses the topic of exhumations as profoundly, and in as many disparate cases in Latin America, Africa, Europe, and Asia. From the chapters herein we learn how exhumations and the reconstructing of past violations are embedded in political movements that ignite political agency and express a newfound sense of citizenship and sovereignty. In recognizing this, we need not lose sight of the fact that the social processes of remembering are often acts of faith and solidarity with the dead, and ways of articulating a sense of dignity and worth among the living. And the anthropological voice and perspective comes through clearly; the empirical documentation and ethnographic analysis presented here should provide activists, scholars, and policymakers alike with new insights into the symbolism and granular-level politics of exhumations. I recommend this book to all those hoping to understand postconflict societies and what happens once they finally address unfinished business, and unearth the grim realities handed down to them from violent historical episodes.

Introduction

The Ethnography of Exhumations

Francisco Ferrándiz and Antonius C. G. M. Robben

Legacies of war and violent conflict are complex and many: traumatized generations and mutilated people, wandering orphans and disappeared persons, unfinished mourning, a destroyed infrastructure, dictatorship and political turmoil, systematic repression of the defeated, a victor's truth that erases historical facts and offends the memory of victims, and the unsettling, horrifying, silent mass graves. Graves containing caches of bones from diverse modalities of extreme violence and destruction are crucial testimony to the wounds of history, and a key element in understanding both the foundations and consequences of violence. The deliberate commingling of human remains in unmarked graves bewilders survivors and heightens the disorder, anxiety, and division of the citizenry. As a sophisticated technology of terror, these types of graves aim to erase the memory of violence, and at the same time consolidate regimes of fear that might last for decades.

But as social and political circumstances evolve in local, national, and transnational contexts, social memory accretes and resurfaces to defy these macabre scenarios of violent death and terror production. The consequences of this recovery of social memory and public space, which frequently involves exhumations, depend on national and international conditions in which the remains are located, exhumed, investigated, and rewoven into local and globalized rituals and narratives, from academic to technical, to political to judicial to everyday. Increasingly, exhumations are becoming crucial to transnational human rights discourses and transitional justice practices, in addition to their local uses. Months, years, or decades after the massacres took place, the remains are excavated and analyzed to reassert their existence and history. While communities confront and struggle with legacies of past violence through contemporary exhumations, the transnational character of these human-rights-related exhumations creates new globalizing tidemarks for coming to terms with history. These tidemarks are no less elusive than the memories being excavated, but the very practice of exhumation helps at least organize the physical and ethereal worlds occupied by the dead as well as reorder the lives of the living.

The growing scholarly debate in anthropology and related disciplines about the meaning of the exhumation of mass graves parallels discussions about its function as an increasingly important tool for the pursuit of human rights and the entitlement to reparations in postconflict situations. Major research projects, such as *Corpses of Mass Violence and Genocide* directed by Anstett and Dreyfus or the more specific *Post-Conflict and Post-Disaster DNA Identification* led by Aronson and Wagner, attest to the rising academic attention to exhumations. This prominence deserves to be understood within its present context.[1] On the one hand, there has arisen a transnational urge to produce both forensic evidence and reparations from the exhumation of skeletal remains in which different types of violence and human rights violations were inscribed. This corpocentric focus demands a new "corporeal epistemology," as Klinenberg (2002:121) has argued, in reference to an "axiomatic principle of human rights workers and truth commissions throughout the world" that consolidates dead bodies worldwide as "the site and surface of essential but otherwise obscured social truths." On the other hand, mass graves should also be analyzed in a much wider context than their local setting. Mass graves are generated under specific political and historical processes and have extensive ramifications in the social and symbolic order.

This book's comparative perspective has been therefore designed with two objectives in mind: one, to understand the disinterment of the remnants of past violence in specific local and national contexts, and two, to analyze and systematize the different cases as the combined result of the *same family of global discourses and practices,* linked to the ongoing development of transnational human rights institutions, humanitarian cultures, and forensic methods. In this respect, the book raises questions about contemporary exhumations not only as a source of personal, historic, and criminal evidence but also as an instrument of redress for victims through transitional justice that in a very fundamental way creates a space for the emergence and reworking of (traumatic) social memory.

Mass graves are much more than sites of forensic exhumation and historical verification. The exhumation sets in motion political, judicial, scientific, symbolic, and commemorative processes that turn the opened mass grave into an anthropological field site, as has been demonstrated by anthropologists worldwide (Binford 1996; Sant Cassia 2005; Robben 2000, 2005; Crossland 2002, 2009; Sanford 2003; Kwon 2008; Wagner 2008; Ferrándiz 2010, 2013; Renshaw 2011; Claverie 2011; Anstett 2012). Forensic investigations of mass graves bring together a myriad of fields and disciplines, such as science and technology, medicine, art, mass media, and in line with this book's disciplinary focus, the anthropologies of violence, death, religion, memory, trauma, social suffering, and human rights. Exhumations, human remains, and their symbolic representations constitute complex ethnographic sites, saturated with meaning and power, in which social traumas and their percolation through the social fabric condense many intertwined processes ranging from deep personal emotions to international politics and transnational memories.

In addition to the ethnographic study of exhumation sites and forensic procedures, researchers need to study the necropolitical tension between "the petrification of the bones and their strange coolness" and "their stubborn will to mean, to signify something" to understand the diverse consequences of mass graves in society (Mbembe 2003). To be sure, necropolitics is a huge topic involving multiple modalities of power deployment over the production and management of dead bodies, while the concept itself is not beyond dispute for its tendency to naturalize sovereignty. Yet in this book we refer to the exercise of necropower only in relation to corpses derived from mass violence and human rights violations. In order to do so, the disinterred remains must be followed on their journey from the unceremonial grave to the morgue's laboratory, the judicial court, and finally the place of reburial. Katherine Verdery's pithy phrase "the political lives of dead bodies" (1999) is invaluable in capturing the transitional complexity of necropolitics. Verdery unpacks the different modalities of "postsocialist necrophilia" in eastern Europe and the former Soviet Union by analyzing the trajectories of cadavers, body parts, mummies, and their representations in statues and mausoleums. The study of such "parade of corpses" demands "attending to political symbolism; to death rituals and beliefs, such as ideas about what constitutes a 'proper burial;' to the connections between the particular corpses being manipulated and the wider national and international contexts of their manipulation; and to reassessing or rewriting the past and creating or retrieving 'memory'" (Verdery 1999:3).

This introduction consists of two main sections: "Mass Violence Exhumed," which discusses critical reflections about increasingly sophisticated forensic procedures and the manner in which mass grave exhumations are interwoven with a repertoire of technical and reparative practices linked to human rights and mechanisms of redress since the late twentieth century; and "Exhumations: Memoryscapes," which touches on the complex links between mass grave exhumations and different types of memory, in particular by examining the relations between the disinterment of victims of past violence and the mobilization of certain categories of corpses through memory politics in contemporary society. By way of conclusion, we will consider the increasingly transnational profile of exhumations that is broadening the field's research horizon. In line with this introduction, we have organized the book into two interrelated parts, "Exhumations as Practice" and "Exhumations as Memory," with a photo essay about the debris of 9/11 to illustrate the entwinement of the practices and memories of exhumations.

Mass Violence Exhumed

The dead of war used to suffer a sorry fate on the battlefields of Western nations. Fallen commanders might be immortalized at home, and their bodies buried with full national honors, but dead soldiers were burned in piles or interred hastily in mass graves. The first military cemetery arose in 1862 during the American Civil War, while the first European burial ground was created during the Franco-Prussian War of 1870–1871. Military cemeteries were instituted throughout Europe during World War I when millions of civilians were drafted into the army, and perished as troops charged against camouflaged machine guns, were shelled by artillery, and were surprised by lethal mustard gas (Capdevila and Voldman 2006:7–10; Mosse 1990:45–50).

The unprecedented battlefield slaughter and rearward repression of World War I—frequently involving exhumations and relocations—cast the management of the war dead in a new light and made the location, reorganization, protection, embellishment, and memorialization of war graves of central concern to the warring countries. As Williams argues, this new focus on war cemeteries "implied at once the democratization, individualization and bureaucratization of death" (2007:39). This was expressed to a different extent in the foundation of the Commonwealth War Graves Commission in 1917 and the German Volksbund Deutsche Kriegsgräberfürsorge (German War Graves

Commission) in 1919 and in the French government's operation to return roughly three hundred thousand soldiers to their relatives in 1922 and 1923, after many tensions and logistical problems, especially because of the chaotic state of affairs at the former battlefields and uncertainty about the identity of many corpses buried there hastily (Winter 1995:22–28). In the first case, the Commonwealth Commission opted for promoting a fellowship of death and rejecting the repatriation of casualties after heated debates in the British Parliament in 1920 in which Winston Churchill played a defining role. It has since focused on designing and keeping cemeteries and memorials identifiable through standard commemorative patterns (including specific horticultural guidelines) at over twenty-three thousand sites and maintaining a thorough casualty database, now online, about the 1.7 million Commonwealth subjects killed during both world wars. The Volksbund also focused on building, repairing, and sustaining cemeteries in Europe and North Africa. Its exhumation division is still functioning today. Current research on corpse management related to the Spanish Civil War (1936–1939), especially with respect to victims of rearguard repression, shows the occurrence of a continued pattern of exhumations during the war, in the early postwar period and thereafter in multiple guises, spanning more than seven decades. Depending on the political circumstances, there were official, unofficial, and clandestine exhumations of mass graves (Dueñas and Solé 2012; Ferrándiz 2013, 2014).

World War II also involved exhumations, Katyn being the most striking case of their use as weapons of war (Paul 1991), performed by the Nazis near the Ukrainian city of Vinnytsia and at other sites on the eastern front (Paperno 2001: 91). Katyn was the eye of a propaganda war of reciprocal finger-pointing between Germany and the Soviet Union for the massacre of around twenty-two thousand people, including over four thousand Polish officers (formerly prisoners of war). The bodies were exhumed in April 1943 by an International Medical Commission, with some involvement of the Polish Red Cross, upon the request and under the supervision of the German army. A team of fourteen representatives from leading forensic medical and criminology schools of different European countries carried out the exhumation, and established a methodical pattern of executing the victims through a shot in the nape of the neck. The German propaganda apparatus then accused the Soviet Union of perpetrating the massacre. After retaking the area a few months later, the Soviets orchestrated a major cover-up operation by creating a Special Commission for Ascertaining and Investigating the Circumstances of the Shootings of Polish Officer Prisoners by the German-Fascist Invaders in the Katyn Forest. The bodies were reexhumed in January 1944, and a counterreport was produced to blame the Nazis. This Soviet report (Document 054-USSR) made it all the way to the Nuremberg Trials. Only in the early 1990s, as a consequence of glasnost, did the Russian government start to acknowledge direct responsibility for these massacres (Paperno 2001).

After World War II, social reconstruction went hand in hand with exhumation, relocation, and reburial (Mant 1987). Current research is unveiling more details about these processes. For example, recent work by Dreyfus (2012) on the French mission from 1946 to 1958 to recover the bodies of French deportees in East and West Germany reveals a remarkable postwar technical and diplomatic effort involving the exhumation of over fifty thousand bodies from mass graves in concentration camps. This mission led to the identification of as many as seven thousand people deported from France, and the repatriation and renationalization of some four thousand of them, first assembled in Strasbourg and then returned to their families. Identified but unclaimed bodies were reburied in French cemeteries or burial grounds established in each camp.

In 1985, another legacy of World War II came to the fore, but now from the side of the perpetrators of the Holocaust, that provided worldwide coverage to forensic investigations. U.S. forensic anthropologist Clyde Snow received a call from the Los Angeles office of the Simon Wiesenthal Center to work with Brazilian and German forensic teams on the identification of a skeleton alleged to be Auschwitz's "Angel of Death," Joseph Mengele, found in the cemetery of the Brazilian town of Embu das Artes. Despite the impossibility of DNA testing at the time and the absence of reliable dental records, the skeleton was identified as Mengele by experts "beyond scientific doubt" (Joyce and Stover 1991; Weizman 2011; Keenan and Weizman 2012). The identification was corroborated in 1992 by British DNA pioneer Sir Alec Jeffreys (Jeffreys et al. 1992). The forensic examination of Mengele was an early example of what Snow calls the osteobiographical method, in which the skeleton is read backward to search for traces of the individual's lifestyle while gradually eliminating alternative identity options (Weizman 2011). This forensic method, linking the life history of individuals with the evidence preserved in the skeletons, proved foundational for scientific research on forced disappearances in the Southern Cone.

Since the mid-1980s, and more specifically in the last two decades, the practice of exhuming mass graves has become widespread in a growing number of countries, involving different historical, social, and institutional contexts. This recent exhumation drive is evidently connected to the global expansion of international human rights discourse and its accompanying institutions and practices, as well as to a parallel and equally transnational trend to display, commemorate, and memorialize atrocities (Williams 2007; Lesley, Chapter 8 here). The origin of various associations of forensic scientists that investigate human rights violations can be traced to the aftermath of several Latin American dictatorships. It is marked by the foundation in 1986 of the Argentine Forensic Anthropology Team or EAAF (Equipo Argentino de Antropología Forense), thanks to the decisive intervention of Clyde Snow (Snow et al. 1984; Keenan and Weizman 2012; Fondebrider, Chapter 1 here).

The end of the Cold War, the fall of the Berlin Wall, and the disintegration of the Soviet Union contributed substantially to unlocking human-rights-related exhumations. In 1991, the precursor of the present Guatemalan Forensic Anthropology Foundation (Fundación de Antropología Forense de Guatemala) was founded. Both the Guatemalan foundation and EAAF have worked incessantly on the exhumation and identification of victims of political violence in their respective countries. The EAAF has furthermore carried out exhumations and forensic identifications in over thirty countries throughout the world, including Haiti, Honduras, Mexico, Angola, Ethiopia, Democratic Republic of Congo, Sierra Leone, Zimbabwe, Morocco, Iraqi Kurdistan, East Timor, Indonesia, Bosnia, and Kosovo. The Argentine and Guatemalan examples were followed in other Latin American countries, either as nongovernmental forensic anthropology organizations (Peru's Equipo Peruano de Antropología Forense) or as part of state institutions (such as the medical-legal services in Chile and Colombia), all of which now belong to the Latin American Forensic Anthropology Association (Asociación Latinoamericana de Antropología Forense).

Since those early days, the emergence of a forensic-led exhumation-of-past-atrocities era has no doubt deeply transformed the ways in which victims and justice are conceived of in the contemporary world. Forensic and legal evidence is constructed, structured, and deployed within this scientific logic, as are the procedures by which the violated dead bodies are found, dug up, processed, identified, and represented. In this unprecedented relationship with human remains, the dead body inscribed by human rights violations of all kinds has taken central stage and become a sort of new scientific memorial relic. As a consequence of the increasing corpocentric importance of the wounded bone in human rights practices and discourses, new legal demands, new reburial claims, new representational styles, and new forms of subjectivity and victimhood have emerged in groups from international organizations to local activists, all deeply conditioned by the predominant necropolitical deployment of forensic logics, procedures, and imageries (Crossland 2013, Epilogue in this volume; Ferrándiz 2014).

The Latin American forensic teams focused first on compiling information about the modus operandi of perpetrators, which could also be useful for criminal prosecution and reparation programs, and paid special attention to technical protocols and their judicial implications (Stover and Shigekane 2002). Their findings were used by truth commissions and achieved a noted presence in national courts, steadily connecting exhumations to transitional justice developments in different parts of the world (Hayner 2002). A second fundamental aim of these forensic teams has been the identification and return of the victims' remains to the affected families or communities, thus underlining the importance of exhumations as spaces for the emergence and reworking of personal, social and political memory (Crossland 2009, 2011; Fondebrider 2002; Robben 2000, 2005; Ferrándiz 2010, 2013, 2014). Overall, their best practices have contributed to the global establishment of a forensic regime of truth and representation in the management of exhumations and historical memory. This standard is based on rigorous methods, evidence-based findings, new forms of technical and digital imaging, scientific custody, electronic archive building, and increasingly standard DNA identification and its associated logics of genetic kinship and statistical probabilities (Laqueur 1989, 2002; Crossland 2011; Wagner 2008; Ríos, Casado, and Puente 2010; Renshaw 2011; Keenan and Weizman 2012).

Owing to the relative novelty of these kinds of exhumation linked to human rights practices, significant gaps still exist in the literature. In outline, we can divide scientific research on these processes of excavating a traumatic past into three partly overlapping categories: (1) those dealing with the technical aspects of exhumations and protocols; (2) those referring to the legal implications, focusing in particular on the coverage offered by international organizations, national authorities, and local or even personal interests; and (3) a broader category encompassing the resulting social, political, and cultural repercussions. Noteworthy is the lack of research that combines the three categories, one of the tasks this book seeks to accomplish.

As far as the technical aspects of mass grave exhumations and the identification of human remains are concerned, a crucial benchmark was the adoption in 1991 by the United Nations of the *Manual on the Effective Prevention and Investigation of Extra-Legal, Arbitrary and Summary Executions* (U.N.

Doc. E/ST/CSDHA/.12), drafted by Advocates for Human Rights (formerly the Minnesota Lawyers International Human Rights Committee). The manual's preliminary work started in the early 1980s. The document responded to the lack of universal standardized procedures for investigating extralegal, arbitrary, and summary executions—producing a response known as the Minnesota protocol—and included a model autopsy protocol and a model protocol for disinterment and the analysis of skeletal remains.[2] This was a major step forward. Yet protocols cannot anticipate unforeseen circumstances or cover all local conditions, and different forensic and human rights teams therefore adjusted this pioneering set of intervention rules to specific contexts, new technologies, and ongoing academic and advocacy debates. Many articles dealing with these technical issues have been published in journals such as *Forensic Science* and *Forensic Science International*.

Most authors agree that exhumations require multidisciplinary cooperation, demand professional intervention in diverse fields, and need the involvement of historians, cultural anthropologists, psychologists, and archaeologists as well as forensic anthropologists, physicians specializing in legal and forensic medicine, forensic odontologists, and biologists with expertise in genetics (Skinner, Alempijevic, and Djuric-Srejic 2003). Current research focusing on the identification of human skeletal remains shows that success depends on a combination of factors, in particular: the number of victims; the conservation status of the skeletal remains and the presence of personal objects (Šlaus et al. 2007; Komar 2003, 2008); the quantity and quality of antemortem data provided by relatives, witnesses, and documentary sources (Baraybar 2008; Jantz, Kimmerle, and Baraybar 2008); the study of remains according to methods accepted by the scientific community (Christensen and Crowder 2009); and the availability of an appropriate laboratory infrastructure combined with the existence of living relatives to supply blood samples for DNA tests (Ríos 2012).

This last aspect is crucial, since genetic analysis became part and parcel of the identification process in the 1990s, adding to existing archaeological, documentary, testimonial, odontological, and osteological findings. This technical development has enabled the identification of large numbers of human remains recovered from mass graves (Wagner 2008, 2011; Ríos, Casado, and Puente 2010; Ríos, García-Rubio, et al. 2012). DNA technology has revolutionized the forensic field, transforming biological identification almost into a fetish of sorts, and is responsible for new cultures and politics of identification and reparation. In contrast to the parallel development of new reproductive technologies that "soften" biological kinship ties, deoxyribonucleic acid matching works the other way by "fixing" and "certifying" those same identities at the molecular level. Beyond the technical debates about bone preservation, mummification, ballistics, and the construction of evidence, there is a growing body of literature that places exhumations, and more broadly the technical treatment of dead bodies after massacres and catastrophes, within science and technology studies. This literature analyzes and questions many interrelated topics, such as the predominance of a necropolitical regime of forensic truths and protocols over the realm of transitional justice after past atrocities and disasters (Klinenberg 2002; Wagner 2008; Renshaw 2011; Crossland 2013; Ferrándiz 2014), the entwinement of and conflicts between forensic practices and religious and funerary practices (Crossland 2011; Stefatos and Kovras, Chapter 6 here), and popular understandings of forensic protocols influenced by what many authors call the CSI effect (Podlas 2005; Tyler 2006; Kruse 2010).

The connection between exhumations and judicial proceedings can be traced to the opening of mass graves since World War II. We have already mentioned the use of the fraudulent Soviet examination of the Katyn massacre during the Nuremberg Trials. A more recent and scientifically proper example is the exhumation campaign of other mass graves from World War II in the Ukraine, conducted in 1990 by the Special Investigations Unit of the Australian War Crimes Commission (Mant 1987; Paperno 2001; Skinner and Sternberg 2005; Crossland 2011). Since the last decade of the twentieth century, this practice has increasingly been deployed and interpreted under the paradigm of transitional justice (Kritz 1995; Minow 1998; Teitel 2000; Fondebrider 2002; Hayner 2002; Sanford 2003; de Greiff 2006; Payne 2008; Hinton 2011; Aguilar 2013). In addition to the Latin American examples already cited, the establishment of two international tribunals by the United Nations Security Council has also been crucial: the International Criminal Tribunal for the Former Yugoslavia in 1993 and the International Criminal Tribunal for Rwanda in 1994.

These international tribunals have entrusted mass grave exhumations and forensic investigations to multidisciplinary teams (archaeologists, anthropologists, and pathologists, many of whom have worked with Latin American teams such as those from Argentina, Guatemala, and Peru) whose reports have been used in judicial proceedings. Other organizations have subsequently been created under the auspices of or in partnership with the United Nations to investigate human rights violations in member states. It is noteworthy that the creation of the International Commission on Missing Persons in 1996 began as a spin-off from the Dayton Peace Accords that ceased hostilities in the former Yugoslavia. Based in Sarajevo, the commission later intervened in the aftermath of the 2004 tsunami, as well as in New Orleans (the Hurricane Katrina catastrophe), Iraq, Kuwait, and Chile. Other instances of the confluence of legal and forensic procedures related to mass violence are the Special Court for Sierra Leone in 1996, the United Nations Mission in Support of East Timor in 1999, and the Extraordinary Chambers in the Courts of Cambodia in 2003. In the tradition of long-standing debates about legal pluralism, recent anthropological studies dwell on the contradictions between the transnational, national, and local dimensions of justice, as well as the different senses of justice surrounding exhumations, in line with what Wilson (2006) labels the social life of rights or Hinton (2011) calls transitional frictions (see also Sanford and Lincoln 2011; Wagner 2011).

Several critical anthropological analyses have been made of the collaboration between the Tribunal for the Former Yugoslavia in the Hague and the Bosnian exhumation efforts at one of the world's principal human-rights-related forensic laboratories (Stover and Peress 1998; Stover and Shigekane 2002; Wagner 2008, 2011, Chapter 5 here). Claverie (2011) has suggested about the Srebrenica case that the empirical evidence accumulated through painstaking exhumations and rigorous lab work had two main consequences. On the one hand, the Commission on Missing Persons' state-of-the-art biotechnical procedures transformed the disappeared into individual victims, and put them on a trajectory from dispersed remains to individualized identities and finally to restoration to their community and family. On the other hand, the procedures show the increasing dominance of a high-tech forensic logic in the production of scientific and legal evidence—the mass grave as crime scene and the body as criminal evidence—as a preamble to the desired prosecution and conviction of war criminals. However, a bottom-up analysis of the techno-legal operations deployed by the Tribunal for the Former Yugoslavia and the Commission on Missing Persons demonstrated the heavy toll that the so-called bureaucracies of transitional justice took on relatives and survivors. Their mourning became conditioned by external rhythms, procedures, and regimes of truth, accountability, and reconciliation that interfered with local cultural forms and distorted social and political postconflict processes in an unstable balance between universalism and particularism (Wagner 2011).

Also in this vein, Theidon's (2012) analysis of the micropolitics of reconciliation in Peru is a major contribution to ongoing debates on postconflict and social repair, based on the ethnographic analysis of transnational influences on community-level reconciliation efforts and the intricate interplay of vertical and horizontal streams of conflict resolution policies. Theidon, who worked with the Peruvian Truth and Reconciliation Commission, eschews simplistic accounts of the aftermath of violence and sets the ground for the development of a more refined and critical understanding of slippery, and at times hard to translate, concepts such as justice, reconciliation, reparation, social memory, transition, truth, victim, terrorist, or even citizenship—all terms with local context-specific meanings. Calling for a sophisticated incorporation of local morality, experiences, perceptions, and concepts in the search for truth and reconciliation, Theidon through a deeply ethnographic perspective on the sequels of violence speaks to the potential of anthropology as a discipline within transnational transitional justice paradigms that are mostly dominated by judicial, technocratic, and bureaucratic approaches to postconflict situations.

In sum, from an ethnographic point of view, research on mass grave exhumations cannot be restricted to technical procedures and their legal implications. Diverse disciplines have turned their attention to the symbolic, social, and political consequences in the context of studies about the management of traumatic memory and memory politics in contemporary society. Although this is still a relatively unexplored field, research is being conducted on the reactions of local populations to international mechanisms and technical protocols (Crossland 2002; Wagner 2008; Renshaw 2011), on their psychological and psychosocial impact (ECAP–GAC–GEZA 2009; Keough, Simmons, and Samuels 2004; Pérez Sales and Navarro 2007), on the diverse rituals and forms of reporting that develop around exhumations (Stover and Shigekane 2002; Sant Cassia 2005; Ferrándiz 2013; Kwon 2008; Hinton 2011), on the political dimensions of exhumations (Verdery 1999; Robben 2000, 2005; Ferrándiz 2006, 2013), on their iconography and technical and media representations (Ferrándiz and Baer 2008; Renshaw 2007; Bernad 2011), and on their influence on the expression and development of certain human rights cultures (Sanford 2003; Ferrándiz 2013).

Exhumations: Memoryscapes

The anthropology of exhumations shares with memory studies an interest in political violence, memory cultures, and transnational circulations of national, local, or even individual representations of memory, violence, and death. Broadly speaking, the term *memory* encompasses the processes of constructing the past in the present. Approaches to the subject of memory are highly diverse and do not always complement one another (Apfelbaum, Alexander, and Barbier 2010). The growing concern for memory in sociology, social anthropology, and cultural studies since the end of the twentieth century is a response to the acceleration of contemporary life, the dwindling of tradition, and a bewilderment in the face of potential oblivion (Jelin 2003; Huyssen 2003). In philosophy, diverse thinkers have positioned themselves in the slipstream of the Frankfurt school with respect to memory as a categorical imperative that calls on us to remember every kind of atrocity, and in essence, the suffering of victims (Mate 1991). Other perspectives, including political theory, have recognized in social memory the considerable potential for a fraudulent or abusive use of the past (Todorov 1995), and have pointed to the conflict-ridden nature of remembrance as opposed to the virtues of forgetting.

For many authors, the current boom in memory studies began with Maurice Halbwachs's influential work (1994) on collective memory in the 1920s. A second wave of academic interest was embodied by historian Pierre Nora (1989) and his conceptualization of *lieux de mémoire* or sites of memory on the one hand and the distinction between communicative memory and cultural memory proposed by Jan Assmann (1995) on the other. This is the backdrop against which the field of memory studies has consolidated its position today, bolstered by an international academic network that boasts numerous conferences devoted exclusively to the question of memory; an impressive list of series produced by academic publishers, including Studies in Memory and Narrative (Routledge, since 1998), Cultural Memory in the Present (Stanford University Press, since 1998), Media and Cultural Memory (De Gruyter, since 2004), and Memory Studies (Palgrave Macmillan, since 2009); and professional journals like *History and Memory* (since 1989) and *Memory Studies* (since 2008).

In the last decade, memory studies have developed a growing interest in what have been called multidirectional memories, transnational memories, global memoryscapes, or cosmopolitan memory cultures in which the experiences and representations of the Holocaust take a central place. The Holocaust has become a universal paradigm of victimhood, evilness, and testimony (Alexander 2002; Huyssen 2003; Levy and Sznaider 2002; Robben 2012; Rothberg 2009; Phillips and Reyes 2011). For example, the Balkan Wars of the early

1990s were clearly framed in these terms, as exemplified by the iconic photograph of a young man behind barbed wire whose visible rib cage evokes images of Nazi concentration camps (Levy and Sznaider 2002). Rothberg (2009:6) has argued that "the emergence of Holocaust memory on a global scale has contributed to the articulation of other histories."

The transnational uses of the Holocaust have revealed the problems and limitations of historiography when tackling a traumatic past. In this area, theories on trauma, and its witnessing and transmission, have all flourished (LaCapra 2001; Caruth 1996; Alexander et al. 2004; Felman and Laub 1992; Hartman 1996; Robben 2005). These theoretical concepts have influenced the study of other traumatic occurrences of mass violence in the twentieth century. Yet recent scholarship warns about the dangers involved in the promiscuous use of trauma paradigms and their associated victimhood politics in the analysis of the violent past (Fassin and Rechtman 2009). Beyond the question of traumatic memory, memory studies cover a wide variety of areas and relate to very different academic disciplines. Examples include sites of memory (Nora 1989); monuments, memorials, and museums (Young 1993; Linenthal 1995; Huyssen 2003; Williams 2007); the representation of the past in cultural industries and their repercussions in the media (Zelizer 1998; Kaes 1990; Hartman 1996; Baer 2001; Hoskins 2009; Erll and Rigney 2009); and celebrations, anniversaries, and commemorative rituals (Gillis 1996; Jelin 2003).

What happens when memory processes intersect with mass graves and exhumations? We believe it fruitful to start with examining the historical production of mass graves and the subsequent exhumations as spatial practices. As such, they can be conceptualized as memoryscapes (Cole 2001:289–293; Phillips and Reyes 2011). Memoryscapes of a very specific kind, though, as they are linked to the burial, unearthing, and reburial of disturbing traces of massive violence. How could mass graves be characterized as landscapes of memory? To be more precise, what is it in mass graves and their exposure that deeply conditions and taints whatever memory processes unfold around them? First, mass graves related to human rights violations are more often than not part of integrated topographies of death and terror. Their analysis is crucial to better understand the logic and symbolism of mass killing and genocide. It is also essential to assess the far-reaching consequences of the foundational production of death and fear by dictatorial, totalitarian, and segregational regimes. Second, as memoryscapes, mass graves are extremely delicate and dangerous lieux de mémoire that contain crucial and uncomfortable evidence of atrocities because contemporary exhumations are increasingly interwoven with the transnational spread of human rights cultures and practices. Global cultures of terror and atrocity display that condition through the readings and interpretations of such evidence. Third, a crucial attribute of mass graves and exhumations as memoryscapes is the predominance of the tissue, bone, and inflicted wounds in the reinterpretation of the past and the body-centered memory necropolitics attached to them. Fourth, the prevalence of bones and potentially criminal evidence in mass graves may engender very specific and sophisticated biotechnologies for deciphering the past in the context of legal prosecution. The increasing predominance of forensic protocols in the management of exhumations establishes technical procedures and laboratory work as almost natural extensions of the mass graves and as integral parts of funerary practices (Crossland 2013), exemplifying the contemporary strength of the sciences of memory (Hacking 1996). Fifth, sites of former mass graves become lieux de mémoire at the same time as communities and families reappropriate the exhumed bodies through mortuary and reburial rituals. Finally, another quality of mass graves as memoryscapes concerns the kinds of testimony and witnessing they elicit, equally attached to the very physical and overwhelming presence of corpses and skeletons.

Exhumations as Practice

Part I focuses mainly on the intertwined first, third, and fourth connection between exhumations and memory processes listed above. Each chapter addresses one or two strands, conceiving mass graves as ethnographic field sites where forensic practices and expectant relatives, destroyed remnants of political violence and memory politics, and contested historical reconstruction and present ideological agendas come together in one location.

The massacre and disappearance of hundreds of thousands of civilians by military regimes in Latin America during the 1970s and 1980s challenged the field of forensic anthropology that had until then dealt mainly with casualties of conventional wars and victims of crimes and accidents. Luis Fondebrider belongs to the first generation of forensic anthropologists who were trained on-site in the investigation of political violence. His mentor Clyde Snow had extensive experience with the examination of criminal cases and aircraft disasters but not with crimes against humanity when he first visited Argentina in 1984 to identify the skeletal remains of people reported as missing. The local trainees may have lacked his technical skills but they were more sensitive to the societal impact of exhumations. They had experienced the ruthless repression themselves, and understood that the forensic investigations not only posed technical but also especially political and emotional problems: Argentina was just emerging from a brutal dictatorship, civil-military relations were tense, a truth commission was investigating whether there were still disappeared people alive, and the junta leaders were being put on trial. Under these trying circumstances, mass graves were opened under the watchful eyes of policemen who might have been complicit in the disappearances, and in the presence of anxious family members who had been searching for their loved ones for years on end.

The enduring contribution of the Argentine exhumations to forensic anthropology has been that the examination of cases of political violence is not a purely technical matter; it is also a proper investigation that requires mutual trust between professionals and family members to overcome their fears of the political implications and convince them of the scientific rigor of forensic work. Relatives are active research participants rather than only providers of DNA and antemortem data. They create public support for opening burial sites, protect mass graves from deliberate destruction, exert political pressure on authorities and the judiciary to allow forensic investigations in a call for truth and justice, and demand the highest scientific standards and technical facilities. Furthermore, forensic anthropologists and relatives may continue their relationship after a successful identification because the presence of the dead and the bereaved in society, and by extension also that of the forensic investigators, changes through time. The pioneering work of the EAAF, as noted founded in 1986, was followed by that of other nongovernmental organizations in several Latin American countries that used similar forensic protocols and established firm relations with the victims' relatives.

The second major application of forensic anthropology to cases of political violence began in 1996 when numerous mass graves were discovered on the Balkans. In particular U.S. and British forensic anthropologists used the most advanced scientific techniques and most sophisticated DNA tests available. They were unaccustomed to dealing with the political complexities of exhumations in postconflict societies and had little experience in cultivating trust with the victims' relatives. The recruitment of Latin American forensic anthropologists improved the quality of their investigations. Fondebrider concludes from his personal experience in dozens of countries, including the Balkans, that better international cooperation among forensic anthropologists with different backgrounds and training is urgently required, that victims' relatives are crucial partners in investigations, and that international protocols should be developed on the basis of a broader range of forensic situations.

The complex relations of exhumations to territoriality and necropower in Chile and Argentina is the main theme of Antonius Robben's contribution to the volume. Necropower and territoriality are the two manifestations of authoritarian sovereignty. The former implies an absolute power over life and death, according to Agamben (1998), whereas the second entails a complete control over territory, according to Mbembe (2003). Mass graves functioned for the military therefore as powerful means to demonstrate their authoritarian sovereignty by allowing them to hide massacres, destroy evidence, avoid the martyrdom of the dead, and deny mourning to the relatives through secret, unceremonial burials. In the military's logic, mass graves were also a victory over the enemy, a mark of territorial reconquest of the motherland, and a tool to send grassroots movements into confusion.

Nonetheless, the junta underestimated the power of mass graves to mobilize searching relatives and oppositional human rights movements that eventually demanded accountability for the crimes against humanity committed by the military. The military's necropower and territoriality were apparently not as absolute as Agamben and Mbembe have made them to be. In fact, as Robben asserts, contemporary exhumations in the two countries have proved their potential to unmake the logic behind military occupation, refurnish national memory, and situate the victims of state terrorism in the framework of international human rights paradigms.

Robben emphasizes also that forensic exhumations should always be analyzed within a wider context that endows scientific procedures with political meaning. The exhumation protocols were similar in Chile and Argentina, but the unburials had very different meanings because they expressed different repressive pasts, civil-military relations, power struggles, legal framings, and memory politics. These are important comparative considerations that cut across most chapters in this book. These divergences between Argentina and Chile are brought to light by the scrutiny of the contexts and consequences of exhumations in Córdoba, Argentina, and Santiago de Chile. Córdoba's San Vicente Cemetery—associated with the secret detention and torture center La Perla—contained the largest mass grave found thus far in Argentina, numbering around four hundred bodies. A hurried partial exhumation carried out with a power shovel in 1984, and without any forensic protocol, destroyed most of the evidence. When it was properly exhumed in 2003 and 2004 by the EAAF, the organization discovered that so-called subversives had been mixed up with abandoned aged persons and even lepers from a neighboring lazaret, a clear statement by the military of their status as expendable nonpersons. The long-term commitment of the EAAF to identify the disappeared, the support of most human rights organizations, and the importance of forensic findings in criminal trials against perpetrators demonstrate the political and judicial significance of exhumations in Argentina. The contrast between Argentina's resolve and Chile's disinterest in exhuming mass graves is remarkable. More than three hundred anonymous bodies were buried in 1973 in Lot 29 at Santiago's General Cemetery, in a perfect example of what the author calls an "in-the-face display of necropower." In 1978 and 1979, the Chilean military became worried about the discovery of incriminating mass graves and engaged in "destructive exhumations," in which bodies were taken from the mass graves and air-dropped at sea or in inaccessible mountain zones. Unlike in Argentina, however, forensic identifications did not carry much weight in Chile when democracy returned in 1990. Former dictator Augusto Pinochet continued as commander-in-chief of the armed forces, and President Patricio Aylwin pursued an agenda of national reconciliation. Lot 29 at the General Cemetery of Chile's capital was exhumed almost perfunctory, and the recovered remains were either placed in a deposit or returned to relatives after rudimentary identification. Gross misidentifications of them became public only in 2003 and caused an uproar in the human rights movement. Reexhumations and forensic restudies were carried out immediately but it was only after Pinochet's death in 2006 that a drastic reorganization of the Medical-Legal Service was undertaken, forensic facilities were improved, a DNA data bank was established, and the exhumed human remains of Lot 29 were finally given their correct identity.

In the first weeks of the Korean War (1950–1953), massacres took place throughout the country. Communists were assassinated preemptively in the South as state enemies, and suspected supporters of the South were massacred in the North. Villages, neighborhoods, and kin groups became poisoned with escalating reciprocal violence carried out by armed political forces on both sides of the ideological divide. The practice of associative culpability—a collective guilt of families and kin groups for the supposed threat to national security by one of its members—resulted in numerous killings of close relatives in North and South that continued well into the Cold War. Anywhere between one to two hundred thousand civilians died violent deaths. They were remembered for decades by the affected families and villages, but their public memory was repressed in South Korea until the 1990s and is still repressed in the North. Heonik Kwon demonstrates the political consequences for the bereaved in South Korea who opened mass graves and reburied their murdered relatives. The state considered these bereaved guilty twice over by defying the ban on exhuming mass graves and by being complicit as relatives of communists executed in the prologue to the Korean War.

The Graves of One Hundred Ancestors and One Descendant on Jeju Island at Korea's southern tip is one such reburial ground. People were barred from attending to the 132 slaughtered and unceremonially buried relatives. The often unidentifiable and incomplete remains were gathered anyway in 1956, and interred in individual anonymous graves accompanied by a collective gravestone rather than individual offering tablets. A national Appeal the Grievance movement arose in 1960 that pursued the exhumation of mass graves and the exoneration of the dead for being innocent civilian victims instead of communist traitors. The movement was proscribed and representatives were detained on the day of the May 1961 military coup d'état. Memorial stones were dismantled, collective tombs were destroyed in many places, and the skeletal remains were cremated. The large memorial stone at Jeju Island was broken and buried by police in June 1961. Many relatives refused to allow the authorities to unearth the coffins without familial and spiritual consent. They were placed under surveillance, discriminated against, and obstructed in their personal ambitions. The democratic opening of 1990 returned the mass graves to public debate, and the national association of bereaved families was resurrected in September 2000. Finally, legislation was passed in 2005 to establish a Truth and Reconciliation Commission to examine the past.

Kwon explains the confrontation of bereaved relatives and police forces as a fundamental conflict between state loyalties and kinship loyalties. The obligation of kinsmen to bury their dead relatives clashed with their obligation as citizens to obey the Korean state. If the state held sway, then both dead and surviving relatives would remain stigmatized as culpable members of society, whereas successful opposition to the state's obstruction of kinship duties would restore the moral identity of the massacred relatives as honorable ancestors and by association elevate the public and political status of the bereaved. Kwon delineates a conflict between family and state as "the confrontation between the ethics of commemoration and the politics of sovereignty" that appears in many other countries, notably Argentina, Chile, and Spain.

The political struggle over mass graves can persist for many decades and reach across generations, as the troubled history of contemporary exhumations in Spain demonstrates. The Spanish Civil War (1936–1939) cost the lives of an estimated 500,000 people, of whom over 200,000 were killed in rearguard executions. Around 150,000 fell among civilians loyal to the Republican government and 55,000 among people supporting Francisco Franco's rebel cause. Francisco Ferrándiz describes sixty years of partisan exhumations during the Franco regime that ruled Spain between 1939 and 1975, followed by twenty-five years of silence during successive democratic governments, and then a new cycle of exhumations. Each of these unburial phases responds to different necropolitical framings that range from becoming a crucial part of the ideological foundation of the dictatorial regime—National Catholicism—to clandestine unburials of the mass graves of the defeated.

The first post–Civil War exhumations were intended to document the crimes committed by the Republican rearguard, legitimize the military regime, honor dead Nationalists with Catholic state reburials, and create a commemorative culture of martyrdom that excluded the vanquished and left their unceremonial burying places untouched. In a parallel space of death, knowledge about Republican mass graves was passed from one generation to the next and occasional exhumations of Republican dead were carried out secretly by bereaved relatives throughout Franco's reign. A second exhumation cycle took place in the late 1950s when over thirty thousand bodies from both sides were reburied at the Valley of the Fallen memorial, ostensibly presented by Franco as a symbol of atonement. After Franco's death in 1975, some relatives opened an unknown number of graves without technical support and limited media coverage during the last decades of the twentieth century. Only since the year 2000 have Republican mass graves been exhumed openly, triggering an intense and bitter public debate.

This last exhumation cycle was sparked by relatives desiring a proper burial for their dead but acquired additional meaning through transnational developments in international law. The author notes the analytical significance of taking into account the temporal disjuncture between the executions—the black and white Spain—and the contemporary reappearance of the bodies—the digital Spain. In this framework, on October 16, 2008, Spanish judge Baltasar Garzón considered the 1977 Amnesty Law for crimes committed during the Civil War not applicable to the disappeared resting in thousands of mass graves, and declared the court competent to investigate the massacres. Based on jurisprudence (and personal prestige) from his international detention order against former Chilean dictator Augusto Pinochet issued on October 16, 1998, Garzón argued that just as Pinochet was responsible for the ongoing crime of the forced disappearance of Spanish citizens in Chile, there was also no statute of limitations on investigating the Spanish mass graves, and at least in theory, prosecuting the aged perpetrators.

The humanitarian right to bury one's massacred relatives became thus infused in 2008 with renewed legal and political meaning, as is shown clearly by Ferrándiz through a detailed analysis of the commotion surrounding the search for five women executed in the hot terror winter of 1936 in the province of Cáceres; a burst of initial mass killing of civilians before kangaroo military courts progressively took over the terror machinery in 1937. In this context, in 2008 the Franco regime was denounced by Garzón for its crimes against humanity, the indiscriminate execution of Republican sympathizers, and its violence against women. The judge's initiative, however, was cut short when he was forced out of office, and exhumations increased their political tone, sometimes against the will of the bereaved relatives.

The halfhearted position of the Spanish government, which financed exhumations between 2006 and 2011 and passed a "memory act" in 2007 that did not assume full administrative responsibility or establish a coordinated supervision of exhumations—resulting in practice in what the author labels a human rights outsourcing scheme—contributed also to a legal vacuum around mass graves, diggings, and reburials. As a consequence, and in the absence of a national forensic protocol until 2011, some diggings took place without proper forensic methods and procedures. Exhumed bodies emerged in contemporary Spain in what amounted to a technical and legal limbo. Despite attempts by the different memorial associations, only very seldom did judges claim competence over these murders, and in no case has this led to the indictment or trial of presumed perpetrators, or even to the legal investigation of the facts.

Indignation with this institutional and legal lack of commitment helped mobilize grassroots support and generated political solidarity among the Left. Many family associations and local memory associations emerged that carried the national exhumation movement forward but at times clashed over the manner in which to proceed. Ferrándiz analyzes the divergence among local exhumations and mortuary and commemoration practices, whether to rebury the dead with a secular, a political or a Catholic funeral or decide to leave mass graves intact and commemorate the interred. Despite these differences, the exhumations were motivated by a shared desire to rehumanize and redignify the dead dumped like dogs in makeshift graves, as a proper way of unmaking the terror legacy of Francoism still inscribed in them. In the case of the exhumation in Villanueva de la Vera, the corpses of the five women were never found, and local activists and relatives improvised "closure" ceremonies under the supervision of Psychologists Without Borders.

The exhumation of mass graves may raise unforeseen technical problems, ethical dilemmas, and ritual complications when human remains are commingled or can only be recovered in part. The mutilation and desecration of the dead through intermixing inflicts additional suffering on the bereaved relatives, whereas the partial recovery of remains may disturb the process of mourning and pose difficult technical and ethical problems for forensic anthropologists. By what standard are human remains considered partial? Should partial remains be handed to the relatives for burial or should all forensic means be exhausted before notifying the bereaved? How should additional remains be treated, and when should they be regarded as identifiable? These questions are addressed by Sarah Wagner in her comparison of the identification of reburied remains of men and boys assassinated in July 1995 in Srebrenica during the Balkan Wars and the identification of the remains of U.S. service members killed during the Korean War that were received from the North Korean government in the early 1990s.

The importance of corporeal integrity after death made the Office of Chief Medical Examiner in New York City do its utmost to identify as many fragmented human remains as possible after 9/11, instead of ceasing DNA testing once all registered victims at the site had been identified. The identification of partial remains from mass graves in Srebrenica—the UN enclave in Bosnia-Hercegovina overrun by Bosnian Serbian troops in 1995—had another complication: the mass graves of around eight thousand men and boys had been opened within weeks of the massacres. The remains were disarticulated, commingled, and finally reburied in secondary mass graves. Painstaking efforts by forensic anthropologists resulted in nearly seven thousand identifications but often without recovering anatomically complete remains, while finding additional fragments at other sites. Exhumation and identification became interminable processes that raised questions about how to communicate this situation to relatives, when to return identified fragments, how to deal with the funerary implications of piecemeal identifications, and what to do with misidentifications. A consent form was developed to give families a choice about what course of action to take with additional human remains, and allow them the possibility to attend reexhumations.

The 208 boxes with the remains of U.S. troops who died during the Korean War have created comparable forensic challenges at the labs of the Joint POW/MIA Accounting Command in Pearl Harbor, Hawaii. The cases contain the commingled and incomplete skeletal remains of an estimated four hundred individuals. Unlike the Srebrenica dead, the Korean dead were recovered by North Korean officials without advanced forensic expertise. Furthermore, the cause of commingling is unknown, and the locations of the exhumations cannot be verified or reexamined due to U.S.-North Korean political tensions. The passage of time raises the stakes of identification as close family members attain old age and burial becomes a transgenerational duty or burden.

Exhuming Ruins: A Photo Essay

Francesc Torres's photo essay on the vestiges of 9/11, stored in Hangar 17 of the cargo area at JFK International Airport in New York, acts as a hinge between this book's two main parts. An acclaimed photographer and conceptual artist, Torres published a book with black-and-white photos of the 2004 exhumation of forty-six bodies from a mass grave at Villamayor de los Montes, Burgos, Spain (Torres 2007, 2008; Ferrándiz 2008). The photographs were exhibited at the International Center for Photography in New York (alongside a concurrent exhibit of war photographs of the Spanish Civil War by Robert Capa and Gerda Taro) and in many other museums and venues. This exhibit was crucial for the international exposure of contemporary Spanish exhumations. Torres's photographic record, undertaken as a "rebellion against oblivion," became actually an integral part of the exhumation by revealing the effects and consequences of mass violence through its most concrete forensic facts (Torchin 2012). In his 2008 text accompanying the photographs, Torres emphasized the importance of both constructing and critically deciphering the pictorial aspects of memory through its visual representations. Memories contain pictures as much as pictures contain memories. This complex process of memories turned images turned memories is not unproblematic, and entails the unavoidable clash among conflicting interpretations of images and icons. He chose analog photography (required for the interruptions and visual silences gone for good with digital technology), and reflexively questioned how to select the proper tone of visual narration, the visual pitch of the images, and how to confront the fear of voyeurism and sensationalism. In all its intricacies, Torres defends photography as a "powerful tool for imprinting and fixing images from the flow of events," while contributing to a "visual consciousness" and emotional anchorage regarding the violent past (Torres 2008:158).

There is a manifest continuity between Torres's Villamayor project and the Hangar 17 photographs presented here. In his text in this volume, Torres places into context the images taken inside the hangar, and defends photography as a powerful exhumation tool, not only of bones, tissue, personal belongings, testimonies, or mortuary practices, such as in Villamayor's mass grave, but also of tragic objects "in a clinically pure state as historical sediment" preceding its museographic interpretation. These tragic objects range from the most quotidian item to conceptually complex and politically controversial materials such as the "magmas," which in fact are compacted floors squeezing within the space of a few inches all the horror from the downfall of the buildings which liberated untamed energies to the scale of atomic fusion. For Torres, what was stored by the Port Authority of New York and New Jersey in a little-known warehouse under its jurisdiction was the result of a sophisticated narrative of the Twin Towers' collapse, a sort of archaeology of the present spread in an accidental protomuseum of memory never to be. Yet he also highlights the practical absence of iconic traces of the 9/11 victims in the public sphere, raising an important debate about the ethics and politics of the display and concealment of terror in the age of information. Torres also points at the importance of assessing the thresholds of tolerance at seeing images of extreme violence and the epistemological status of the victim's body—a discussion no doubt crucial for experts, researchers, politicians, lawyers, artists, activists, and relatives witnessing mass grave exhumations in one capacity or the other.

Exhumations as Memory

The chapters in Part II attend to the second, fifth, and sixth strand of the connection between exhumations and memory processes. Rather than focusing on the dynamics of exhumations as sites of ethnographic inquiry, these chapters situate mass graves and their disinterred remains in the bereaved society. Political processes of grassroots resistance against state manipulation and appropriation become visible, and official memorialization politics clash with the emotional, social, and cultural needs of the mourning relatives and communities. The site of memory becomes a source of political contestation about who owns the human remains and how their violent death should be remembered.

Greek Orthodox funerary culture maintains elaborate rituals to accompany the deceased's soul to the afterworld. Katerina Stefatos and Iosif Kovras explain that relatives wash the body, dress it, and bury it while the soul wanders near the corporeal remains during forty days. Elaborate rituals are held and women lament the deceased with mortuary songs. The exhumation of the bones after a period of three to seven years symbolizes a negation of death by returning the ossified remains to home and family. The bones are greeted, kissed, and honored before they are finally confined to an ossuary. Considering such elaborate mortuary process, it is surprising that the tens of thousands of dead of the 1946–1949 Greek Civil War have not been exhumed and reburied.

The Greek Civil War between the Greek Democratic Army of the Communist Party and the official National Army broke out two years after the 1941–1944 German occupation. The U.S. government supported the Greek national government with extensive military and economic aid to win one of the first proxy confrontations of the Cold War, but without resolving the deep political tensions between communists and nationalists. After the 1967–1974 military dictatorship was toppled and the deposed colonels put on trial, a national reconciliation was undertaken that included symbolic and economic reparations but not exhumations. A blanket of silence was cast over the past so as not to resuscitate unresolved animosities and uncover inconvenient truths. Even relatives did not dare disturb the dead, except in Lesvos.

More than one hundred guerrillas, communist sympathizers, and political prisoners were killed or executed by paramilitaries and members of the gendarmerie on Lesvos during the Civil War. Stefatos and Kovras emphasize that official nonexhumations may reveal an interesting perspective about national memory construction and how people contest the state's attempt to monopolize the past. Their analysis of an inconclusive exhumation on the island of Lesvos demonstrates that people from Lesvos ruptured the state's hegemonic silence since the early 1950s by intermittent exhumations of guerrilla insurgents. These exhumations were carried out secretly at first by relatives and by the 1980s were conducted informally by local communities in the spirit of national reconciliation, without, however, government support. Stefatos and Kovras analyze the search in 2009 for the remains of thirteen guerrillas killed on New Year's Eve of 1948 when their female host destroyed the hut by detonating the ordnance placed there. The dead were besmirched by local authorities and put on display in village squares. The principal reason for the 2009 exhumation was not political but motivated by a desire for a dignified ritual reburial to undo the unceremonial and corrupted interment five decades earlier. The 2009 exhumation proved unsuccessful because the remains had already been exhumed and reburied by relatives in 1952. The attempt demonstrates that national agendas and local experiences diverge, and that the exhumations on Lesvos were primarily personal and not politically motivated to break the official silence about the Greek Civil War.

Isaias Rojas-Perez explores the role of exhumations, and especially reburials, in the aftermath of Peru's twenty years of internal war (1980–2000) between the Peruvian Armed Forces, the Peruvian Communist Party–Shining Path, and the Tupac Amaru Revolutionary Movement (Movimiento Revolucionario Tupac Amaru). From late 2000 to 2012, more than 2,200 bodies were recovered, and 1,238 of them have been identified, of which over 1,000 were returned to their relatives. Yet numbers only tell a very small part of the story. In his chapter, Rojas-Perez focuses on the involvement by the Peruvian Truth and Reconciliation Commission (Comisión de la Verdad y Reconciliación or CVR) in the exhumation of mass graves, and more particularly on the moral framing of these forensic and legal interventions. For the author, there are three crucial points in the critical analysis of the CVR's role in mass grave management within its larger mandate. First, it is important to decipher how the CVR formulated the issue, and why reburials eventually were established, with the encouragement of the commission, as a powerful justice mechanism in contemporary Peru. Second, Rojas-Perez explores how this focus on clandestine mass graves was connected to the state's absorption of global human rights and humanitarian discourses and practices, especially as it related to the Peruvian translation of the "right to truth." Finally, it is necessary to evaluate the results in terms of nation building and reconciliation policies. In particular, the focus is on the extent to which these officially promoted exhumations and reburials, and the political and moral grounds underlying them, contributed toward fostering a more inclusive political community that transcends racism and still prevalent notions of the "internal enemy."

After a scrutiny of how the CVR's decisions and actions regarding mass graves implied a nuanced shift from the category of the "unknown dead" to that of the "unacknowledged dead," Rojas-Perez analyzes the three exhumations and reburials at Chuschi, Totos, and Lucanamarca in Ayacucho District in 2002, jointly managed by a rather unstable ensemble of the commission and the Attorney General's Office. The first two mass graves involved army killings of respectively eight and nineteen Quechua-speaking peasants, while the last one concerned a Shining Path massacre of sixty-nine peasants. Chuschi had a highly symbolic value as this was the community where Shining Path had launched its revolutionary struggle in May 1980. The reburial in the village was presided over by a local representative of the attorney general and two CVR commissioners who were priests and who celebrated the Catholic funeral. It remained a local event that was largely unnoticed by the national elites. Totos's case shows the increasing importance of exhumations, and in particular re-burials, in the work of the CVR. Its institutional presence and public visibility were scaled up: the reburial rituals started in Ayacucho city with the participa-tion of the district attorney, four commissioners, members of the Ombuds-man's Office, and representatives of Peruvian human rights organizations.

The author considers Lucanamarca the most telling exhumation—a great opportunity to remind the nation and the world of Shining Path's atrocities. The political and symbolic location of the public commemorations was trans-ferred from Ayacucho to Peru's capital, Lima, where the bodies had previously been sent for forensic analysis. President Alejandro Toledo participated in the dignification ceremonies, where the dead were hailed as heroes. In the name of the Peruvian nation, Toledo asked relatives for forgiveness, not for the bru-tality of the armed forces during the conflict, but for the state's inability to protect those murdered by terrorists. Peruvian political elites were quite visi-ble and comfortable at the place of ceremony, publicly showing that they iden-tified much more with this exhumation and reburial than with the former ones. To Rojas-Perez, these developments show that the CVR failed to incor-porate the Spanish-speaking political elites into a politics of recognition of the suffering by Quechua-speaking Peruvians. After these politically and morally charged early exhumations and reburials, the CVR procedure has been con-tinued, while losing a good part of its high political and exemplary profile and becoming more of a bureaucratic affair.

The tower of skulls at the "killing fields" outside Phnom Penh, Cambodia, and the mummified human remains at the former technical school at Mur-ambi, Rwanda, have become icons of post-Holocaust genocides. The Choeung Ek Memorial stands at a former Chinese cemetery, containing more than one hundred mass graves with thousands of dead. In her comparative analysis, Elena Lesley describes how the first exhumations were carried out by Viet-namese forensic specialists who preserved the skeletal remains before placing them in a wooden memorial. The memorial was erected in part to justify the December 1978 invasion of Cambodia by Soviet-backed Vietnam, strongly condemned by China and the United States. The commemoration of the Cambodian dead as alternatively war heroes or genocide victims was modeled after Vietnamese memorial practices, even though most Cambodian dead had neither died in combat nor belonged to a targeted national, racial, religious, or ethnic group. Upon the initiative of a Vietnamese general, a Buddhist memorial stupa was erected in 1988 at Choeung Ek in which the skeletal remains of Khmer Rouge victims were put on display. The disintegration of the Soviet Union in the late 1980s and the détente among the three world powers made the United States withdraw political support from the Khmer Rouge leadership in exile. The Vietnamese forces withdrew, and the Cambodian government distanced the memorial from its Cold War rhetoric. Lesley demonstrates that these official state narratives exist alongside, and clash with, popular spiritual beliefs and mortuary practices related to the notion of bad death. Choeung Ek is believed to be haunted, and there is concern about the preservation of uncremated human remains. Relatives make frequent offerings to compensate for the ritual losses, and seem to find some comfort in the reincarnation of the dead.

The Murambi Genocide Memorial Center is a former technical school perched on a hill, located in southern Rwanda. Tens of thousands of Tutsis and Hutu sympathizers had taken refuge on school grounds during the invasion by the Rwandan Patriotic Front, but were assassinated by local militia and government troops in April 1994. Twenty-seven thousand bodies were exhumed and reburied during a 1996 ceremony. Mummified human remains were displayed on wooden frames in the school's classrooms together with piles of skulls and ribs. The Patriotic Front government and international agencies took the lead in organizing the Murambi memorial to denounce the genocide, fight denial of it, and make the international community come face to face with its failure to halt the indiscriminate killings. Conservation efforts have been made to preserve the human remains but some have suggested that they should be buried properly.

The chapter by Lesley raises uncomfortable questions about the tensions between the care for the displayed human remains of people who suffered while alive and continue in spiritual limbo while dead. The ritual and spiritual needs of the dead and their surviving relatives may clash with the state's interests and its desire to create a national memory about past genocides for the sake of authenticity, accountability, prevention, and nation rebuilding. State agendas simplify historical pasts and political realities and reduce social and religious complexities existing among its diverse population. People seem to approve or give in to state pressure to set aside their personal misgivings because of the magnitude and moral burden of the genocides, but many would

still prefer cremation or burial rather than the public display of human remains. Lesley's reflections on Cambodia and Rwanda appeal to the more generalized contemporary drive for atrocity display and commemoration, and to
its correlate terror tourism, in the framework of memorial practices—the exhibition of human remains as irreducible evidence (Williams 2007:38–50).
This tendency, today inseparable from new communication technologies and
the society of spectacle, is connected to the current popularity of
exhumations—as a scientifically mediated modality of wounded bone display
and elaboration—as truth-seeking and dignifying tools within transnational
human rights discourses and practices.

Exhumations in Transnational Perspective

The combination of research and analytical frameworks from the anthropology of exhumations and memory studies examines the struggle of different
social agents to find meaning in violent and traumatic atrocities through forensic evidence and the study of the social, political, and cultural processes that
such excavations touch off (Hodgkin and Radstone 2003; Aguilar 2008; Ferrándiz 2013). The processes of reevaluating the past, such as those derived
from the registration and scientific exhibition of bodies exhumed from mass
graves, not only correct existing knowledge of historical circumstances but also
pose the crucial question of who holds the power to represent the past in the
present, and on the basis of what repertoires and referents they construct their
narratives in a globalized world. To this end, the pioneering work of Katherine
Verdery's *The Political Lives of Dead Bodies* (1999) is a vital contribution that
provides a road map for analyzing the crossroads of exhumations and the politics of memory. Moreover, the analysis of contemporary exhumations as transnational practices linked to human rights and of their impact on the
constitution of global cosmopolitan memory cannot stem solely from the study
of specific cases but must come from probing the similarities and differences
between diverse processes. This compelling issue relates to Michael Rothberg's
category of multidirectional memory, which does not interpret the different
memories circulating in the public sphere as competitive but rather as engaged
in ongoing negotiations, full of cross-referencing and borrowing (2009:3).
        Several chapters briefly refer to the intersection of exhumations and glo-
balization processes, specifically those linked to the expansion of international human rights paradigms, but its study remains a pending research

agenda. Globalization processes, as described in an extensive literature (see, e.g., Appadurai 1990, 1991; Featherstone 1990; Castells 1996; Hannerz 1996; Beck 1999; Inda and Rosaldo 2002), have had a major impact on spaces, iconographies, circuits, and communities of memory worldwide. In her recent book *Memory in Culture* (2011), Astrid Erll reviews the field of cultural memory studies and points to the proliferation of transnational memory sites, such as those connected with the attacks of 9/11. She emphasizes that cultural memory is gradually breaching local boundaries and the limits of the nation-state to become a global phenomenon. Indeed, recent memory studies indicate a change of direction toward the exploration of a transnational or transcultural dimension, emphasizing an increasing flow, interconnection, and interdependence between countries (Rothberg 2009; Assmann and Conrad 2010; Cronshaw 2011; Levy and Sznaider 2010; Phillips and Reyes 2011). The movement of people, the global influence of political stakeholders and nongovernmental organizations, but above all the impact of the media and social networks have led to memorialist discourses, practices, and repertoires that are becoming ever more interconnected. Local events can have a global impact, while transnational discourse finds local expression. *The Holocaust and Memory in the Global Age* (2006) by the sociologists Daniel Levy and Natan Sznaider is a pioneering work in the field of transnational memory and the theorization of what the authors call cosmopolitan memory. They point to the gradual globalization of memory, holding up as their paradigm the global dissemination and reworking of memory discourse related to the Holocaust. In their view, the Holocaust has become in the early twenty-first century a central political and cultural referent, facilitating the formation of transnational memory cultures with the potential of becoming the cultural cornerstone of a global human rights policy.

Similar considerations can be applied to the increasing interest in unearthing mass graves in different parts of the world, as described in this introduction. The very same globalized processes that affect the nature of the production, circulation, and consumption of social memory are also transforming contemporary human-rights-related exhumations into an increasingly transnational practice. Local processes in Spain, Bosnia, or Argentina resonate with one another, technical protocols backed by the UN and the Red Cross have gained global currency, and unearthing mass graves has become part of diverse but interrelated repertoires of reparation and truth seeking across the world within the transitional justice framework. Also, in iconographic terms, just as pictures of victims prior to their victimization—the images of the *missing*—have become "a widespread, almost epidemic image of tragedy and defiance that is just as much a part of our planetary imagination as the all-pervasive brands and logos, which obviously convey a very different sort of message" (Dorfman 2006: 255; Ferrándiz and Baer 2008), images of exhumed corpses and their postexhumation funerary and political handling in different parts of the world—such as Torres's 2004 Villamayor photographs—are also becoming an integral part of the global visualization of terror.

In the same vein, the anthropological study of specific cases in a comparative model and from a transnational perspective permits the exploration of the interface between global mechanisms and local realities in different historical, social, and cultural contexts, all associated with past violence and in line with the concept of transitional frictions formulated by Hinton (2011) to express the tension between local and global processes of justice. According to Susannah Radstone (2011), it is located engagement with transnational memory that endows memory processes with meaning. Radstone highlights two dimensions of local engagement: first, the location of the researcher and second, the location of memory transmission. Any analysis of the production and circulation of social memory derived from exhumations must recognize the privileged perspective we as scholars gain from the evidence unearthed in these excavations and the processes they set in motion, ranging from the most intimate feelings to the whole repertoire of global justice and redress procedures. This unique perspective on memory politics entails a critical analysis of the negotiation of the bonds between personal and collective memory, private and public, local and embodied, as well as transnational and ephemeral.

This book brings together experts working on mass grave exhumations in different parts of the world to foster comparative and interdisciplinary reflection on these ghastly traces of war and violent conflict. Significantly, we also explore the international tidemarks of exhumations. The book speaks therefore to three overarching issues that require more attention in the ethnography of exhumations: (1) the bifocal conceptualization of contemporary exhumations, both in their local politics and meanings and in the context of transnational human rights practices and transitional justice paradigms; (2) the critical analysis of the role of social, cultural, physical, and forensic anthropology and archaeology in the various processes taking shape around mass grave exhumations; and (3) the exploration of the types of interdisciplinary and collaborative work needed to effectively and critically unpack mass graves' potential for constructing sustainable peace, prominently including memory, reparation, and justice.

Notes

1. See *Corpses of Mass Violence and Genocide* at http://www.corpsesofmassviolence .eu/; accessed on 21 June 2013. See "Post-Conflict and Post-Disaster DNA Identification," *Center for Human Rights Science, Carnegie Mellon University* at http://www.cmu.edu/ chrs/postconflict-postdisaster-dna/, accessed on 21 June, 2013.

2. See the Advocates for Human Rights' web page at http://www.theadvocatesfor humanrights.org/4Jun20046.html, accessed on 3 June, 2013.

Bibliography

Agamben, Giorgio. 1998. *Homo Sacer: Sovereign Power and Bare Life*. Stanford: Stanford University Press.

Aguilar, Paloma. 2008. *Políticas de la memoria y memorias de la política*. Madrid: Alianza.

———. 2013. Judiciary Involvement in Authoritarian Repression and Transitional Justice: The Spanish Case in Comparative Perspective. *International Journal of Transitional Justice* April 23. doi:10.1093/ijtj/ijt008.

Alexander, Jeffrey C. 2002. On the Social Construction of Moral Universals: The "Holocaust" from War Crime to Trauma Drama. *European Journal of Social Theory* 5(1): 5–85.

Alexander, Jeffrey C., et al., eds. 2004. *Cultural Trauma and Collective Identity*. Berkeley: University of California Press.

Anstett, Élisabeth. 2012. La longue vie des fosses communes: Enjeux symboliques et sociaux du traitement des restes humains du Goulag en Russie postsoviétique. In *Cadavres impensables, cadavres impensés: Approches méthodologiques du traitement des corps dans les violences de masse et les génocides*, ed. Élisabeth Anstett and Jean-Marc Dreyfus, 119–132. Paris: Petra.

Anstett, Élisabeth and Jean-Marc Dreyfus, eds. 2012. *Cadavres impensables, cadavres impensés: Approches méthodologiques du traitement des corps dans les violences de masse et les génocides*. Paris: Petra.

Apfelbaum, Erica, Sally Alexander, and Amanda Barnier. 2010. *Memory: Histories, Theories, Debates*. New York: Fordham University Press.

Appadurai, Arjun. 1990. Disjuncture and Difference in the Global Cultural Economy. *Public Culture* 2(2): 1–24.

———. 1991. Global Ethnoscapes: Notes and Queries for a Transnational Anthropology. In *Recapturing Anthropology: Working in the Present*, ed. Richard G. Fox, 191–210. Santa Fe: School of American Research Press.

Assmann, Aleida and Sebastian Conrad. 2010. *Memory in a Global Age: Discourses, Practices and Trajectories*. Basingstoke: Palgrave Macmillan.

Assmann, Jan. 1995. Collective Memory and Cultural Identity. *New German Critique* 65: 125–134.

Baer, Alejandro. 2001. Consuming History and Memory Through Mass Media Products. *European Journal of Cultural Studies* 4(4): 491–501.

Baraybar, José Pablo. 2008. When DNA Is Not Available, Can We Still Identify People? Recommendations for Best Practice. *Journal of Forensic Sciences* 53(3): 533–540.

Beck, Ulrich. 1999. *What Is Globalization?* Cambridge: Polity Press.

Bernad, Clemente. 2011. *Desvelados*. Pamplona: Alkibla.

Binford, Leigh.1996. *The El Mozote Massacre: Anthropology and Human Rights*. Tucson: University of Arizona Press.

Capdevila, Luc and Danièle Voldman. 2006. *War Dead: Western Societies and the Casualties of War*. Edinburgh: Edinburgh University Press.

Caruth, Catherine. 1996. *Unclaimed Experience: Trauma, Narrative and History*. Baltimore: Johns Hopkins University Press.

Castells, Manuel. 1996. *The Information Age: Economy, Society and Culture*. Vol. 1: *The Rise of the Network Society*. Oxford: Blackwell.

Christensen, Angie M. and Christian M. Crowder. 2009. Evidentiary Standards for Forensic Anthropology. *Journal of Forensic Sciences* 54: 1211–1216.

Claverie, Élisabeth. 2011. Réapparaître: Retrouver les corps des personnes disparues pendant la guerre en Bosnie. *Raisons Politiques* 41: 13–31.

Cole, Jennifer. 2001. *Forget Colonialism? Sacrifice and the Art of Memory in Madagascar*. Berkeley: University of California Press.

Cronshaw, Richard, ed. 2011. *Transcultural Memory*. Special issue of *Parallax* 17 (4).

Crossland, Zoë. 2002. Violent Spaces: Conflicts over the Reappearance of Argentina's Disappeared. In *Matériel Culture: The Archaeology of Twentieth Century Conflict*, ed. John Schofield, William Gray, and Collen M. Beck, 115–131. New York: Routledge.

———. 2009. Of Clues and Signs: The Dead Body and Its Evidential Traces. *American Anthropologist* 111(1): 69–80.

———. 2011. The Archaeology of Contemporary Conflict. In *The Oxford Handbook of the Archaeology of Ritual and Religion*, ed. Timothy Insoll, 285–306. Oxford: Oxford University Press.

———. 2013. Evidential Regimes of Forensic Archaeology. *Annual Review of Anthropology* 42: 121–137.

de Greiff, Pablo, ed. 2006. *The Handbook of Reparations*. Oxford: Oxford University Press.

Dorfman, Ariel. 2006. The Missing and Photography: The Uses and Misuses of Photography. In *Spontaneous Shrines and the Public Memorialization of Death*, ed. Jack Santino, 255–260. New York: Palgrave Macmillan.

Dreyfus, Jean-Marc. 2102. Une renationalisation des corps? La Mission française de recherches des cadavres de déportés en Allemagne, 1946–1958. In *Cadavres impensables, cadavres impensés: Approches méthodologiques du traitement des corps dans les violences de masse et les génocides*, ed. Élisabeth Anstett and Jean-Marc Dreyfus, 67–78. Paris: Petra.

Dueñas, Oriol and Queralt Solé. 2012. *El jutge del cementiris clandestins: Josep M. Bertran de Quintana, 1884–1960*. Maçanet de la Selva: Editorial Gregal.

ECAP—GAC—GEZA. 2009. *International Consensus on Minimum Standards for Psychosocial Work in Exhumation Processes for the Search for Disappeared Persons / Consenso Internacional sobre Estándares Mínimos en Trabajo Psicosocial en Procesos de Exhumación y Búsqueda de Personas Desaparecidas.* Guatemala City: ECAP—GAC—GEZA.

Erll, Astrid. 2011. *Memory in Culture.* Basingstoke: Palgrave Macmillan.

Erll, Astrid and Ann Rigney. 2009. *Mediation, Remediation and the Dynamics of Cultural Memory.* Berlin: de Gruyter.

Fassin, Didier and Richard Rechtman. 2009. *The Empire of Trauma: An Inquiry into the Condition of Victimhood.* Princeton: Princeton University Press.

Featherstone, Mike. 1990. *Global Culture: Nationalism, Globalization and Modernity.* London: Sage.

Felman, Shoshana and Dori Laub. 1992. *Testimony: Crises of Witnessing in Literature, Psychoanalysis and History.* New York: Routledge.

Ferrándiz, Francisco. 2006. The Return of Civil War Ghosts: The Ethnography of Exhumations in Contemporary Spain. *Anthropology Today* 22(3): 7–12.

———. 2008. Cries and Whispers: Exhuming and Narrating Defeat in Spain Today. *Journal of Spanish Cultural Studies* 9(2): 177–192.

———. 2010. The Intimacy of Defeat: Exhumations in Contemporary Spain. In *Unearthing Franco's Legacy: Mass Graves and the Recovery of Historical Memory in Spain*, ed. Carlos Jerez-Farrán and Samuel Amago, 304–325. Notre Dame: University of Notre Dame Press.

———. 2013. Exhuming the Defeated: Civil War Mass Graves in 21st-Century Spain. *American Ethnologist* 40(1): 38–54.

———. 2014. *El pasado bajo tierra: Exhumaciones contemporáneas de la Guerra Civil.* Barcelona: Anthropos/Siglo XXI.

Ferrándiz, Francisco and Alejandro Baer. 2008. Digital Memory: The Visual Recording of Mass Grave Exhumations in Contemporary Spain. *Forum Qualitative Sozialforschung/ Forum: Qualitative Social Research* 9(3): Art. 35.

Fondebrider, Luis. 2002. Reflections on the Scientific Documentation of Human Rights Violations. *International Review of the Red Cross* 84(848): 885–891.

Gillis, John R., ed. 1996. *Commemorations: The Politics of National Identity.* Princeton: Princeton University Press.

Hacking, Ian. 1996. Memory Sciences, Memory Politics. In *Tense Past: Cultural Essays in Trauma and Memory*, ed. Paul Antze and Michael Lambek, 67–87. London: Routledge.

Halbwachs, Maurice. 1994 [1925]. *Les cadres sociaux de la mémoire.* Paris: Albin Michel.

Hannerz, Ulf. 1996. *Transnational Connections: Culture, People, Places.* London: Routledge.

Hartman, Geoffrey. 1996. *The Longest Shadow: In the Aftermath of the Holocaust.* Bloomington: Indiana University Press.

Hayner, Priscilla B. 2002. *Unspeakable Truths: Facing the Challenges of Truth Commissions.* New York: Routledge.

Hinton, Alex, ed. 2011. *Transitional Justice: Global Mechanisms and Local Realities After Genocide and Mass Violence.* New Brunswick: Rutgers University Press.

Hodgkin, Katharine and Susannah Radstone, eds. 2003. *Memory, History, Nation: Contested Pasts.* New Brunswick: Transaction.

Hoskins, Andrew. 2009. The Mediatization of Memory. In *Save as . . . Digital Memories,* ed. Joanne Garde-Hansen, Andrew Hoskins, and Anna Reading, 27–44. Basingstoke: Palgrave Macmillan.

Huyssen, Andreas. 2003. *Present Pasts: Urban Palimpsests and the Politics of Memory.* Stanford: Stanford University Press.

Inda, Javier and Renato Rosaldo, eds. 2002. *The Anthropology of Globalization: A Reader.* Oxford: Blackwell.

Jantz, Richard, Erin Kimmerle, and José Pablo Baraybar. 2008. Sexing and Stature Estimation Criteria for Balkan Populations. *Journal of Forensic Sciences* 53(3): 601–605.

Jeffreys, Alec, Maxine J. Allen, Erika Hagelberg, and Andreas Sonnberg. 1992. Identification of the Skeletal Remains of Josef Mengele. *Forensic Science International* 56(1): 65–76.

Jelin, Elizabeth. 2003. *State Repression and the Labors of Memory.* Minneapolis: University of Minnesota Press.

Joyce, Christopher and Eric Stover. 1991. *Witnesses from the Grave: The Stories Bones Tell.* Boston: Little, Brown.

Kaes, Anton. 1990. History and Film: Public Memory in the Age of Electronic Dissemination. *History and Memory* 2(1): 111–129.

Keenan, Thomas and Eyal Weizman. 2012. *Mengele's Skull: The Advent of Forensic Aesthetics.* Berlin: Stenberg Press.

Keough, Mary E., Tal Simmons, and Margaret Samuels. 2004. Missing Persons in Post-conflict Settings: Best Practices for Integrating Psychosocial and Scientific Approaches. *Journal of the Royal Society of the Promotion of Health* 124(6): 271–275.

Klinenberg, Eric. 2002. Bodies that Don't Matter: Death and Dereliction in Chicago. In *Commodifying Bodies,* ed. Nancy Scheper-Hughes and Loïc Wacquant, 121–132. London: Sage.

Komar, Debra. 2003. Lessons from Srebrenica: The Contributions and Limitations of Physical Anthropology in Identifying Victims of War Crimes. *Journal of Forensic Sciences* 48: 1–4.

———. 2008. Is Victim Identity in Genocide a Question of Science or Law? The Scientific Perspective, with Special Reference to Darfur. *Science and Justice* 48: 146–152.

Kritz, Neil J. 1995. *Transitional Justice: How Emerging Democracies Reckon with Former Regimes.* 3 vols. Washington: U.S. Institute of Peace Press.

Kruse, Corinna. 2010. Producing Absolute Truth: *CSI* Science as Wishful Thinking. *American Anthropologist* 112(1): 79–91.

Kwon, Heonik. 2008. *Ghosts of War in Vietnam.* Cambridge: Cambridge University Press.

Lacapra, Dominick. 2001. *Writing History, Writing Trauma.* Baltimore: Johns Hopkins University Press.

Laqueur, 1989. Bodies, Details, and the Humanitarian Narrative. In *New Cultural History*, ed. Lynn Hunt, 176-204. Berkeley: University of California Press.

———. 2002. The Dead Body and Human Rights. In *The Body*, ed. Sean T. Sweeney and Ian Hodder, 75-93. Cambridge: Cambridge University Press.

Levy, Daniel and Natan Sznaider. 2002. Memory Unbound: The Holocaust and the Formation of Cosmopolitan Memory. *European Journal of Social Theory* 5(1):87-106.

———. 2006. *The Holocaust and Memory in the Global Age*. Philadelphia: Temple University Press.

———. 2010. *Human Rights and Memory*. Philadelphia: University of Pennsylvania Press.

Linenthal, Edward T. 1995. *Preserving Memory: The Struggle to Create America's Holocaust Museum*. New York: Viking Penguin.

Mant, Arthur K. 1987. Knowledge Acquired from Post-War Exhumations. In *Death, Decay and Reconstruction: Approaches to Archaeology and Forensic Science*, ed. Andrew Boddington, Andrew N. Garland, and Robert C. Janaway, 65-78. Manchester: Manchester University Press.

Mate, Reyes. 1991. *La razón de los vencidos*. Barcelona: Anthropos.

Mbembe, Achille. 2003. Necropolitics. *Public Culture* 15(1): 11-40.

Minow, Martha. 1998. *Between Vengeance and Forgiveness: Facing History After Genocide and Mass Violence*. Boston: Beacon Press.

Mosse, George L. 1990. *Fallen Soldiers: Reshaping the Memory of the World Wars*. New York: Oxford University Press.

Nora, Pierre. 1989. Between Memory and History: *Les Lieux de memoire*. *Representations* 26: 7-25.

Paperno, Irina. 2001. Exhuming the Bodies of Soviet Terror. *Representations* 75: 89-118.

Paul, Allen. 1991. *Katyn: Stalin's Massacre and the Seeds of Polish Resurrection*. Annapolis: Scribner.

Payne, Leigh A. 2008. *Unsettling Accounts: Neither Truth nor Reconciliation in Confessions of State Violence*. Durham: Duke University Press.

Pérez-Sales, Pau and Susana Navarro. 2007. *Resistencias contra el olvido: Trabajo psicosocial en procesos de exhumaciones*. Barcelona: Gedisa.

Philips, Kendall R. and G. Mitchell Reyes, eds. 2011. *Global Memoryscapes: Contesting Remembrance in a Transnational Age*. Tuscaloosa: University of Alabama Press.

Podlas, Kimberlianne. 2005. "The CSI Effect": Exposing the Media Myth. *Fordham Intellectual Property, Media and Entertainment Law Journal* 16(2): 429-465.

Radstone, Susannah. 2011. What Place Is This? Transcultural Memory and the Locations of Memory Studies. *Parallax* 17(4): 109-123.

Renshaw, Layla. 2007. The Iconography of Exhumation: Representations of Mass Graves from the Spanish Civil War. In *Archaeology and the Media*, ed. Timothy Clack and Marcus Brittain, 237-251. Walnut Creek: Left Coast Press.

———. 2011. *Exhuming Loss: Memory, Materiality and Mass Graves of the Spanish Civil War*. Walnut Creek: Left Coast Press.

Ríos, Luis. 2012. Identificación de restos óseos exhumados de fosas comunes y cementerios de presos del periodo de la Guerra Civil española (1936–1939). PhD thesis. Madrid: Universidad Autónoma de Madrid.

Ríos, Luis, José Ignacio Casado, and Jorge Puente. 2010. Identification Process in Mass Graves from the Spanish Civil War I. *Forensic Science International* 199: e27–e36.

Ríos, Luis, Almudena García-Rubio, Berta Martínez, Andrea Alonso and Jorge Puente. 2012. Identification Process in Mass Graves from the Spanish Civil War II. *Forensic Science International* 219: e4–e9.

Robben, Antonius C.G.M. 2000. State Terror in the Netherworld: Disappearance and Reburial in Argentina. In *Death Squad: The Anthropology of State Terror*, ed. Jeffrey A. Sluka, 91–113. Philadelphia: University of Pennsylvania Press.

———. 2005. *Political Violence and Trauma in Argentina*. Philadelphia: University of Pennsylvania Press.

———. 2012. From Dirty War to Genocide: Argentina's Resistance to National Reconciliation. *Memory Studies* 5(3): 305–315.

Rothberg, Michael. 2009. *Multidirectional Memory: Remembering the Holocaust in the Age of Decolonization*. Stanford: Stanford University Press.

Sanford, Victoria. 2003. *Buried Secrets: Truth and Human Rights in Guatemala*. New York: Palgrave Macmillan.

Sanford, Victoria and Martha Lincoln. 2011. Body of Evidence: Feminicide, Local Justice and Rule of Law in "Peacetime" Guatemala. In *Transitional Justice: Global Mechanisms and Local Realities After Genocide and Mass Violence*, ed. Alex Hinton, 67–91. New Brunswick, NJ: Rutgers University Press.

Sant Cassia, Paul. 2005. *Bodies of Evidence: Burial, Memory and the Recovery of Missing Persons in Cyprus*. Oxford: Berghahn.

Skinner, Mark, Djordje Alempijevic, and Marija Djuric-Srejic. 2003. Guidelines for International Forensic Bio-archaeology Monitors of Mass Grave Exhumations. *Forensic Science International* 134:81–92.

Skinner, Mark and Jon Sterenberg. 2005. Turf Wars: Authority and Responsibility for the Investigation of Mass Graves. *Forensic Science International* 151(2–3): 221–232.

Šlaus, Mario, Davor Strinovic, Nives Pecina-Slaus, Hrove Brkic, Drinko Balicevic, Vedrana Petrovecki, and Tatjana C. Pecina. 2007. Identification and Analysis of Human Remains Recovered from Wells from the 1991 War in Croatia. *Forensic Science International* 171(1): 37–43.

Snow, Clyde, et al. 1984. The Investigation of the Human Remains of the Disappeared in Argentina. *American Journal of Forensic Medicine and Pathology* 5(4): 297–299.

Stover, Eric and Gilles Peress. 1998. *The Graves: Srebrenica and Vukovar*. Zurich: Scalo.

Stover, Eric and Rachel Shigekane. 2002. The Missing in the Aftermath: When Do the Needs of the Victims' Families and International War Crimes Tribunals Clash? *International Review of the Red Cross* 84(848): 845–866.

Teitel, Ruti G. 2000. *Transitional Justice*. Oxford: Oxford University Press.

Theidon, Kimberly. 2012. *Intimate Enemies: Violence and Reconciliation in Peru*. Philadelphia: University of Pennsylvania Press.

Todorov, Tzvetan. 1995. *Les Abus de la mémoire*. Paris: Arléa.

Torchin, Leshu. 2012.*Creating the Witness: Documenting Genocide on Film, Video, and the Internet*. Minneapolis: University of Minnesota Press.

Torres, Francesc. 2007. *Dark Is the Room Where We Sleep/ Oscura en la habitación donde dormimos*. Barcelona: Actar.

———. 2008. The Images of Memory: A Civil Narration of History. *Journal of Spanish Cultural Studies* 9(2): 157–175.

Tyler, Tom R. 2006. Viewing *CSI* and the Threshold of Guilt: Managing Truth and Justice in Reality and Fiction. *Yale Law Journal* 115: 1052–1085.

Verdery, Katherine. 1999. *The Political Lives of Dead Bodies*. New York: Columbia University Press.

Wagner, Sarah E. 2008. *To Know Where He Lies: DNA Technology and the Search for Srebrenica's Missing*. Berkeley: University of California Press.

———. 2011. Identifying Srebrenica's Missing: The "Shaky Balance" of Universalism and Particularism. In *Transitional Justice: Global Mechanisms and Local Realities After Genocide and Mass Violence*, ed. Alex Hinton, 25–48. New Brunswick, NJ: Rutgers University Press.

Weizman, Eyal. 2011. Osteobiography: An Interview with Clyde Snow. *Cabinet* 43: 68–74.

Williams, Paul. 2007. *Memorial Museums: The Global Rush to Commemorate Atrocities*. Oxford: Berg.

Wilson, Richard A. 2006. Afterword to "Anthropology and Human Rights in a New Key": The Social Life of Human Rights. *American Anthropologist* 108(1): 77–83.

Winter, Jay. 1995. *Sites of Memory, Sites of Mourning: The Great War in European Cultural History*. Cambridge: Cambridge University Press.

Young, James. E. 1993. *The Texture of Memory: Holocaust Memorials and Meaning*. New Haven: Yale University Press.

Zelizer, Barbie. 1998. *Remembering to Forget: Holocaust Memory Through the Camera's Eye*. Chicago: University of Chicago Press.

PART I

EXHUMATIONS AS PRACTICE

Chapter 1

Forensic Anthropology and the Investigation of Political Violence

Lessons Learned from Latin America and the Balkans

Luis Fondebrider

The development of forensic anthropology in the investigation of political violence can be attributed in substantial part to systematic case work carried out in Latin America since 1984 and in the Balkans since 1996.[1] The scientific advances were made mostly independently rather than in conjunction because of the different national backgrounds of the investigators, other professionals, and contrasting personal experiences with political violence. Most anonymous and mass graves in Latin America were exhumed by Latin American forensic anthropologists who had personal knowledge of military repression under dictatorial rule. They were taught through hands-on training at home, learned the importance of interviewing the relatives of the victims, and were profoundly formed as professionals by navigating the political perils of their investigations. Sensitized to the complex circumstances, ethics, and politics of forensic work in postauthoritarian societies, they applied their professional insights elsewhere in the world. In contrast, the forensic studies on the Balkans were conducted mainly by English-speaking practitioners who lacked knowledge of the Latin American experiences, and did not have a comprehensive understanding of the unique humanitarian, judicial, and political dimensions of forensic work in postconflict societies. These professionals had until 1996 excavated only individual graves in their own countries, and had therefore little experience with the nuances and implications of investigations in contexts of political violence, which are alternatively designated as humanitarian, human rights, war crimes, or genocide investigations, all of which are but partial and incomplete names that simplify the complexities of such forensic work.

The literature on the origins and current status of the application of forensic anthropology to political violence has increased substantially in the past decade (Haglund 2001; Hunter et al. 2001; Doretti and Fondebrider 2001; Fondebrider 2004; Haglund 2002; Haglund, Connor and Scott 2001; Skinner, Alempijevic, and Djuric-Srejic 2003; Steadman and Haglund 2005; Skinner and Sterenberg 2005; Simmons and Haglund 2005), but the contributions made by Latin American and Anglo-Saxon practitioners are only rarely integrated. One clear example of such lack of coordination is the parallel development of protocols for field practices, laboratory work, and the collection of antemortem data by Latin American and Anglo-Saxon professional communities. Practitioners could build on existing protocols instead of developing procedures anew in each situation. Another example of the absence of international professional communication is that the practices developed in the Balkans are taken as the paramount model for other parts of the world, while the Latin American experiences could have contributed substantially to improve forensic studies in postauthoritarian countries such as Iraq (Bernardi and Fondebrider 2007).

This chapter compares the breakthroughs of Latin American practitioners, in particular by the Argentine Forensic Anthropology Team (EAAF), with later developments by forensic investigators in the Balkans, to demonstrate how a better attunement of the separate professional cultures could further advance forensic anthropology for the investigation of cases of political violence.

Political Violence and the Rise of Forensic Anthropology in Latin America

Figures are tangible evidence and hard to dispute: more than two hundred thousand people were disappeared or were murdered (or both) in Guatemala between 1960 and 1996; fifteen thousand in Argentina between 1976 and 1983; seventy thousand in El Salvador between 1981 and 1991; seventy thousand in Peru between 1980 and 2000; three thousand in Chile between 1973 and 1989; and thousands in Colombia, an estimate that increases daily. These abstract figures refer to real human beings with first and last names, with families and friends still longing to know what has happened to them and, if applicable, demanding to know where the remains are buried, who killed them, and when justice will be brought to those responsible for the crimes.

What were the prevailing modes of operation in these Latin American countries when the massacres occurred? It mainly involved three scenarios: (1) the victim's illegal detention, immediate extrajudicial killing, and disappearance of the body; (2) the victim's kidnapping, transfer to a legal or clandestine detention center, torture, extrajudicial killing, and disappearance of the body; or (3) a confrontation between state security forces and a guerrilla group, resulting in the theft and disappearance of the remains of dead guerrillas. More often than not, the state was the main perpetrator (with the exception of killings in Colombia and Peru). As a result, entire families and communities were terrorized. Families were unable to ascertain the fate of their loved ones and failed to obtain a response from the state to their claims for truth, justice, and reparation, while community members feared that they might also become victims of state terror.

What happened to the remains? The bodies were buried in official cemeteries as John Does; buried in clandestine cemeteries without any identification on the grave, or on croplands, in military compounds, or in ravines; thrown into empty water wells; hurled into the sea or volcanoes from airplanes; incinerated or destroyed with explosives or chemicals.

When Clyde Snow arrived in Argentina in 1984 as part of a scientific delegation organized by the American Association for the Advancement of Science, he knew nothing of this situation. He traveled to Argentina to help family members find and identify the remains of their disappeared loved ones, and thus pioneered the forensic anthropological approach to cases of political violence that soon spread throughout Latin America. Since this initial trip, Clyde Snow repeatedly visited several countries in the same spirit, training young scientists, building a bridge between scientists and searching relatives, and raising an awareness among public authorities that their interests were not at odds with those of the relatives (Joyce and Stover 1991; Snow et al. 1984).

At that time, it was most unusual to speak of forensic anthropology in Latin America because the discipline was largely unknown to judges and prosecutors. Forensic physicians were acquainted with some general forensic notions through legal medicine publications, which used to include a small section with tables and measurements drawn from late nineteenth-century European publications. Physical anthropologists, instead, were better positioned to make osteological analyses of skeletons but were only seldom consulted by official authorities, and there was little interest in incorporating them into forensic circles.[2] The procedure of recovering remains was even less developed since this task was left to police, firefighters, and gravediggers.

To fully grasp the professional context of exhumations in Latin America during the mid-1980s, one must understand the political situation at the time. The same countries that had undergone political violence, causing massive human rights violations, were gradually returning to democracy. The transition to democracy was a complex process during which those responsible for "the disappearances" were free or, in some cases, occupying political positions in the new government. Forensic investigations were therefore from their very beginning conditioned by the following factors: (1) a strong presence of human rights organizations, particularly those involving the relatives of victims; (2) few or no independent forensic institutes, as many had been complicit in the crimes;[3] (3) a lack of information about burial sites; (4) an almost complete disinterest of the academic world in participating in the forensic investigations; (5) a decline of the state's interest in continuing with the investigations after an initial period of support; and (6) an ensuing decline of support from the international community.

Clyde Snow was faced with this political situation at the time of his arrival in Argentina, even though he received ample support from the Argentine authorities and the international community. He began to work with a group of students in archaeology, anthropology, and medicine who later founded the EAAF (Joyce and Stover 1991). Snow's seminal work extended to Chile in 1989 and Guatemala in 1992, thus contributing significantly to the training of independent forensic anthropologists in these three Latin American countries.

The birth of forensic anthropology in Latin America was not the result of an administrative decision or a desire by an anthropology department eager to fulfill its civic duty. On the contrary, the academic community was not interested, and turned its back on the urgent demands of social sectors hit hardest by political violence. This origin is one of the most striking differences between the development of forensic anthropology in Latin America and that in the United States and Europe.

Forensic anthropology in Argentina, Chile, Guatemala, and later Peru was initially promoted to expand its traditional role of identifying skeletons into the forensic examination of victims of political violence. This extension proved to be too limited because there was not only a requirement to recover bodies using a correct procedure but also a need to respond to the demanding political and legal context. Forensic interventions required proper logistics and security, and in particular a harmonious working relation with the victim's relatives and their communities. The awareness that the relatives, rather than the judge or the anthropologists, were the true protagonists of forensic investigations was and continues to be hard for many scientists to understand. Given all these considerations, Latin American forensic anthropologists had to broaden the scope of their investigations, and slowly establish ties with the searching relatives based on mutual trust.

How to build an atmosphere of trust is a capability that goes well beyond the skill of collecting antemortem data, and is generally not taught in forensic training. As apprentice practitioners in the mid-1980s in Argentina, we had to learn how to interact with relatives, understand their doubts and uncertainties, and respect their need for time to come to terms with the exhumation procedure. For example, not all family members were willing to allow an investigation. Sometimes, people were afraid of the political consequences. On other occasions, the perpetrators were still living in the same community, and asking a relative or a witness to point out the gravesite might place the person in danger. For these reasons, we think that it is a mistake to regard the relatives as simple providers of antemortem data or blood samples for DNA analysis. It is a much more complex procedure, entailing hours spent with the relatives to describe the exhumation process, to honestly assess the probability of finding any remains, and to explain the difficulties of identification, but also to listen to their life histories and try to understand how the disappearance of their loved ones affected the family and changed their lives. All these issues are unrelated to the traditional field of forensic anthropology but were important capabilities we had to learn along the way (Doretti and Fondebrider 2004; Doretti and Snow 2003; Stover and Shigekane 2002).

For Latin American forensic anthropology organizations like the EAAF, the preliminary investigation became essential to the case work. The lack of interest of the Argentine judiciary to investigate properly, the absence of state support, and the reluctance of perpetrators to provide information required that from the very start we constructed our own hypotheses about the location of the remains of disappeared people. We could not ask the police or criminal investigators for assistance. They were in many cases part of the same system that had carried out the disappearances. Based on the assumption that perpetrators, especially when they were state officials, left a paper trail of their actions, we started searching cemetery records, death certificate archives, court records, press information, and intelligence reports produced by the army or police. In addition, we interviewed not only the relatives of the victims but also witnesses who had participated in or had seen the killings and burials (Bernardi and Fondebrider 2007; Doretti and Snow 2003; Snow and Bihurriet 1992).

This procedure of investigating cases of political violence has been refined by the EAAF over the last thirty years through forensic work in thirty-five countries and through the creation of a laboratory where dozens of remains are analyzed each year. The Argentine team has since 1992 been recognized by the United Nations as a leader in the field, trained forensic teams and professionals in seven countries, and maintained lasting contact with the victims' relatives. The Guatemalan Forensic Anthropology Foundation (Fundación de Antropología Forense de Guatemala) has been modeled after the EAAF. It is staffed by a large number of full-time anthropologists, equipped with a laboratory, and has two decades of experience in excavating highly complex mass graves and analyzing hundreds of skeletons a year (Steadman and Haglund 2005; and see www.eaaf.org and www.fafg.org).

In Latin America, forensic anthropology is applied to these cases: domestic crimes, mass disasters (aircraft accidents, earthquakes, car bombs, and so on), and political violence (kidnapping or disappearance of persons and executions). The first two scenarios involve forensic anthropologists working for official institutes, for example medico-legal services, judicial police, offices of prosecutors, and police detectives. A number of Latin American countries have incorporated forensic anthropologists in these services. In general, they focus on the analysis of skeletal remains rather than their recovery but they have undoubtedly acquired important case-based knowledge.

The third type has been largely left in the hands of nongovernmental organizations, with notable exceptions such as in Peru and Chile. Why are most of the initiatives from private and not state-run organizations? The two most important reasons are that searching relatives mistrust public agencies to conduct forensic investigations, despite the new democratic wind blowing in the region, and that states have a lack of interest in digging deep into the past.

In addition to the Argentine EAAF and the Guatemalan foundation, there are other organizations that investigate political violence in Latin America, namely the Guatemalan Center for Forensic Analysis and Applied Sciences (Centro de Análisis Forense y Ciencias Aplicadas), the Peruvian Forensic Anthropology Team (Equipo Peruano de Antropología Forense), and the Andean Center for Forensic Anthropology Research (Centro Andino de Investigaciones Antropológico Forenses) in Peru. Similar activities are undertaken by the Specialized Forensic Team (Equipo Forense Especializado) of the Institute of Legal Medicine in Peru under the purview of the Public Ministry. In Colombia, these activities are performed by the Legal Medicine Institute and the Prosecutor's Office, with their own anthropologists, and recently an independent organization was formed called Colombian Interdisciplinary Team for Forensic Work and Psychosocial Services (Equipo Colombiano Interdisciplinario de Trabajo Forense y Asistencia Psicosocial).

This extensive Latin American expertise has developed partly independent of and partly alongside forensic investigations in the Balkans after the violent disintegration of Yugoslavia. In the last fifteen years, many forensic anthropologists of different nationalities have worked in the Balkans, acquiring skills in exhuming and analyzing skeletal remains as well as understanding the importance of developing good working relations with the relatives of the victims.

International Forensic Investigations in the Balkans

The scientific progress made since 1996, when the International Criminal Tribunal for the Former Yugoslavia (ICTY) started its intensive forensic investigations of mass graves in Bosnia, has been enormous on all counts. Hundreds of archaeologists and anthropologists have worked long hours excavating graves and analyzing remains. A great number of these professionals, particularly those from countries lacking experience in this kind of massive investigation of political violence, had to start from basics. They had never seen a real mass grave before or had exhumed only individual graves associated with criminal cases at home. Some had a master's degree in forensic archaeology but were not prepared for fieldwork. They had very seldom worked with contemporary skeletons or were much used to *per mortem* injuries caused by gunshot. They had also been more accustomed to interacting with forensic pathologists. There were nevertheless professionals arriving in Bosnia, and later in Croatia and Kosovo, with experience in cases of political violence. These were professionals (particularly from the United States) who had worked in the recovery of missing U.S. citizens in wars and professionals (from Argentina, Guatemala, and Colombia) for whom working in mass graves and analyzing remains were ordinary rather than exceptional experiences.

The contributions to forensic anthropology made by the exhumations in the Balkans began in 1996 with the involvement of Physicians for Human Rights (PHR). PHR had been founded in 1986 after U.S. physicians had successfully intervened on behalf of political prisoners during human rights missions to Chile, Guatemala, South Korea, and the Philippines.[4] Its forensic program was directed initially by Robert Kirshner and later by William Haglund. Eric Stover had participated in the 1984 delegation of the American Association for the Advancement of Science to Argentina and played a major role in developing its international forensic program as executive director of PHR until his retirement in 1995. By 1996, PHR had conducted forensic missions to Croatia, Mexico, Guatemala, Honduras, and Rwanda. Instead of using its own team of forensic anthropologists, PHR's forensic program is presided over by a forensic specialist who recruits anthropologists and other professionals from different countries for each specific mission. Once the mission is finished, specialists return to their countries of residence. PHR began its longest and most significant project in 1996 in Bosnia upon the request of the ICTY.

PHR recruited a large group of experts from different countries, including me and other Latin American forensic anthropologists. For most forensic anthropologists who traveled to Croatia and Bosnia in 1996 and 1997, however, this was their first confrontation with a mass grave and their first analysis of the skeletal remains of different populations. Many of the pathologists, radiologists, and crime-scene investigators had never investigated these kinds of cases where the state was responsible for the killing of large numbers of people. It was not a typical mass disaster, such as an airplane crash. Here, the perpetrators went free, the bodies were hidden in mass graves, and thousands of families were involved. Very few of these scientists realized that they were not properly prepared for the investigation of cases of political violence. In contrast to what Clyde Snow had emphasized in Latin America since 1984, these first years in Bosnia were characterized by a very technical approach, almost without cultivating contacts between practitioners and families. Some time later, the ICTY decided to contract its own forensic specialist, José Pablo Baraybar from Peru, who opened the path for another important contingent of anthropologists, mainly from Latin America, the United States, and the United Kingdom, to work in the Balkans.

Also in 1996, the International Commission on Missing Persons was created, with a strong emphasis on the use of DNA analysis to identify remains. Several years later, it began to hire anthropologists for the recovery and identification of remains from mass graves. A synergy developed in the late 1990s among forensic anthropologists working at the same time for the ICTY, PHR, and the International Commission in Bosnia that produced some of the most interesting articles about the exhumation and analysis of mass graves (e.g., Baraybar and Marek 2006; Haglund 2002; Komar 2003; Skinner et al. 2003; Skinner and Sterenberg 2005; Tuller and Duric 2006; Tuller, Hofmeister, and Daley 2008).

In 2001, the British NGO Inforce was founded to provide forensic expertise to organizations and governments (www.inforce.org.uk). This organization is staffed mostly by British scientists who have been trained in forensic anthropology and archaeology, and who gained practical experience in the Balkans between 1996 and 2001 working for PHR, ICTY, or the International Commission. To date, Inforce has worked in the Balkans, Cyprus, and Iraq, and one of its members participated in a mission to the Democratic Republic of Congo in 2003 coordinated by EAAF.

In 2002, the United Nations Interim Administration Mission in Kosovo created the Office on Missing Persons and Forensics at the Department of Justice, with the objective of determining the whereabouts of missing persons, identifying their remains, and returning these to their families. The office was also assigned to establish a medical examiner's office to provide medico-legal forensic examinations according to international standards and to build local institutional capacity to carry out this work.[5] Aside from the major advances in forensic anthropology because of the concentration of international experts in the region, there were also several negative experiences, including ill-prepared local and international agencies that applied ad hoc protocols.

The lack of coordination among the multiple forensic groups in the Balkans resulted in numerous problems with the identification and reanalysis of the remains. This regrettable and even unethical situation created uncertainty among the relatives about the forensic investigations. As a result, the International Committee of the Red Cross launched the Missing Project.[6] This important initiative promotes *the right to know* by relatives of deliberately disappeared people around the world, and promotes the raising of standards of the legal, humanitarian, psychological, and scientific aspects of forensic work. It draws important lessons from experiences gained in the Balkans and other parts of the world, such as Latin America, where forensic science has been used for three decades to investigate cases of missing people.

This brief historical overview illustrates that, with the exception of the EAAF and PHR, the above-mentioned organizations have focused their activities mainly on the Balkans. Consequently, the great majority of forensic anthropologists who have been working for the last fifteen years in applying their disciplines to cases of political violence have done so almost exclusively in this region of the world.[7] Many influential publications on the application of forensic anthropology to political violence are therefore limited to this local experience. The combination of forensic insights from the Balkans with those of Latin America would yield a major step forward.

Conclusion

Forensic anthropology first began to be applied to investigations of political violence in Argentina in 1984, an approach that then spread to other countries in Latin America, to Asia, Africa, and the Balkans. Due to the characteristics of the Latin American situation, forensic anthropology amplified from a confined technical profile (recovery and analysis of human remains) common in countries such as the United States and the United Kingdom into a much broader discipline that encompassed the three main subfields of anthropology: social anthropology, archaeology, and physical anthropology.

This approach offered a much wider perspective to the investigator whose principal achievement was the incorporation of the relatives of the disappeared and their communities into the forensic investigation. Legal proceedings began to take cultural and religious aspects into account, and thus paid attention to the wishes of those affected by violence, and provided more credibility and transparency. This involvement of family members and survivors of violence in legal and forensic investigations is perhaps the most important contribution made by Latin American forensic anthropologists to the discipline.

Notes

1. Forensic investigations began in the Balkans in 1992 when the United Nations appointed the Commission of Experts, assisted by Physicians for Human Rights (PHR), but extensive investigations did not start until 1996 when the International Criminal Tribunal for the Former Yugoslavia (ICTY) commissioned PHR to conduct the forensic exhumations and allow the recruitment of large numbers of scientists.

2. In this brief summary, the pioneering work of José Vicente Rodríguez from Colombia deserves to be mentioned for his training of young generations of Colombian forensic anthropologists.

3. In most Latin American countries, forensic experts form part of the judicial system, the prosecutor's office, and the security forces.

4. See http://physiciansforhumanrights.org/about/history.html, accessed on February 22, 2013.

5. Also it should be mentioned that apart from the organizations mentioned above, local governments in Bosnia, Croatia, and Republica Srpksa exhumed graves, in some cases with advice or participation of foreign scientists.

6. See http://www.icrc.org/eng/resources/documents/publication/p0897.htm, accessed on February 22, 2013.

7. One of the exceptions is the participation of several forensic anthropologists since 2001 in investigations in East Timor, under the direction of the United Nations Serious Crimes Investigation Unit.

Bibliography

Baraybar, José Pablo and Gasior Marek. 2006. Forensic Anthropology and the Most Probable Cause of Death in Cases of Violations Against International Humanitarian Law: An Example from Bosnia and Herzegovina. *Journal of Forensic Sciences* 51(6):103–108.

Bernardi, Patricia and Luis Fondebrider. 2007. Forensic Archaeology and the Scientific Documentation of Human Rights Violations: An Argentinean Example from the Early 1980s. In *Forensic Archaeology and the Investigation of Human Rights Abuses*, ed. R. Ferllini, 205–232. Springfield, IL: Charles C. Thomas.

Doretti, Mercedes and Luis Fondebrider. 2001. Science and Human Rights: Truth, Justice, Reparation and Reconciliation: A Long Way in Third World Countries. In *Archaeologies of the Contemporary Past*, ed. V. Buchli and L. Gavin, 138–144. London: Routledge.

———. 2004. Perspectives and Recommendations from the Field: Forensic Anthropology and Human Rights in Argentina. *Proceedings of the 56th Annual Meeting of the Academy of Forensic Sciences*, Feb. 16–21, Dallas, Texas.

Doretti, Mercedes and Clyde Snow. 2003. Forensic Anthropology and Human Rights: The Argentine Experience. In *Hard Evidence: Case Studies in Forensic Anthropology*, ed. D. W. Steadman, 290–310. Upper Saddle River, NJ: Prentice Hall.

Fondebrider, Luis. 2004. *Uncovering the Evidence: The Forensic Sciences in Human Rights*. Minneapolis: Center for Victims of Torture.

Haglund, William D. 2001. Archaeology and Forensic Death Investigations. *Historical Archaeology* 35:26–34.

———. 2002. Recent Mass Graves, an Introduction. In *Advances in Forensic Taphonomy: Method, Theory and Archaeological Perspectives*, ed. W. D. Haglund and M. H. Sorg, 243–262. Boca Raton: CRC Press.

Haglund, William D., Melissa Connor, and Douglas D. Scott. 2001. The Archaeology of Contemporary Mass Graves. *Historical Archaeology* 35:57–69.

Hunter, John R., M. B. Brickley, J. Bourgeois, W. Bouts, L. Bourguignon, F. Hubrecht, J. DeWinne, H. van Haaster, T. Hakbijl, H. de Jong, L. Smits, L.H. van Wijngaarden, and M. Luschen. 2001. Forensic Archaeology, Forensic Anthropology and Human Rights in Europe. *Science and Justice* 4:173–178.

Joyce, Christopher and Eric Stover. 1991. *Witnesses from the Grave: The Stories Bones Tell.* Boston: Little, Brown.

Komar, Debra. 2003. Lessons from Srebrenica: The Contributions and Limitations of Physical Anthropology in Identifying Victims of War Crimes. *Journal of Forensic Science* 48(4):713–716.

Simmons, Tal and William D. Haglund. 2005. Anthropology in a Forensic Context. In *Advances in Forensic Archaeology*, ed. J. R. Hunter and M. Cox, 159–176. New York: Routledge.

Skinner, Mark, Djordje Alempijevic, and Marija Djuric-Srejic. 2003. Guidelines for International Forensic Bio-archaeology Monitors of Mass Grave Exhumations. *Forensic Science International* 134:81–92.

Skinner, Mark and Jon Sterenberg. 2005. Turf Wars: Authority and Responsibility for the Investigation of Mass Graves. *Forensic Science International* 151:221–232.

Snow, Clyde, et al. 1984. The Investigation of the Human Remains of the Disappeared in Argentina. *American Journal of Forensic Medicine and Pathology* 5(4): 297–299.

Snow, Clyde and Maria Julia Bihurriet. 1992. An Epidemiology of Homicide: Ningun Nombre Burials in the Province of Buenos Aires 1970 to 1984. In *Human Rights and Statistics: Getting the Record Straight*, ed. T. B. Jabine and C. P. Claude, 328–363. Philadelphia: University of Pennsylvania Press.

Steadman, Dawnie Wolfe and William D. Haglund. 2005. The Scope of Anthropological Contributions to Human Rights Investigations. *Journal of Forensic Sciences* 50(1):1–8.

Stover, Eric and Rachel Shigekane. 2002. The Missing in the Aftermath of War: When Do the Need of Victims' Families and International War Crimes Tribunals Clash? *International Review of the Red Cross* 84(848):845–866.

Tuller, Hugh and Marija Duric. 2006. Keeping the Pieces Together: A Comparison of Mass Grave Excavation Methodology. *Forensic Science International* 156:192–200.

Tuller, Hugh, Ute Hofmeister, and Sharna Daley. 2008. Spatial Analysis of Mass Grave Mapping Data to Assist in the Re-association of Disarticulated and Commingled Human Remains. In *Recovery, Analysis, and Identification of Commingled Human Remains*, ed. B. Adams and J. Byrd, 7–30. Totowa, NJ: Humana Press.

Chapter 2

Exhumations, Territoriality, and Necropolitics in Chile and Argentina

Antonius C. G. M. Robben

"The people of Santiago must remain inside their homes to avoid [being] innocent victims"; so ordered the Chilean military authorities on September 11, 1973, the day of the coup d'état against President Salvador Allende (Montealegre Iturra 2003:21). Hours before daybreak a naval uprising had taken place in the port of Valparaiso but Allende and fifty loyal supporters remained inside the presidential palace in Santiago, unwilling to surrender. Traffic barriers were placed in the city center, tanks surrounded the building by ten o'clock, and Hawker-Hunter jets began firing missiles at La Moneda Palace shortly before noon. Allende had been offered a safe conduct abroad by General Augusto Pinochet but he decided to take his own life instead. A state of siege was declared. The army raided locations where suspected guerrilla insurgents and leftist opponents might be hiding, and tens of thousands of civilians were penned up in soccer stadiums after being detained in factories, universities, slums, and government buildings; others were disappeared (Ensalaco 2000:23–30; National Commission 1993 1:130–131, 147–149).

A similar scenario unfolded in neighboring Argentina two and a half years later on March 24, 1976, when at 3:21 A.M. the news media announced: "It is communicated to the population that starting from today the country is under the operational control of the Junta of General Commanders of the Armed Forces. . . . All inhabitants must abstain from gathering in public places" (Graham-Yooll 1989:417). President María Estela Martínez de Perón had been detained two hours earlier. The presidential palace and Congress were taken over by army units, and the military authorities declared a nocturnal curfew, travel restrictions, roadblocks, and sealed national borders (Dearriba 2001:257–268).

The Chilean and Argentinean dictatorships territorialized state repression. Chile was divided into thirteen security regions, and the military took control of the nation's capital with roadblocks, street patrols, and helicopter surveillance. The repression in Argentina was organized into five defense zones, which were further divided into subzones, areas, and subareas. This control emanated from the adaptation of the three fundamental Clausewitzean objectives of classical warfare to counterinsurgency warfare and state terrorism, namely the destruction of enemy forces, the occupation of territory, and the breaking of the enemy's will (Clausewitz 1984 [1832]:90). Guerrilla combatants and their supporters, militant unionists, government employees, and members of the heterogeneous political left were executed, imprisoned, disappeared, assassinated, or forced into exile, while torture and a culture of fear served to discourage armed violence and political activity. National territories were occupied with regular troops, while specialized task forces conducted abductions and inflicted terror on the population, true to the etymological origins of the word *territory*.

The word *territory* derives not only from the root *terra*, soil, indicating why Romans talked about a township as a *terrātōrium*, but also from *terrēre*, to frighten and terrorize. Combining these two etymological roots, the word *territōrium* referred to "a place from which people were warned off" (*OED* 2nd ed., s.v. "territory"). An area becomes a territory through the exercise of power. In the Chilean and Argentinean political context, this meant that the national territory was to be cleansed of so-called subversives. On the day of the Chilean coup, the air force commander, General Gustavo Leigh Guzmán, said about the Allende government that the armed forces had been "bearing the Marxist cancer" for three years but "that the great majority of the Chilean people is with us, that it is ready to fight communism, that it is ready to extirpate it, whatever the cost" (Ensalaco 2000:49). In Argentina, the military junta declared that the coup "is aimed at ending misrule, corruption, and the scourge of subversion" (Loveman and Davies 1989:197), while General Díaz Bessone compared the guerrilla organizations to "strange bodies" that had to be extirpated "however hard the surgery may be" (*La Nación*, October 23, 1976). Subversives had to die to make life safe and worthy again for ordinary law-abiding citizens and protect national interests against foreign domination and alien ideologies, so went the reasoning.

If state sovereignty is defined in terms of necropower, or the power to rule over life and death in exceptional situations (Agamben 1998:8; Foucault 1998:135; Mbembe 2003; Das and Poole 2004), then its counterpart is territoriality, or the absolute dominion over national territory. "Space was therefore the raw material of sovereignty and the violence it carried with it," Mbembe argues (2003:26). The Argentinean and Chilean dictatorships were concerned with cleansing the country of contaminating political and cultural forces, represented as cancers and viruses. The repressive state powers were manifested in the ubiquitous penetration of public, political, and domestic space by the armed forces, and the ensuing extermination of armed and political opponents. Graves filled with the enemy dead literally embodied the relationships between territory, necropower, and sovereignty for the military rulers, including the sovereignty over territorial waters in which bodies were dropped.

The Chilean and Argentinean dictatorships seem to be exemplary illustrations of sovereignty operating with unlimited power during a "state of exception." Under the influence of Agamben (1998, 2005), this conceptualization of sovereignty, framed in a critical discourse, has become hegemonic in the anthropological interpretation and representation of the state. Jennings (2011) has persuasively questioned this naturalization of sovereignty and its assumption that a political life independent of sovereign authority is ultimately impossible. He emphasizes that the sovereign state is a product of modernity, and finds a conceptual alternative in the political philosophy of Hannah Arendt, who "understood that it is only in a political community that there exists the possibility for people to live outside of subjecthood, whether to private power, tyranny or sovereignty" (Jennings 2011:43). Arendt (1958:198) regarded the Greek polis as such a political community free from the coercion of sovereign power: "The *polis*, properly speaking, is not the city-state in its physical location; it is the organization of the people as it arises out of acting and speaking together, and its true space lies between people living together for this purpose, no matter where they happen to be." The creation of a political community curbs the sovereign's power, defined mistakenly by Agamben as boundless, because "power springs up between men when they act together and vanishes the moment they disperse" (Arendt 1958:200). The Chilean and Argentinean military tried therefore to prevent people from uniting, acting, and communicating beyond their authoritarian reach by means of the supervision of schools, the media, and the arts, the control of the national territory, and the prohibition of public gatherings other than military parades, religious masses, and pilgrimages (Robben 2005b:81–85).

Having won the violent dispute over sovereign power with the guerrilla insurgency and having silenced and disbanded the leftist opposition, the dictatorship felt confident about being able to control human rights protests. Instead, the moral appeal to information about the disappeared, and the incessant demand for the right of habeas corpus, forged an unstoppable social movement that based its public claims on the affectional bond of blood relatives. This movement did not recognize the dictatorship's legitimacy, was ultimately not intimidated by state terror, and negated its necropolitical sovereignty. This essay argues therefore that the exhumation of mass graves reclaimed national territory from military occupation and undermined the dictatorship's power over life and death. The forensic identification of the exhumed acknowledged the victims of state terrorism and crimes against humanity, reframed national memory, and dismantled necropower by holding perpetrators accountable.

The forensic methodologies in Chile and Argentina hardly vary, but exhumations have different meanings in the two countries because of other repressive pasts, power configurations, civil-military relations, and memory politics.[1] Mass graves generated different power struggles, and exhumations led to other political and legal consequences. This chapter analyzes the incompatible political and symbolic meanings of mass graves for the military, the state, and bereaved relatives of the Southern Cone, and demonstrates how democratic state sovereignty and citizenship are reclaimed by dissolving the territoriality and necropolitics exercised by the military through the exhumation of the burial places of disappeared and executed civilians. Territoriality and necropower were the Janus-faced manifestations of lawless sovereignty that intended to control the circulation of people and ideas in and also between the two countries. Here, I will elaborate territoriality in Argentina and necropower in Chile, rather than analyzing them together in both countries, to be able to enter into more detail about their devastating impact on society.

Mass Graves and State Sovereignty

The discovery in 1979 of fifteen bodies at an abandoned limestone quarry in Lonquén, Chile, and the opening in 1982 of a mass grave near Buenos Aires with hundreds of bodies were shocking events.[2] These mass graves made "visible a formerly neglected cartography of terror and repression that encompasses many landscapes and localities throughout the country," as Francisco Ferrándiz (2010:311–312) has written about mass graves from the Spanish Civil War. Mass graves in the Southern Cone also functioned to occult massacres, destroy incriminating evidence, prevent martyrdom, and deny the bereaved relatives their mourning and their dead a proper mortuary ritual. Ferrándiz argues further that each opened mass grave confronted people with violated human remains, resignified the past through extensive media coverage, reordered national space through the creation of commemorative landmarks, and redrew collective memory with the testimonies of witnesses and survivors. Rojas and Silva Bustón (2009:618) aptly call this process "the territorialization of memory" in their analysis of the transformation of a Chilean torture center into a national monument. Or as Victoria Sanford (2003:18) has written about Guatemalan mass graves: "The exhumation demands a coming to terms with space: physical space for the excavation, public space for memory, political space created by the exhumation, and the individual and collective giving of testimonies, each of which creates new space." Mass graves carry different meanings and memories for perpetrators and bereaved relatives, and their exhumation resignifies them. The three principal symbolic meanings of mass graves and anonymous burials mirrored for the Chilean and Argentinean military the Clausewitzean objectives of war: the annihilation of the insurgency and political Left, the reconquest of national territory, and the incapacitation of political agency.

The dead and disappeared symbolized for the authoritarian regimes first of all a victory over an enemy regarded as a threat to state sovereignty. The anonymous burial of the executed and disappeared entailed their physical, social, political, legal, and spiritual eradication. They were not acknowledged as fellow citizens, as legitimate members of the polity, or as interlocutors about the country's future. They were therefore not entitled to a ritual that would reincorporate them into society as deceased members. Evil deserved to be buried in anonymity, thus epitomizing the inhumanity of the dead. In fact, the coexistence in space of anonymous graves and ordinary grave sites in cemeteries enhanced the classification of the dead into opposed groups.

This symbolic meaning evoked a countersymbolism among bereaved relatives. The clandestine graves manifested the commitment and sacrifice of loved ones fighting with political and military means against poverty and social inequality, irrespective of the risks involved. The unceremonial abandonment of these patriots in unhallowed soil was emotionally and politically intolerable, and mobilized deep feelings of trust and protection. If parents harbored any guilt feelings about having been unable to protect their children from abduction or execution, and could not comfort them in the hour of death, then the only obligation pending was to give them an honorable burial (Robben 2005a). It was therefore important for relatives to support national genetic data banks, collect blood samples, and allow for the exhumation of anonymous graves.[3] Exhumations uncover a deliberately buried past by showing the forensic evidence of violently broken ribs or skulls impacted by bullets. Recovered remains could then be restored to their proper place in human society through mortuary rituals. The offer of Chilean and Argentinean forensic anthropologists to lay out an identified skeleton anatomically on a table in the presence of the bereaved family symbolizes the restoration of the body in rest before being awakened on resurrection day (Caiozzi 1998).

The second symbolic meaning of mass graves for the military was to mark the territorial reconquest of Chile and Argentina. Judeo-Christian culture defines the relation between territory and death by burying the dead in cemeteries. Cemeteries have "four interlinked features: physical characteristics; ownership and meaning; the site's relationship to personal and community identities; and sacredness" (Rugg 2000:272). The mausoleums of the patriotic men and women who died for national causes, located in Santiago's General Cemetery and La Recoleta in Buenos Aires, are the most prominent expressions of such connection to native soil. Clandestine graves invert this relationship. They are invisible, lack property rights, negate spiritual, religious, and political meanings about death and resurrection, destroy individual and group identities through the jumble of skeletal remains, and withhold the dead their ritual burial and enduring remembrance. Paradoxically, the symbolic significance of anonymous graves as territorial markers rested for the military regimes thus precisely on being known to perpetrators and hidden to the rest of society (Robben 2011).

The disappeared and unclaimed dead in Chile and Argentina were for the perpetrators enduring reminders of their territorial hold. Some perpetrators might have been troubled by remorse or, with the distance of time, regarded the assassinations as a stain on their military honor. Others might have taken refuge in denial, and some were openly content, while many probably rejoiced privately about the successful extermination. Perpetrators would be reminded of their past deeds as they drove by the hidden mass graves on their way to work or on vacation. The secret burial sites are therefore inconspicuous monuments to the country's reconquest. This interpretation of mass graves derives from the earliest Spanish meaning of the word *monument* (*el monumento*) as a place of burial (*el sepulcro*) or a memorial to a heroic act (*OED* 2nd ed., s.v. "monument"). Just as the severed heads and limbs of defeated war lords were displayed in town squares throughout Chile and Argentina to mark victory during the nineteenth-century civil wars (Robben 2000), so the mass graves during the military juntas of the 1970s and 1980s staked their claim to the fatherland. The burial of the dead in marked anonymous graves in cemeteries and the secret burials in undisclosed mass and individual graves express the two sides of sovereignty: necropower and territoriality. The appropriation of life and land through secret inhumations were mnemonic markers of an authoritarian sovereignty that even included remote corners of the Chilean Andes and the tributaries and waters of the Atlantic and Pacific Oceans where dead bodies or sedated disappeared were dropped.

The human rights organizations of the Southern Cone undermined the military's necropolitics as short of being absolute, and undid the appropriation of national territory deemed total, by reburying exhumed remains and erecting hundreds of memorials and monuments to the victims of state terrorism. Sites of memory narrate people's suffering and reinsert the remembrance of past repression in the public domain. Hundreds of memorial plaques, street, square, and park names, school, library, and hospital names, murals, crosses, photographs, monoliths, and monuments are now dotting Chile and Argentina to show that the military's political hold over national territory has ended (Hoppe 2007; Memoria Abierta 2009).

Finally, the mass graves symbolized for the military a disabling of the political movements, grassroots organizations, and armed insurgencies. The disappearance of guerrilla combatants was intended to demoralize the insurgents because they did not know whether their missing comrades had deserted, had defected, were being tortured for information, or had been assassinated. The disappearance of political opponents served to restructure Chilean and Argentinean society and spread a culture of fear intended to terrorize people into political paralysis. Furthermore, the military also assumed that relatives of the disappeared would either remain passive not to endanger other family members or would be so occupied by the search that they would refrain from any political activity. The mass graves symbolized for perpetrators therefore the subjection of civil society to the authoritarian state.

The Chilean and Argentinean military did not foresee that the disappearances would give rise to oppositional human rights movements they could not dominate, and that the discovery of mass graves would lead to persistent calls for accountability. The emotional bond between parents and children proved stronger than military repression. Protest was more than reactive resistance but employed both proven and new forms of political action. Organized protest began in Chile with the founding of the Group of Families of Detained-Disappeared in 1974, while the Argentinean mothers of the Plaza de Mayo became in 1977 the public face of a human rights movement that had been working in less visible ways since 1975 (Garcés and Nicholls 2005; Robben 2005b). Not to let down the struggle for truth and justice was an emotional, moral, and political imperative. Their fight for accountability proved eventually successful because hundreds of perpetrators have been convicted in Chile and Argentina since 2006.

Chile and Argentina have had on the one hand secret individual and mass graves in and beyond cemeteries, and on the other hand individual and mass graves in cemeteries marked by visible signs or registered in cemetery records. Anonymous graves marked with the initials "NN" (*Nomen Nescio* or No Name) differ from concealed graves by their state of suspended reburial until the known remains can be exhumed and identified. These two types of burial sites have other meanings for the military and the bereaved relatives in the two countries. Both countries used the existing necroadministration of cemeteries to bury or cremate bodies for functional reasons, such as accessibility and the requirements of infrastructure. Occasionally, bodies were interred in mass graves beyond cemeteries, while the disposal of bodies through air drops was common in both countries.

The next two sections analyze territoriality in Argentina and necropower in Chile. I first describe the exhumation of a mass grave in Córdoba, and then analyze how the 1989 exhumation and identification of the disappeared adolescent Norberto Morresi disintegrated this dominion through relentless memory politics and calls for accountability. The second section analyzes the troubled exhumation and sabotage of the marked burial site Patio 29 in Santiago, Chile, and the botched identification of Fernando de la Cruz Olivares Mori as prolongations of authoritarian necropolitics during democratic times.

Territoriality and Clandestine Graves in Argentina

Dead bodies marked by signs of violence began appearing along streets, roads, riverbanks, and beaches of Argentina immediately after the military took power on March 24, 1976. Mutilated bodies washed ashore along the Uruguayan coast and were recovered from the Paraná River. Some dead had been killed in armed confrontations between insurgents and the military but most had been assassinated in secret torture and detention centers, such as La Perla in Córdoba. In Córdoba, Francisco Rubén Bossio witnessed in 1976 the delivery of large numbers of dead by police and military at the Judicial Morgue: "These corpses had the following characteristics: they had bullet wounds, some with a lot of perforations, sometimes so many as eighty, sometimes seventeen, for example. They all had painted fingers and bore clear marks of torture. They had marks on their hands as if they had been tied with cords. From time to time one would appear completely torn to pieces, split open" (CONADEP 1986 [1984]:232). So many bodies arrived at the Córdoba morgue that mass transfers to San Vicente Cemetery were undertaken (Cohen Salama 1992:125).

The disappearance, death, and disposal of abducted captives from the Córdoba region through La Perla, the Judicial Morgue, and San Vicente Cemetery illustrate the territorialization of repression. La Perla was housed at the Fourth Airborne Transport Company base, near Córdoba, and pertained to Area 311 located in Subzone 31 of Defense Zone 3 (Mittelbach 1986:89–94). Argentina had been organized into five defense zones (*zonas de defensa*); four were commanded by the four army corps commanders, while the nation's capital, Buenos Aires, was the fifth zone that fell under Military Institutes that housed the officers' academies. The five defense zones were divided into nineteen subzones and these were subdivided into 117 areas, and some even further into subareas. Areas and subareas were the operational terrain of task forces that abducted the disappeared (Robben 2005b:193–197). Each area had one or more secret detention centers, and the disposal of the dead generally took place in the corresponding area or subarea. Most of the assassinated disappeared were interred in marked anonymous individual graves and a few mass graves at cemeteries. Only three mass graves have been located on military and police premises, but no mass graves are known to exist in open fields. When the decision was taken not to bury the assassinated disappeared, the bodies were cremated at cemeteries or incinerated in pits and oil drums. Other disappeared destined to die were sedated and dropped alive from planes flying over the Atlantic Ocean (CONADEP 1986 [1984]:221–225; Dandan 2010; interview with Luis Fondebrider on July 1, 2011). Around ten thousand assassinated disappeared persons have been documented. Forensic anthropologists assume that fifteen thousand people were assassinated, but the Argentinean human rights movement claims that as many as thirty thousand disappeared were murdered.

The December 1983 turn to democracy made room for many exhumations ordered at the request of courts, but these early exhumations were frustrating for the relatives because they were carried out without the proper forensic techniques that could have yielded positive identifications. In 1984, the American forensic anthropologist Clyde Snow trained a group of Argentinean anthropology and medical students who founded the Argentine Forensic Anthropology Team or EAAF (Equipo Argentino de Antropología Forense) in 1986 (Cohen Salama 1992:147–150; CONADEP 1986 [1984]:311).

The first exhumation at Córdoba's San Vicente Cemetery was conducted in March 1984. It turned out to be Argentina's largest mass grave, measuring 25 by 2.5 meters and 3.5 meters deep and containing a roughly estimated 400 dead. The exhumation was done with a power shovel. The skeletal remains were put into bags, separate from the skulls. Snow examined twenty skulls and the dental records deposited at the Judicial Morgue in May 1984, but he was only able to identify twenty-five-year old Cristina Costanzo (Cohen Salama 1992:124–130). The San Vicente mass grave was finally exhumed properly by the EAAF in 2003 under trying forensic circumstances. The 1984 excavation had destroyed part of the mass grave, and thirty-three bags with remains were missing. The new exhumation recovered 123 bodies, of which around one-third corresponded to mostly young persons assassinated during the 1976–1983 dictatorship. The remaining two-thirds consisted of much older anonymous persons without signs of violent death, including four bodies with signs of leprosy who came most likely from a lazaret adjoining the cemetery. The tossing together of assassinated captives, abandoned aged, and lepers in the San Vicente mass grave demonstrates how the "subversives" were categorized as nonpersons who did not require any mortuary ritual. The exhumations continued into 2004, recovering over 300 bodies, of which 56 were most likely disappeared persons. A total of 14 individuals had been identified by 2009 (EAAF 2007:40–52, 2011:68; Olmo 2005).

The reburial of identified remains was a mortuary ritual for family members, the commemoration of all disappeared for the mourners, and a political act for human rights activists motivating them to fight for the accountability of perpetrators and demonstrate that the assassinations had been politically motivated. Exhumations and reburials thus undermined the three symbolic military meanings of mass graves, namely victory, territorial control, and the incapacitation of political agency. The following analysis of the disappearance, assassination, and clandestine inhumation in 1976 of Norberto Morresi, and his forensic exhumation, positive identification, and reburial in 1989 demonstrate the three countersymbolic meanings that increasingly took their place.

Norberto Morresi was a seventeen-year-old noncombatant member of the forbidden Union of High School Students (Unión de Estudiantes Secundarios) linked to the Montoneros guerrilla organization. He was caught in Buenos Aires on April 23, 1976, by troops of the First Army Corps, together with the thirty-four-year old Luis María Roberto, when they were distributing the illegal magazine *Evita Montonera*. They were executed on the spot, placed in their Chevrolet station wagon, and set ablaze. The police found the car with the partially torched bodies, took fingerprints, and buried them as unidentified persons (Robben 2005b:267). Argentinean forensic anthropologists exhumed and identified the remains in June 1989.

The Roman Catholic funeral on July 7, 1989, demonstrates the first symbolic meaning of mass graves for the parents of Norberto Morresi and the widow of Luis María Roberto. The two dead were incorporated into society as deceased members and the transition from their earthly existence to the hereafter was accomplished through a mortuary ritual. The political significance of this reburial was revealed not only by the presence of many members of the human rights movement but especially by the joint burial of the skeletal remains in one niche of a large raised tomb at the Bajo Flores Cemetery (Cohen Salama 1992:228–232). When I interviewed Julio Morresi in 1991 he spoke of his son's idealism, how he had worked in the slums of Buenos Aires and had convinced teenagers to abandon their drug use and attend school again. The identification and reburial of their son had given Julio and Irma Morresi peace of mind, and allowed them to extend parental care to their dead son. "I know," said Julio Morresi, "unfortunately we have this little heap of bones at the Flores cemetery, no? It is like a ritual that we go there every Sunday to bring him even if it is only one flower. It is completely useless, but it helps spiritually. . . . We go there, we kiss the photo that is hanging on the niche, and it makes us feel good" (interview, March 29, 1991).

On April 23, 1990, one year after Norberto Morresi's identification, a documentary about the exhumation was shown in the José Hernández Community Center in Buenos Aires. It was standing room only as around 450–500 persons gathered to remember Norberto Morresi and Luis María Roberto. "This is a sad occasion but also an occasion of vindication," said Julio Morresi. "This is not a homage because Norberto lives on in the ideals which we continue to carry through." These words manifest the third symbolic countermeaning of mass graves, namely that the exhumations and forensic identifications gave an impetus to the human rights struggle and undid the political paralysis intended by the dictatorship. Furthermore, such activism belied the argument of one faction of the Mothers of the Plaza de Mayo, which claimed that reburials set a mourning process in motion that will depoliticize the bereaved relatives.

In 1986 and 1987, President Raúl Alfonsín secured the legislative passage of two amnesty laws that freed suspects of human rights violations from prosecution, and President Carlos Menem pardoned hundreds of military officers and former guerrillas in 1989 and 1990, including five junta commanders convicted in 1985. With the impunity legislation in place, perpetrators could not be brought to trial. The construction of sites of memory became a priority for the human rights movement, and exhumations became of heightened importance to make visible the state terror. The ongoing exhumations and the creation of memorials, monuments, and sites of memory unveiled the hidden infrastructure of state repression and helped dismantle the second symbolic meaning of mass graves as concealed territorial markers.

Just when Argentinean society seemed to resign itself to the impunity of the perpetrators, army general Martín Balza declared in June 1998 that the military had separated guerrillas from their children by standard operating procedure and given them to childless military couples. Child theft had been excluded from the amnesty legislation, so now pardoned officers could be held responsible. A chain of events was set in motion that was accelerated when President Néstor Kirchner took office in 2003. The amnesty laws were derogated in 2005, and the presidential pardons in 2007 by the Supreme Court. By January 2014, there were 927 persons in detention, of whom 520 had been convicted of human rights violations (Dandan 2014; Robben 2010).

The Monument to the Victims of State Terrorism was inaugurated in November 2007. It carries the names of those who had been disappeared and assassinated between 1969 and 1983. The five walls contain 8,727 names, including those of Norberto Morresi and Luis María Roberto. The memorial is a countermonument to the hidden graves of the disappeared and a place of acknowledgment of their disappearance for the searching and bereaved relatives, such as Julio and Irma Morresi.

Julio and Irma still visit the Flores Cemetery every Sunday, but their sentiment has changed. When I spoke with Julio Morresi in March 2010, he said that the visits continue to fill him with spiritual energy and give relief to his emotions, but his sentiments changed after the memorial wall was erected at the Memory Park along the banks of the River Plate: "He [Norberto] is more present for us at the Memory Park because he is there with his comrades. Only his bones are at the cemetery, and even though they are mine, they are still only bones and not really Norberto for me" (interview, March 22, 2010). Norberto's name and his age at the day of his disappearance are engraved on the memorial wall. There is no mark that distinguishes him from the more than ten thousand documented disappeared who have not yet been exhumed and identified, as if to share their continued liminality in solidarity. Julio and Irma Morresi are more attracted by to the presence of Norberto's political spirit felt at the memorial amid so many others who had died for a better Argentina than by the senseless waste of life experienced at the Flores Cemetery. Julio Morresi's changing sentiments with respect to the remains of his son are telling illustrations of the changing significance of the three symbolic meanings of mass graves for bereaved relatives and Argentinean society.

Necropolitics and Marked Anonymous Graves in Chile

Within days of the Chilean military coup, people found corpses lying in the streets and saw bodies floating in the Mapocho River that winds its way through Santiago. Bodies that were not recovered by relatives were taken to the Medical-Legal Institute (Instituto Médico Legal). Elsewhere in the country, the dead were taken to morgues where some bereaved succeeded in recuperating their executed relatives (Corporación Nacional 1996:31). The number of executed and disappeared between 1973 and 1990 has been established at nearly thirty-two hundred persons by two truth commissions but some human rights organizations believe that the number might be as high as forty-five hundred (Corporación Nacional 1996:535). Unclaimed bodies were buried in cemeteries as unidentified persons in marked graves together with those who had been brought there secretly in army trucks after they had been disappeared and assassinated. Destitute persons who had died of natural causes were also interred there.

As in Argentina, Chile harbored concealed mass and individual graves. In December 1978, fifteen bodies were found in the abandoned kilns of a limestone mine at Lonquén, near Santiago, followed in October 1979 by the exhumation of nineteen corpses buried secretly at the cemetery of Yumbel (Bustamante and Ruderer 2009:61–62). There were also many marked anonymous graves. Santiago's General Cemetery distinguished mass interments by crosses bearing the initials "NN." Lot 29 (Patio 29) at the cemetery's northern side received during a three-month period more than three hundred bodies—some of which were crammed into one coffin (Wyndham and Read 2010:34–35). These graves were an in-the-face display of necropower. They showed that the military junta possessed a power over the living by assassinating them at will, and over the dead by denying them an identity and a proper burial. Whereas hidden mass graves were the inversion of general cemeteries by situating the dead outside society, the marked anonymous gravesites at cemeteries revealed a hierarchical relation between victims and perpetrators.

The authoritarian state's hold on Chilean society is exemplified by the so called Caravan of Death. The Caravan of Death was a series of visits to five towns in October 1973 by General Sergio Arellano Stark as Pinochet's delegate to lay down the law about how to deal with the regime's opponents. Commanders considered too softhearted were decommissioned, sidelined, or imprisoned. Seventy-five political prisoners already under indictment were taken from their prison cells and executed by the general's entourage. The deaths were announced publicly yet many bodies were not handed to the relatives for burial. Some were interred in sealed graves, while others were disappeared (Verdugo 2001). Whereas necropower in Argentina was parceled out through a network of task forces operating in semiautonomous areas and subareas that fell under the five fiefdom-like defense zones headed by army corps commanders, the Chilean military state installed a top-down system of repression with a clear chain of command deriving from President and Commander-in-Chief Pinochet.

The discovery of mass graves in Lonquén and Yumbel in 1978 and 1979 attracted so much media attention that the Chilean military decided to empty a number of mass graves, including those of Lot 29 at Santiago's General Cemetery, and disappear the dead for the second time by air-dropping the remains at sea or over remote mountain regions (Bustamante and Ruderer 2009:62–63). These destructive exhumations served obviously to obliterate incriminating evidence, but also reinforced the first meaning of mass graves as signifying a military victory, and affirmed the regime's necropolitical power by condemning the relatives to an interminable search for their twice disappeared loved ones.[4]

Analyzed in terms of authoritarian sovereignty, the destructive exhumations showed the power to decide about the life and death of Chilean citizens through the presence of marked anonymous burials in cemeteries and the prohibition of forensic identifications. Visitors left flowers and prayers at NN crosses but could not ascertain whether or not their relatives were buried there. The dead had been declared untouchable. The clandestine exhumation and scattering of skeletal remains by the military intended to remove the anonymous dead from public view and obliterate their existence.

The official search for the disappeared began when Patricio Aylwin took the presidential office in March 1990 after winning the December 1989 elections. Aylwin was Chile's self-pronounced president of reconciliation. National reconciliation did not imply emotional or ideological harmony among the strongly divided Chilean people but a tacit agreement to avoid painful memories in public, to accept unbridgeable political differences, and to advance pragmatically toward the future (Loveman and Lira 2007:50).

Given President Aylwin's emphasis on reconciliation and the military's continued political influence, the exhumation of mass graves did not carry the same political and judicial weight as in Argentina, and therefore soon ceased to be a national priority. The exhumed bodies from the mass graves of Lonquén, Yumbel, and Lot 29 were left untouched in the depots of the Medical-Legal Institute. It was only after pressure from the human rights lawyer Pamela Pereira that the identification process was accelerated (Bustamante and Ruderer 2009:38). The institute was, however, poorly equipped and the staff lacked professional experience. Despite misgivings about the reliability of the identifications by the judge who had ordered the exhumations, the institute began handing remains to relatives in 1993 and 1994. They included peasants from Paine and people detained at La Moneda presidential palace on September 11, 1973 (Bustamante and Ruderer 2009:81). Eventually, ninety-six bodies were identified, of which a substantial number were returned to the relatives, while the remains of thirty unidentified persons were stored at the institute.

In the absence of DNA testing capabilities in Chile, mitochondrial material of twenty-one provisionally identified persons was sent in 1994 to the University of Glasgow for confirmation. The Scottish lab concluded in a 1995 report that there was not a match between the DNA of sixteen persons and the blood samples of their presumed relatives. Only one identification was correct. Three of the misidentified remains had already been handed to the relatives but they were not notified. The report was not sent to the court or the human rights organizations, and neither was a 2002 evaluation of the 1995 report by the University of Granada, Spain, which placed serious doubts on all identifications.

Apparently, the Chilean government was more interested in memorializing than stirring up the past. Mass graves were left untouched but a commemorative monument at Santiago's General Cemetery was planned to manifest Chile's reconciliation by listing all persons who had died from political violence during military rule. Relatives of the disappeared and executed protested with success against this equivalence of victims and perpetrators. The Memorial of the Detained-Disappeared and Political Victims was inaugurated in February 1994 (Wilde 1999:485).

Even though the memorial wall listed the disappeared and dead separately, its location at the General Cemetery redefined the ambiguous status of the disappeared. The category of detained-disappeared persons was dissolved symbolically by commemorating them among the dead and constructing niches for the interment of exhumed ossified remains. Searching relatives who wanted to commemorate their disappeared had to enter the cemetery and were thus faced with the daily rituals of death. The first and second symbolic countermeanings of reincorporating the exhumed dead into society and creating memorials to undo the concealed military symbols of victory and territorial control were thus compromised by the memorial's positioning at the General Cemetery. The military's ongoing necropolitics became visible in a contradictory memorial—intended by the state to bring about national reconciliation—which shared space with the unidentified disappeared of Lot 29.

The October 1998 arrest of Augusto Pinochet in Great Britain brought the unresolved issue of the unidentified exhumed individuals from Lot 29 again to light, and obliged the government to consider the dictator's prosecution in Chile. In a reconciliatory initiative, the armed forces revealed in January 2001 the fate of 200 disappearances, and admitted that 151 disappeared had been thrown into Chile's open waters. Several indicated burial sites, however, turned out to be empty while the remains of one disappeared declared to have been thrown in the sea were found several months later. The list of 200 seemed intended to demonstrate that the Chilean military continued to exercise power over the dead and hold the searching relatives hostage indefinitely. Many people who had received the remains of relatives buried in Lot 29 were shocked to find that their names were on the list of 130 disappeared who had been thrown into the sea. Efforts to undo the symbolic meanings of mass graves bestowed by the military through exhumations were thus frustrated.

In 2003 Judge Sergio Muñoz was assigned to resolve the identification of the 30 bodies from Lot 29 still in the Medical-Legal Institute's custody. After discovering the Glasgow and Granada reports about the improper identifications of 96 exhumed persons, he ordered a thorough investigation of all 126 bodies and the exhumation of the reburied remains. The new exhumations proved hard on the relatives. They had buried their loved ones ceremonially after searching for many years, and were now faced with the fact that they continued to be disappeared after all.

The most notorious misidentification concerned the remains of Fernando de la Cruz Olivares Mori, a member of the Movement of the Revolutionary Left. He had been taken to the Ministry of Defense on October 5, 1973, and disappeared. Twenty-five years later, the Medical-Legal Institute identified him among the bodies buried in Lot 29. His presumed widow, Ágave Díaz, was shown the skeleton by two forensic anthropologists who explained that all his ribs had been broken when he was alive and that he was assassinated with gunshots to the back of his head. His remains were placed in a family niche on April 22, 1998, during a funeral at Santiago's General Cemetery. The reburial was filmed by Silvio Caiozzi (1998) and released under the title *Fernando Has Returned*. Fernando's brothers did not have the heart to tell their ninety-four-year old mother, Juana, that her son was missing again. In April 2010, the remains attributed to Fernando Olivares Mori were identified as belonging to Francisco Arnaldo Zúñiga Aguilera (*La Nación* 2010; National Commission 1993 1:207; Valencia 2006).

The Medical-Legal Institute declared in April 2006 that of a total of 96 identified bodies, 48 remains had been misidentified and there were doubts about 37 bodies (Bustamante and Ruderer 2009:105). An additional 30 bodies had continued on deposit at the institute from 1991. The government of President Michelle Bachelet decided to reorganize the institute and rename it the Medical-Legal Service (Servicio Médico Legal), appointed a new director, brought the facilities up to international standards, and in August 2007 created a genetics bank that stores DNA samples of relatives. These samples were joined with DNA material extracted from the 126 skeletal remains originally exhumed, and sent in June 2008 to the University of North Texas to ascertain once and for all their identity with the most sophisticated technology available. By January 2014, of the 124 exhumed persons, 53 had been identified.

The official policy change toward exhumations resulted from a fresh political climate in 2006. Newly elected President Bachelet, herself a survivor of torture and disappearance, mustered the political courage to prosecute perpetrators, and Pinochet's death in December 2006 accelerated the desire for accountability. By October 2013, courts had convicted 839 officers, soldiers, policemen, and civilians, albeit they received mild sentences compared to perpetrators in Argentina (Instituto de Investigación en Ciencias Sociales 2014).

What does the botched identification of the disappeared buried in Lot 29 and the change of course in 2006 toward thorough forensic investigations indicate about the way Chile has dealt with mass graves? Seen from the perspective of searching relatives and human rights organizations, it revealed the continued necropolitical hold of the military on Chilean society and the weakness of the state in fighting this power. The three countermeanings of mass graves hardly materialized in Chile, as compared to Argentina. Relatives and human rights activists had to jump-start the exhumation and proper identification of the disappeared in Lot 29 time and again. The Chilean state paid lip service to their needs but pursued a political agenda of reconciling Chilean society, inspired by fear of the military and the indifference of large segments of Chilean society. The successive governments of Presidents Patricio Aylwin, Eduardo Frei, and Ricardo Lagos ignored the known problems at Lot 29 for the sake of national reconciliation until the Bachelet government finally undertook decisive action by reforming the Medical-Legal Institute and establishing a DNA data bank.

In July 2006, only weeks after the misidentifications of Lot 29 became known, the state's National Monuments Council declared the burial ground as the seventh national monument of historical sites associated with human rights violations to serve as a reparative act and homage to the hundreds of people buried there illegally, as a place of historical memory to be preserved, and a national symbol of atrocity and suffering (Bustamante and Ruderer 2009:113–114). The monument status of Lot 29 shows the changing political and symbolic significance of mass graves in Chilean society, the dissolution of the Chilean military's necropower, and a redirection of the state's reconciliation agenda toward constructing a national memory based on the prosecution of perpetrators and the public recognition of the disappeared through exhumation, identification, and reburial.

Conclusion

In 2005, Argentinean anthropologists exhumed the remains of twelve individuals at General Lavalle Cemetery who had been interred in anonymous graves after their bodies had washed ashore along the banks of the River Plate in 1978. Forensic examinations of the bone fractures determined that five individuals had fallen on open water from a large height. This finding was the first forensic proof of the death flights that dropped sedated disappeared persons from airplanes (EAAF 2006). The establishment of the identity and cause of death of human remains that had floated in seawater for weeks, if not months, and then been buried for more than twenty-five years, demonstrates how advanced forensic techniques have become. It shows at the same time that many Chilean and Argentinean disappeared will never be found. The permanently disappeared constitute therefore an ongoing field of tension in both societies. Exhumations have undercut the three symbolic military meanings of mass graves and substituted for them the countermeanings of bereaved relatives with every identified person and each reburial and memorial, without ever succeeding completely.

The forensic discoveries are also a demonstration of countervisuality, namely "the assertion of the right to look" in defiance of sovereign authority (Mirzoeff 2011:25). The broken bones not only make visible what the Chilean and Argentinean military tried so hard to hide but expose as well an authoritarian sovereignty that manipulated the visuality of its necropolitical and territorial power. The checkpoints, uniformed troops, and televised speeches of military juntas were camouflaging civilian-clad special forces, secret detention centers, and mass graves whose existence was denied in public but known in private by commanders and perpetrators. The manipulative power of visuality could also be shamelessly blatant, as in the case of sealed graves and marked anonymous graves in Chile whose exhumation was prohibited.

The mothers who carried photographs of their disappeared children during protest marches challenged the military's representation of guerrilla insurgents and political opponents as cancerous bodies that had to be removed and destroyed to prevent the contamination of the nation. The exhumation of mass graves reinserted the extirpated dead into postdictatorial society, wrested control of the visualization of repression from the military, and confirmed a hidden reality that had been described by searching relatives and former disappeared all along.

The efforts of human rights organizations to denounce state terrorism during the dictatorship, and to pursue the exhumation of mass graves during democracy, confirm that political freedom may be constricted by authoritarian sovereignty but not eliminated. The conceptualization of sovereignty by Agamben, Foucault, and Mbembe in terms of necropower and territoriality has been an important advance in our understanding of state power, but their neglect of countervailing forces and their emphasis on the omnipresence and omnipotence of sovereign power require correction. As Arendt and Jennings have argued, political communities can arise beyond the powers that be because people possess a natural ability to form groups that can corrode sovereignty and even authoritarian regimes, as was shown so clearly in Chile and Argentina.

Notes

This essay was written with support from Spain's Ministerio de Economía y Competitividad (project MINECO CSO2012-32709), and has benefited greatly from the inspiring discussions with its members and the astute critique of two anonymous reviewers. Research in Argentina would not have been possible without the friendship of the anthropologists who founded the EAAF (Argentine Forensic Anthropology Team) and have been sharing their knowledge and expertise with me since their inception.

1. There are differences between the two countries in the record keeping at the time of the disappearances, the forensic expertise, and the means made available by the two governments to assist forensic examinations, but the scientific labor of opening a mass grave and conducting a skeletal analysis has been largely the same in Chile and Argentina. The similar operating procedure was born from the supervision of Chilean exhumations by the Argentine Forensic Anthropology Team.

2. Forensic scientists disagree about the definition of a mass grave. Even a general description as "a demonstrable place of deliberate disposal of multiple death within the same grave structure" is qualified with the caveat that "the term cannot be applied meaningfully without additional contextual definition" (Cox, Flavel, and Hanson 2008:11). Jessee and Skinner (2005:56) distinguish between archaeological definitions that focus on the number of dead and the condition of intermingled bodies in one burial site and legal definitions that emphasize the unlawful execution of civilians and their joint internment as specific of mass graves. I define mass graves in the legal sense because the unceremonial burial and anonymity of the interred bodies are most essential to mass graves in the Southern Cone. I therefore subsume anonymous individual burials under the mass grave category, unless stated otherwise.

3. Exhumations and memorials do not necessarily go together. Ferrándiz (2006:9) describes how certain memory groups, founded to remember the disappeared of Spain's Civil War, oppose exhumations and "promote *above-ground* commemorative and symbolic markers" at mass graves.

4. The only confirmed destruction of a mass grave in Argentina took place at the Arsenal Battalion of Azcuenaga in Tucumán Province (interview with Luis Fondebrider, July 1, 2011).

Bibliography

Agamben, Giorgio. 1998. *Homo Sacer: Sovereign Power and Bare Life*. Stanford: Stanford University Press.

———. 2005. *State of Exception*. Chicago: University of Chicago Press.

Arendt, Hannah. 1958. *The Human Condition*. Chicago: University of Chicago Press.

Bustamante, Javiera and Stephan Ruderer. 2009. *Patio 29. Tras la cruz de fierro*. Santiago: Ocho Libros Editores.

Caiozzi, Silvio. 1998. *Fernando ha vuelto*. Santiago: Andrea Films Production.

Clausewitz, Carl von. 1984 [1832]. *On War*. Princeton: Princeton University Press.

Cohen Salama, Mauricio. 1992. *Tumbas anónimas: Informe sobre la identificación de restos de víctimas de la represión ilegal*. Buenos Aires: Catálogos Editora.

CONADEP (Comisión Nacional sobre la Desaparición de Personas). 1986 [1984]. *Nunca Más: The Report of the Argentine National Commission on the Disappeared*. New York: Farrar, Straus and Giroux.

Corporación Nacional de Reparación y Reconciliación. 1996. *Informe sobre calificación de víctimas de violaciones de derechos humanos y de la violencia política*. Santiago: Corporación Nacional de Reparación y Reconciliación.

Cox, Margaret, Ambika Flavel, and Ian Hanson. 2008. Introduction and Context. In *The Scientific Investigation of Mass Graves: Towards Protocols and Standard Operating Procedures*, ed. Margaret Cox et al., 1–35. Cambridge: Cambridge University Press.

Dandan, Alejandra. 2010. El trabajo de nombrar a los desaparecidos. *Página/12* November 17.

———. 2014. La hora de revisar el rol de la Justicia. *Página/12* January 2.

Das, Veena and Deborah Poole. 2004. State and Its Margins: Comparative Ethnographies. In *Anthropology in the Margins of the State*, ed. Veena Das and Deborah Poole, 3–33. Santa Fe: School of American Research Press.

Dearriba, Alberto. 2001. *El golpe: 24 de marzo de 1976*. Buenos Aires: Editorial Sudamericana.

EAAF (Equipo Argentino de Antropología Forense). 2006. *2006 Mini Annual Report: Covering the Period January to December 2005*. Buenos Aires: EAAF.

———. 2007. *2007 Annual Report: Covering the Period January to December 2006*. Buenos Aires: EAAF.

———. 2011. *2007–2009 Triannual Report*. Buenos Aires: EAAF.

Ensalaco, Mark. 2000. *Chile Under Pinochet: Recovering the Truth*. Philadelphia: University of Pennsylvania Press.

Ferrándiz, Francisco. 2006. The Return of Civil War Ghosts: The Ethnography of Exhumations in Contemporary Spain. *Anthropology Today* 22(3):7–12.

———. 2010. The Intimacy of Defeat: Exhumations in Contemporary Spain. In *Unearthing Franco's Legacy: Mass Graves and the Recovery of Historical Memory in Spain*, ed.

Carlos Jerez-Farrán and Samuel Amago, 304–325. Notre Dame: University of Notre Dame Press.

Foucault, Michel. 1998 [1976]. *The Will to Knowledge*. Vol. 1 of *The History of Sexuality*. Harmondsworth: Penguin.

Garcés, Mario, and Nancy Nicholls. 2005. *Para una historia de los derechos humanos en Chile: Historia institucional de la Fundación de Ayuda Social de las Iglesias Cristianas FASIC 1975–1991*. Santiago: LOM Ediciones.

Graham-Yooll, Andrew. 1989. *De Perón a Videla*. Buenos Aires: Editorial Legasa.

Hoppe, Alejandro. 2007. *Memoriales en Chile: Homenajes a las víctimas de violaciones a los derechos humanos*. Santiago: Flacso.

Instituto de Investigación en Ciencias Sociales. 2014. *Cifras Causas DDHH Chile*. Universidad Diego Portales. Http://www.icso.cl/observatorio-derechos-humanos/cifras -causas-case-statistics/#causas. Accessed on January 21, 2014.

Jennings, Ronald C. 2011. Sovereignty and Political Modernity: A Genealogy of Agamben's Critique of Sovereignty. *Anthropological Theory* 11(1):23–61.

Jessee, Erin and Mark Skinner. 2005. A Typology of Mass Grave and Mass Grave-Related Sites. *Forensic Science International* 152(1):55–59.

La Nación (Chile). 2010. Concluye rectificación de errores del patio 29. April 2.

Loveman, Brian and Thomas M. Davies, Jr., eds. 1989. *The Politics of Antipolitics: The Military in Latin America*. 2nd ed. Lincoln: University of Nebraska Press.

Loveman, Brian and Elizabeth Lira. 2007. Truth, Justice, Reconciliation, and Impunity as Historical Themes: Chile, 1814–2006. *Radical History Review* 97:43–76.

Mbembe, Achille. 2003. Necropolitics. *Public Culture* 15(1):11–40.

Memoria Abierta. 2009. *Memorias en la ciudad: Señales del terrorismo de estado en Buenos Aires*. Buenos Aires: EUDEBA.

Mirzoeff, Nicholas. 2011. *The Right to Look: A Counterhistory of Visuality*. Durham: Duke University Press.

Mittelbach, Federico. 1986. *Punto 30: Informe sobre desaparecidos*. Buenos Aires: Ediciones de la Urraca.

Montealegre Iturra, Jorge. 2003. *Frazadas del Estadio Nacional*. Santiago: LOM Ediciones.

National Commission on Truth and Reconciliation. 1993. *Report of the Chilean National Commission on Truth and Reconciliation*. 2 vols. Notre Dame: University of Notre Dame Press.

Olmo, Darío, ed. 2005. *Cementerio de San Vicente: Informe 2003*. Equipo Argentino de Antropología Forense. Córdoba: Ferreira Editor.

Robben, Antonius C. G. M. 2000. State Terror in the Netherworld: Disappearance and Reburial in Argentina. In *Death Squad: The Anthropology of State Terror*, ed. Jeffrey A. Sluka, 91–113. Philadelphia: University of Pennsylvania Press.

———. 2005a. How Traumatized Societies Remember: The Aftermath of Argentina's Dirty War. *Cultural Critique* 59:120–164.

———. 2005b. *Political Violence and Trauma in Argentina*. Philadelphia: University of Pennsylvania Press.

———. 2010. Testimonies, Truths, and Transitions of Justice in Argentina and Chile. In *Transitional Justice: Global Mechanisms and Local Realities After Genocide and Mass Violence*, ed. Alexander Laban Hinton, 179–205. New Brunswick: Rutgers University Press.

———. 2011. Silence, Denial and Confession About State Terror by the Argentine Military. In *Violence Expressed: An Anthropological Approach*, ed. Maria Six-Hohenbalken and Nerina Weiss, 169–186. Farnham: Ashgate.

Rojas, María Fernanda and Macarena Paz Silva Bustón. 2009. Espacio público y políticas de memoria en Chile. In *El estado y la memoria: Gobiernos y ciudadanos frente a los traumas de la historia*, ed. Ricard Vinyes, 605–622. Barcelona: RBA Libros.

Rugg, Julie. 2000. Defining the Place of Burial: What Makes a Cemetery a Cemetery? *Mortality* 5(3):259–275.

Sanford, Victoria. 2003. *Buried Secrets: Truth and Human Rights in Guatemala*. New York: Palgrave Macmillan.

Valencia, Antonio. 2006. La herida no deja de sangrar. . . . *La Nación* April 25, Argentina.

Verdugo, Patricia. 2001. *Chile, Pinochet, and the Caravan of Death*. Coral Gables: North-South Center Press.

Wilde, Alexander. 1999. Irruptions of Memory: Expressive Politics in Chile's Transition to Democracy. *Journal of Latin American Studies* 31:473–500.

Wyndham, Marivic and Peter Read. 2010. From State Terrorism to State Errorism: Post-Pinochet Chile's Long Search for Truth and Justice. *Public Historian* 32(1):31–44.

Chapter 3

Korean War Mass Graves

Heonik Kwon

On a gentle hillside south of Jeju Island is a local cemetery with a unique name and history. The cemetery overlooks the open Pacific Ocean and is framed at the back by extensive fields of reeds, which are abundant on this beautiful island near Korea's southern maritime border. The cemetery consists of a large stone-walled compound in which approximately ten dozen modest mound-shaped and well-tended graves lie in neat order. A tall granite memorial stands in the middle of the compound. Visitors to this cemetery easily recognize that it is not an ordinary burial ground. The place is different from the traditional hillside family ancestral graveyards familiar to mainland Korea or from the stone-fenced individual and family tombs that reflect the Jeju Islanders' burial tradition. There are simply too many graves concentrated in one place for it to be deemed a family graveyard. Moreover, none of the graves has the benefit of a gravestone or a stone-made tablet where the visiting family can place food and alcohol offerings to the dead in accordance with local custom. The graves in this place are nameless; they stand in a strangely structured fashion of tidily organized lines—an orderliness that one would expect to encounter in a military graveyard, such as the military cemeteries on the mainland or the many smaller district-based cemeteries of fallen soldiers and police personnel scattered around the island, but not in a village burial ground.

The locals call the cemetery, according to the inscription on the dark granite memorial written in Chinese script, the "Graves of One Hundred Ancestors and One Descendant" (*baekjo ilson jimyo*). On top of the script, engraved on white granite, the image of South Korea's national flag is visible. The image is confusing, again making the place seem like an organized national military cemetery. The name of the cemetery is also unusual, going against the conventional notion of genealogical continuity and prosperity, which is emphasized in Korea's traditional commemorative culture. In ordinary circumstances, this continuity would be expressed in the opposite order, in the language of reproductive prosperity and family expansion from one ancestor to many descendants. The name does not correspond to the forms of genealogical order familiar to anthropological research either, which usually take the shape of a pyramid, with a single apical ancestral figure followed by increasingly numerous members of the genealogical group in descending lines.

How is it possible that only a single descendant survives from the historical community of a hundred ancestors? What happened in this community's past that its order of descent has fallen to the uncommon situation of a single entity today? The answer lies in the fact that the people buried in this cemetery are all casualties of the Korean War. What then does the particular structure of the cemetery and the related anomaly in the community's genealogical order say about the reality of this war?

The Other Korean War

The Jeju cemetery was established as a result of the destruction of the Korean War (1950–1953); yet it relates to a specific and a hitherto largely unknown part of this formative regional and international crisis, which took place in the early years of the Cold War. The Korean War was not a single war but rather a combination of several different kinds of wars. It was a civil war, of course, waged between two mutually hostile postcolonial political forces, each of which aspired to build a common, larger, singular, and united modern nation-state. It was also an international war, fought between, among others, two of the most powerful states in the contemporary world, the United States and China. Furthermore, it was a global war waged between two international political, moral, and economic forces, each with different visions of modernity, which we commonly call, for want of a better term, the Cold War (Kwon 2010). Hidden beneath these well-known characteristics of the Korean War, however, was another kind of war that commenced on the Korean peninsula in 1950.

The Canadian historian Steven Lee (2001) calls this war the Korean War's war against the civilian population. Lee argues that the reality of the Korean War is unintelligible if it is approached only from the perspective of conventional military history, which focuses on the interaction between organized armed groups (60). The important recent study by the South Korean sociologist Kim Dong-Chun (2000:282) makes a similar point: "The violence against civilians was 'another war' within the military conflict of the Korean War. This was primarily a war against civilians. As such, this was the war that was actually experienced by the masses; and it is what stays in their memories." The historian Park Chan-Sung (2010) calls it "the war that went into villages," highlighting the disparity between the Korean War history as a national narrative and as a narrative of village history. Within this context, Park details how the violence of the civil war seeped deeply into traditional communities, resulting in vicious reciprocal violence carried out by people from neighboring villages, between sections within a residential community, and even between competing kin groups within the same line of descent. Kim Seong-Nae, a distinguished South Korean anthropologist, discusses political violence against civilians, especially in the context of Jeju and drawing on René Girard's idea of generative violence, as being constitutive of the order of South Korea's early postcolonial Cold War state (S. Kim 1999:240–241; Girard 1977). What these scholars try to draw our attention to is the fact that the Korean War was not necessarily or primarily a violent struggle between contending armed forces. Instead, they show that the war was centrally about the struggle for survival by unarmed civilians against the generalized, indiscriminate violence perpetrated by the armed political forces on all sides.

In the early days of the war, the South Korean state committed preemptive violence against people who they suspected were harboring sympathy for communism and were, therefore, hypothetical collaborators with the enemy, and this set in motion a vicious cycle of violence against civilians in the ensuing chaos of war. The initial violence committed by the South Korean authorities radicalized the punitive actions perpetrated under North Korean occupation against the individuals and families who were classified as supporters of the southern regime, which in turn escalated the intensity of retaliatory violence directed against the so-called collaborators who had sided with the communist occupiers when the tide of war changed. When the North Korean forces left their briefly occupied territory in the South, they did the same thing as the South had done before and committed numerous atrocities of preemptive violence against people whom they considered to be potential collaborators with the southern regime.

The reality of the Korean War's war against civilians became a taboo subject once the war was over. South Koreans were not able to recall this reality publicly until recently, while continuing to live in a self-consciously anticommunist political society. The story of this war also remains untold among North Koreans who, living in a self-consciously revolutionary political society, are obliged to follow the singular official narrative of war: a victorious war of liberation against American imperialism. Nevertheless, the stories of the Korean War's "other war" existed throughout the postwar years in numerous communities and families: in whispered conversations among family and village elders, in quiet talk among trusted relatives during family ancestral death-day ceremonies, in the silent agony of parents who couldn't tell their children the true stories of how their grandparents died and where their bodies were buried, in the anxieties of aging parents who didn't know how to meet death without knowing about or hearing from their children whom they still wanted to believe were surviving on the other side of the bipolar border, and in the furious self-expression of some forgotten ancestral spirits who intruded into shamanic rites to express the terror of summary killings and the agony of an afterlife in a mass grave. These stories make up only a tiny fragment of the gigantic iceberg of the Korean War in which human dramas exist and are still unfolding in Korea.

The history of the One Hundred Ancestors and One Descendant cemetery is emblematic of these dramas. The memorial stone in the cemetery is dedicated to the victims of a tragic event that took place immediately after the Korean War broke out in June 1950. The island's police and military forces, under orders from a higher authority, arrested several hundred islanders and executed them, without trial, in several remote locations. Similar orders were carried out widely throughout the central and southern regions of mainland South Korea, as the country's military forces failed to stop the advance of the North Korean invasion, and the South Korean government was forced to flee southward, having abandoned the capital, Seoul. These atrocious actions targeted mainly those whom the government had earmarked before the war as communist sympathizers or potential collaborators with North Korea. An estimated one to two hundred thousand civilians are believed to have been killed by this extraordinary state-of-emergency measure taken in the first few weeks of the Korean War. The dead included inmates of national and provincial prisons, who had been held there on charges of political crimes relating to the social unrest and political conflicts of postcolonial Korea since the nation's liberation from Japan's colonial rule in August 1945 at the end of the

Pacific war during World War II and the subsequent division of the nation between the Soviet-occupied north and the U.S.-occupied south.

The killings were conducted in remote hill areas, in abandoned mines, or on unpopulated islands. Also reported are cases in which the victims were thrown into the coastal waters with their hands tied behind their backs and heavy objects attached to their bodies. After the killings, the massacre sites became forbidden places. For a period after the war ended in 1953, families of the victims were forbidden from going to the sites to identify and recover the bodies of their relatives from the shallow mass graves. The state authority branded the bodies in these mass graves as the bodies of traitors so, by extension, the act of touching these bodies (especially for the purpose of giving the victims a burial) constituted treason. Despite these harsh measures, a number of families secretly recovered the bodies of their relatives, and this was often done through a wider communal effort involving several bereaved families. The grave site on Jeju was prepared in this way in 1956 based on a shared initiative of bereaved families. By that time, the corpses had decomposed, and the families found it nearly impossible to identify the remains that they had excavated from a valley where an old munitions depot of the Japanese colonial army had existed before 1945. The villagers joined hands to separate the entangled remains and to put them back together, according to a village elder who participated in the exhumation, in the hope of helping the dead have a "minimal human shape with a head, two arms, and two legs." This communal excavation activity resulted in over one hundred more or less complete skeletal sets. The bereaved families then prepared 132 graves, buried the remains separately in these nameless graves and, a few years later, erected a collective gravestone.

Today this gravestone is kept in broken pieces inside a glass cabinet on the cemetery premises. According to the annals prepared by a local scholar, they were unearthed from the bushes near the cemetery a few years after the current memorial stone was built in 1993 (D. Lee 2000:76). The local annals relate how, in June 1961, shortly after a military coup took place in Seoul, the families who had taken part in erecting the original gravestone were summoned by the district's police chief, who ordered them to remove the stone. When the families protested against the order, the police sent a convoy of officers and hired laborers to destroy and bury the stone (D. Lee 2000:46–47). The police also intended to obliterate the graves and ordered the families to unearth the remains from the graves and then to cremate them. Several families felt threatened by the situation and removed the coffins of their relatives from the gravesite while other families continued protesting against the orders. They contended that the police order was a blatant violation of the customary laws, which prohibited the act of opening someone's grave without obtaining consent from the entombed person's close relatives (and also from the spirit of the dead through an appropriate rite). The district police chief argued that this order had come from a high state authority and also that the construction of the cemetery and the memorial stone violated state law, posing threats to public security. For many years after this incident, the police forces in the area were given a distinct and disreputable identity by many locals—as the desecraters of ancestral graves.

Such confrontations between the public authorities and families on the question of burial were not unusual at the time. On July 28, 1960, a large number of people gathered at the public square of Daegu's central railway station in South Korea's southeast region. They arrived from all corners of the town and many from the near and far countryside, following the rumor that on that day, people like them, the bereaved families of the Korean War, were invited to attend a public assembly. By early afternoon, the station's public square was crammed with many hundreds of women in their traditional white dresses, eagerly waiting for the meeting to start. The meeting began with a schoolgirl who, standing on the podium, read her letter to her deceased father, which caused a tremendous stir in the crowd. This was followed by a ritual address by a young widow: "You, broken names—the names that departed to the empty air, names belonging to the unknown, names I must keep calling upon until I myself meet death—here I am calling your names."[1] On hearing this invocation of invitation to the souls of the dead, several white-clothed women in the crowd took up an audible lamentation, which soon became, when the initial group was joined by hundreds of others, one of deafening proportions.

Based on this meeting, the town's bereaved families of the Korean War civilian massacres later initiated what was then called the Appeal the Grievance movement. "Appeal the Grievance" is a concept originating from Korea's premodern Confucian dynastic rule, which refers to the state institution that allowed the sovereign's subjects to appeal to the sovereign authority with respect to their grievances, such as those resulting from an abuse of power by local officials or powerful local notables. The Appeal the Grievance movement in 1960 focused on changing the names of the victims of the Korean War civilian massacres from communist suspects to innocent civilian victims, *yangmin*. *Yangmin* is another traditional concept coming from the dynastic era, meaning literally "virtuous subjects." The locally based Appeal the Grievance movement soon developed into a broad national organization comprising representatives of local family associations. The movement also focused on the excavation of the suspected killing sites in several areas. Undertaken primarily by the victims' families, this included several sites in Daegu and other parts of the southeastern region. The local press in Daegu followed this development closely, reporting on the wartime realities of violence against civilians within the province and the current activities of the victims' families. Evidence suggests that the activities of the bereaved families had broad support from local society. In Daegu, for instance, the plan of the local bereaved families' association to excavate three killing fields in the town's environs was endorsed by the provincial governor, the mayor, the town's high court judges, the chief of police, and the town's major newspapers, as well as the local Red Cross and chief of the railway station.

These initiatives advanced during the brief yet critical transitional period of postwar South Korea, when its political order changed from the previous anticommunist regime headed by the Princeton-educated civilian leader Rhee Syng-Man to an administratively more effective anticommunist regime led, in subsequent decades, by the military elite. The transition between these two forms of authoritarian politics was made possible by the student-led mass uprisings in April 1960, which brought down Rhee. The uprisings subsequently paved the way to a short-lived democratic government before the latter was toppled by a military coup, on May 16, 1961, which ended the brief period of political democracy and bought an abrupt halt to the activity of the Korean War–bereaved families. One of the first acts of the so-called military revolutionary authority after seizing political power was, in fact, to outlaw the activities of the Appeal the Grievance movement. Commencing May 18, 1961, the authorities arrested the representatives of the bereaved families' associations and later took them to a military court, accusing them of having committed an "extraordinary anti-state activity" under the newly established "special law against extraordinary crimes" (see K. Kim 2002: 363–364). Fifteen representatives of various local family associations received severe sentences, including the death sentence for a delegate of the Daegu family association. The prosecutor's evidence against the accused, which was submitted to the military court, included the newsletters and petitions issued by the associations, the list of victims, testimonies by the victims' families, and documents detailing the progress of the excavations.

The punishment against the families, whom the military authorities deemed to have challenged the sacred principle of anticommunism, also extended to the remains of their dead relatives. While the court proceedings were in progress, and even before, the political authority ordered the dismantling of the collective tombs and memorial stones that the bereaved families had collaboratively prepared a short while before. The stones were broken into pieces or buried underground, the tombs were desecrated, and the remains found in them were forcibly removed to other venues or taken to crematoriums. When interviewed, the survivors of the 1960 Appeal the Grievance movement commonly mentioned the desecration of graves as the most tragic, unforgettable occurrence of the era when they spoke about their high hopes at the time and their bitter memories. The movement's main objective, stated in one public communiqué, was "to obtain the liberty to attend to the bones . . . scattered in the hills and valleys without a grave."[2] It was this freedom to bury the dead that the country's reinvigorated anticommunist political regime chose as an exemplary public crime to demonstrate and build up its integrity.

The assault against these local sites of memory was, as mentioned, one of the first major policy directives, among other disciplinary actions against society, undertaken by the coup leaders. The Jeju police chief understood the urgency and gravity of these actions when he ordered the removal of the One Hundred Ancestors and One Descendant gravesite, and he argued that the existence of this site of memory was not a private matter for the families involved but constituted a question of state and national security. The coup leaders subsequently declared a new constitutional order for South Korea based on the principle of anticommunism; this order had to be demonstrated first in the culture of commemoration—just as the local grievances against the militant anticommunist political rule had been expressed through this cultural form.

The fate of the Korean War's civilian mass graves was subsequently relegated to nonhistory under the military-ruled authoritarian regimes that lasted until the late 1980s. By contrast, since the early 1990s, these hidden histories of mass death have become one of the most heated and contested issues of public debate, and their emergence into public discourse is, in fact, a key feature of Korea's political democracy. Benefiting from the atmosphere of political liberalization, various locally based family groups began to raise their voices again and, in some cases (such as the families related to the people of the One Hundred Ancestors and One Descendant site), gather their strength again to attend to the graves of their relatives. Similar communal initiatives arose across South Korea during the 1990s. In September 2000, the national association of the bereaved families of the Korean War civilian massacres, which had been outlawed in 1961, was revitalized and reborn as the Committee for the Investigation of Civilian Massacres Before and During the Korean War. Consisting of family representatives, civil rights activists, and concerned public figures, this nongovernmental organization aimed to achieve "legislation that permits the investigation of the Korean War civilian massacres" and thereby "to contribute to consoling the grievances of the dead and their families and to building a society free from the specter of state terror."[3] In November 2000, the South Korean National Assembly held a public hearing on "the problem of the Korean War civilian massacres" and discussed the idea of a legislative act for the purpose of investigating such events. These important proceedings successfully developed into the legislation of what is now called "The Basic Law for the Clarification of Past History" in May 2005 and, by the end of the year, the establishment of the Truth and Reconciliation Commission formally in charge of the work of "clarification of past history."[4] By the second half of the decade, investigative activity regarding the locations of the mass killings and the excavation of the Korean War mass graves spread to virtually all corners of the country, resulting in the shocking revelation that a vast number of hidden, unacknowledged mass graves existed across the territory of South Korea.[5]

Guilty by Association

The civil war's extraordinary violence against its civilians left shattering, enduring wounds in intimate communal relations. The depth of these wounds was not merely a reflection of the intensity of the physical violence but also of the particular nature and character of the political violence. Remarkable in this respect, according to testimonial histories recently made available in South Korea, is the practice of so-called substitutive death. Widely observed during wartime civilian killings, this practice entailed the killing of an individual's close relations in place of that individual if the latter was unavailable. Although the dreadful logic of this practice had several facets, it was fundamentally based on the idea of associative culpability that purported the sharing of guilt by the guilty individual's family and kin group.

The logic continued to hold sway even after the war was over, at which time it turned into a shadowy legal and political rule called *yŏnjwaje*. The broad definition of this system is, according to the definition provided in the 1980 Basic Laws of the Republic of Korea that banned the practice, that a person experiences disadvantages due to the actions committed not by him or her but by someone else related to the person. In a narrower definition, which is how the term has been used in postwar Korea, the rule of *yŏnjwaje* refers to the specific domain of civic life in which the culpability for an individual's criminal actions, if these are judged to threaten national security, may be shared by the culpable individual's close relations. The rule has been in practice in both Koreas since the war ended, although the specific ways in which it was implemented are different between the two societies. This is due, above all, to North Korea's liberal use of labor camps for containing politically subversive individuals and their families, an institution that North Korea borrowed from the Soviet Union. This is unlike the South Korean context, where the containment took a more socially diffused technical form (Szalontai 2005:221–223). In postwar South Korea, *yŏnjwaje* means, in popular understanding and according to Balázs Szalontai (2005:222), primarily "a type of guilt-by-association in which one leftist in a family could subject all relatives to surveillance." In the literature of law and ethics, similar institutional or customary practices appear under the rubric of collective responsibility, contrasting with the principle of individual rights and responsibility sanctified in modern society and law (see Barkan 2004:309). They also appear in the idiom of being "guilty by association"—"a deplorable ethical concept, a carryover from our barbaric, tribal past," according to legal historian Larry May (1987:8; see also Barkan 2004:311).

Korea was not the only place where family and other intimate communal relations became the subject of political control and punitive actions during the era of the global Cold War. Speaking of the impact of the anticommunist terror unleashed in Java and Bali in 1965–1966, historian Geoffrey Robinson (1995) describes how the terror campaign distorted the moral fabric of Balinese communities. He observes that the widespread practice of punishing the chosen victims together with their families and close relatives left deep scars on the affected communities. People of the war generation in Vietnam are familiar with the idiom of *hat going do*. Meaning that a "red plant" comes from "red seeds," the idiom justified the Vietnam War's prolific acts of violence against rural communities, which were believed to harbor subversive elements (Kwon 2006). In a broadly similar light, Greg Grandin (2004:14) investigated the alleged "susceptibility of Mayans to communism" during the 1981–1983 terror campaigns in Guatemala against indigenous communities.

Anthropologist Stephan Feuchtwang (2011) examined the state terror in Taiwan in the early 1950s (which was in fact closely related to the outbreak of war on the Korean peninsula), focusing on how the experience of state violence is transmitted across generations. During the Greek Civil War, according to Polymeris Voglis (2002:7–8), "the line between legality and illegality was drawn along the lines of nationalism versus communism. Ideas, intentions, and even family relations during the Civil War were labelled as 'antinational' and thus became new forms of illegality and new objects of punitive practices." Voglis describes how family relations became "new objects of punitive practices" and how the terrifying label "antinational" exerted enormous pressure on prisoners and their families.

The post–Korean War politics of associative guilt should be considered in this broad comparative historical perspective as a particular local manifestation of global Cold War political modernity. Yŏnjwaje is associated most prominently with the prevailing wartime and postwar conditions in which the punishment of an individual, whom the state defined as an enemy of the political community, might fall onto the individual's family and kindred. Criminalization of the family was nominally against the law: the practice of collective responsibility was unconstitutional and was banned as early as 1894 when the first modern constitutional rule was established in Korea. Nevertheless, it became an integral element of the state's penal practice throughout much of the twentieth century. Although there were several attempts to eradicate the practice of collective culpability, which included the 1980 Basic Law mentioned above, the draconian practice actually lasted until very recently.[6]

The existence of yŏnjwaje goes a long way back in Korean history. In premodern times, collective culpability was an explicit, legitimate element of the penal institution of the feudal dynastic system in which those who were judged to have challenged the authority of the sovereign were punished not only with their death but also with the death (or enslavement or banishment to remote areas) of their entire families. The term *yŏnjwa*, meaning literally "relations seated together," refers to the structure of the feudal court where the judgment against the accused was pronounced in the presence of his dependents and descendants gathered behind him. Although the yŏnjwa system has a long history in Korea, its modern ramifications in the forms briefly described above are not to be considered merely in terms of historical continuity or deplorable cultural survival as the legal historian cited earlier argues. The "barbaric" institution of collective punishment existed in twentieth-century Korea not merely as a remnant of its backward past but primarily because the institution was a highly effect instrument of social control in a particular condition of political modernity and crisis. Moreover, the institutional practice of collective culpability proliferated in Cold War–era Korean politics and society despite clear public awareness that the practice was unwarranted in modern life.

The important point about the yŏnjwa system is, therefore, that, in practice, this punitive system existed both outside the rule of law and inside the legal order. It was in part a feudal legacy outlawed in Korea's modern constitutional history. Nevertheless, the system has had a powerful and shadowy presence in the country's modern political and legal history. Its existence in modern life became a source of suffering and bitterness for numerous families and individuals, and it continued to exist until the geopolitical structures of the Cold War began to crumble in the late 1980s. Therefore, it is possible to imagine that the system of collective culpability has both premodern and modern origins. The fact that the institution was in practice in modern Korea, in spite of general public awareness of its unlawful status within modern politics, shows the limits and distortions of political modernity at the outposts of the global Cold War.

Recovering the Normativity of Kinship

The commemorative efforts undertaken by families, such as those who built the Jeju cemetery, are to be considered partly in light of the state's disciplinary power based on familial relations. The efforts these families made to take the bodies of their tragically killed relatives out of their mass graves may be an expression of what Hegel calls "the law of kinship" (the rights and obligation of kinship to attend to the death of members). However, they also relate to the fact that the nonnormative status of the dead had direct consequences for the political and moral life of their surviving families. In other words, just as the logic of associative guilt postulated the sharing of an individual's political culpability by that individual's family relations, so did the prospect of breaking the power of this logic and attaining a normative status within the political community for the surviving families of these individuals involve efforts to restore the moral identity of their dead relatives as family ancestors, away from the stigmatizing negative political identity imposed on them. In this context, the hope to further individual civil and human rights in wider society becomes inseparable from the communal right to attend to the plight of the dead.

Hegel explored the philosophical foundation of the modern state both through ethical questions involving remembrance of the war dead and by drawing on the legend of Antigone from the Theban plays of Sophocles (see Stern 2002:135–45; Sant Cassia 2005). Antigone was torn between the obligation to bury her war-dead brothers according to "the divine law" of kinship on one hand and, on the other, the reality of "the human law" of the state, which prohibited her from giving burial to enemies of the city-state (Stern 2002:140). She buried one brother, who died as a hero of the city, and then proceeded to do the same for another brother, who died as an enemy of the city. The latter act violated the edict of the city's ruler, and she was subsequently condemned to death as punishment. Invoking this powerful epic tragedy from ancient Greece, Hegel reasoned that the ethical foundation of the modern state is grounded in a dialectical resolution of the clashes between the law of the state and the law of kinship. For Judith Butler (2000:5), the question is about the fate of human relatedness when it is suspended between life and death and forced into the torturous condition of having to choose between the norms of kinship and subjection to the state. Similar predicaments confronted the families connected to the One Hundred Ancestors and One Descendant cemetery. Many of them experienced discrimination in public life, restrictions in social mobility, and regular surveillance by state security agencies. They were thus victimized, not because they had committed anything that could be deemed to threaten public order, but purely because of their ties of kinship with the victims of state terror during the war. If an individual is deemed guilty of a political crime by virtue of his or her communal kinship ties, the proper emancipatory political actions must involve practices that aim to free the relational ties from the logic of persecution, not merely the individual subject.

Considering this background, the cemetery's unusual organization and name appear to be less mysterious. Rather than an anomalous, upside-down genealogical condition, the name of the place points to the norms of kinship to commemorate the dead and, when the commemoration concerns a mass grave, the imperative for the concerned families to unite beyond the narrow unity of consanguinity. Although the 132 human remains were buried in the cemetery individually, they all shared the same fate and tragic circumstances of death, and their bodies were in actuality intertwined with one another (most of the victims were males aged from eighteen to thirty). In this sense, the name of the cemetery reflects the interconnectedness of the bereaved families to one another, making a single community of mourners despite their differences in genealogical identity and separate consanguine ties to the dead.

Also notable is the fact that the ancestral memorial stone is not a solitary object. The stone does not merely represent the desire of the bereaved families to commemorate their tragically dead relatives but also testifies to the fact that formidable obstacles existed to thwart their commemorative effort. Standing next to the broken remains of the old memorial, as described earlier, the stone shows that it itself has a history of death and regeneration of life. It speaks of the fact that the rights of kinship to commemorate the dead can be negated by powerful political forces and that the assertion of these rights is inseparable from the progression of a democratic political order. The history of Korea's political democracy is then, partly yet crucially, about the struggle to confront the destruction of war in truthful ways and about the right to grieve and re-member the victims of that destruction without having to fear the negative consequences of doing so.

At the same time, the excavation of the Korean War civilian mass graves has been an act of opening up the hitherto untold history of the war and the yet unresolved issues of Korea's modern political history. At the heart of this important process are the claims of the Korean War–bereaved families, some public and explicit and others raised and heard only in local contexts, to find a rightful place in history for their civil war dead. These contemporary claims for political and civil rights to grieve for the war dead keep the distant echo of the early 1960s in current memory: the publicly expressed aspirations of the bereaved families to grieve for the dead without fearing the consequence of doing so—the fear that a family's act to remember the dead may make the family as a whole an outcast from the political community by virtue of its identification with the dead. The distant echo still rings true today, and the confrontation between the ethics of commemoration and the politics of sov-ereignty is not over yet two generations after the end of the brutal civil war.

Notes

The research for this essay received generous support from the Academy of Korean Stud-ies (AKS-2010-DZZ-3104).

1. *Daegu Maeil Sinmun* (Daegu Daily Gazette), July 29, 1960. The funerary address of that day was based on the poem *Ch'ohon* (Calling the souls), composed by the well-known South Korean literary figure Kim So-Wŏl in 1925. The poem's title derives from the traditional Korean mortuary custom of calling the soul of the dead to the deceased person's funerary clothing before the person was buried.

2. From a document entitled *Bisŏkgŏnlipch'wijisŏ* ("Appeal for memorial stone"), pri-vate publication of a former member of the Daegu association of bereaved families.

3. From a book published by the Hangukjŏnjaengjŏnhu minganinhaksal jinsanggyu-jmyŏng bŏmgukminwiwŏnhoi (National association for the truth of civilian massacres before and during the Korean War), *Da jukyŏra da ssŭlŏbŏryŏra* (Kill them all, waste them all), published in Seoul by Wuinmidia in 2003, p. 193.

4. From a publication of the Jinsil hwahaerŭluihan gwagŏsajŏngliwiwŏnhoi (Truth and reconciliation commission), *2007 nyŏn habangi josabogosŏ* (Investigation report, second half of 2007), published in Seoul by the commission in 2007, p. 15.

5. Hangukjŏnjaengjŏnhu, pp. 14–36.

6. Yŏnjwaje formally ended in South Korea in 1988. The outlawing of this institutional practice was one of the first legal reforms undertaken by the democratically elected legislative body after the fall of the military regime in 1987. Commentators in Korea hailed the reform as historic progress in the country's legal history. However, the penalization of family relations continued even in the 1990s, although less intensively and systematically than in previous postwar decades. The difficulty in identifying the end of the institutional practice relates to the practice's dubious legal status. Formally yŏnjwaje had always been an unconstitutional practice in postcolonial Korea. The 1948 constitution of the Republic of Korea includes an article that specifically abolishes the system. In subsequent decades, various political leaders again promised the abolition of yŏnjwaje.

Bibliography

Barkan, Elazar. 2004. Individual Versus Group Rights in Western Philosophy and the Law. In *Collective Guilt: International Perspectives*, ed. Nyla R. Branscombe and Bertjan Doosje, 309–319. Cambridge: Cambridge University Press.

Butler, Judith. 2000. *Antigone's Claim: Kinship Between Life and Death*. New York: Columbia University Press.

Feuchtwang, Stephan. 2011. *After the Event: The Transmission of Grievous Loss in Germany, China and Taiwan*. Oxford: Berghahn.

Girard, René. 1977. *Violence and the Sacred*. Baltimore: Johns Hopkins University Press.

Grandin, Greg. 2004. *The Last Colonial Massacre: Latin America in the Cold War*. Chicago: University of Chicago Press.

Kim Dong-Chun. 2000. *Jŏnjaengwa Sahoi* (War and society). Seoul: Dolbege.

Kim Ki-Jin. 2002. *Gukminbodoyŏnmaeng* (National guidance alliance). Seoul: Historical Criticism Press.

Kim Seong-Nae. 1999. Gŭndaesŏnggwa pokryŏk: Jeju 4.3 damronchôngch'i (Modernity and politics: the discursive politics of Jeju April Third incident). In *Jeju 4.3 yŏngu* (Studies of Jeju April Third incident), ed. Jeju 4.3 Research Instutitute, 238–267. Seoul: Historical Criticism Press.

Kwon, Heonik. 2006. *After the Massacre: Commemoration and Consolation in Ha My and My Lai*. Berkeley: University of California Press.

———. 2010. *The Other Cold War*. New York: Columbia University Press.

Lee Do-Young. 2000. *Jukŭmŭi yebigŏmsok: yangminhaksal jinsangjosa bogosŏ* (The deadly preventive custody: Investigative report of [the Korean War] civilian massacres [in Jeju]). Seoul: Mal.

Lee, Steven Hugh. 2001. *The Korean War*. Harlow, England: Longman.

May, Larry. 1987. *The Morality of Groups: Collective Responsibility, Group-Based Harm, and Corporate Rights*. Notre Dame, IN: University of Notre Dame Press.

Park Chan-Sung. 2010. *Maŭlro gan hankukjŏnjaeng* (The Korean War that went into the villages). Seoul: Dolbege.

Robinson, Geoffrey. 1995. *The Dark Side of Paradise: Political Violence in Bali*. Ithaca, NY: Cornell University Press.

Sant Cassia, Paul. 2005. *Bodies of Evidence: Burial, Memory and the Recovery of Missing Persons in Cyprus*. Oxford: Berghahn.

Stern, Steve. 2002. *Hegel and the Phenomenology of Spirit*. New York: Routledge.

Szalontai, Balázs. 2005. *Kim Il Sung in the Khrushchev Era: Soviet-DPRK Relations and the Roots of North Korean Despotism, 1953–1964*. Washington, DC: Woodrow Wilson Center Press.

Voglis, Polymeris. 2002. *Becoming a Subject: Political Prisoners During the Greek Civil War*. Oxford: Berghahn.

Chapter 4

Mass Graves, Landscapes of Terror

A Spanish Tale

Francisco Ferrándiz

On October 30, 2008, the search began for the bodies of five women in the area known as Las Albarizas, located in the municipality of Villanueva de la Vera in the province of Cáceres. Florentina Quintana Huertas and her two daughters, Ángela and Ana Tornero Quintana, Úrsula Sánchez Mate, and Bernarda García Hernández were killed on September 26, 1936, by a paramilitary group supporting Francisco Franco's rebellion against the legitimate Republican government—otherwise known as the Spanish Civil War (1936–1939). They were executed in the midst of what historians call the "hot terror" phase of rearguard repression, a burst of initial mass killing of civilians before kangaroo military courts progressively took over the terror machinery applied to civilians in 1937 (Chaves 1995:96–104; Casanova 1999:159–177). The war left behind hundreds of thousands of dead, as many as 500,000 victims—300,000 persons killed in the frontlines and up to 200,000 civilians executed behind the lines. Regarding the execution of civilians throughout the country, contemporary historiography places the numbers at 55,000 executed in the Republican rearguard action, and as many as 150,000 in the rebellious or "Nationalist" army rearguard action and repression of civilians, both during the war and in the early postwar years (Rodrigo 2008; Preston 2012; Ferrándiz 2013).

Since the end of the Civil War, there have been different exhumation cycles in Spain, each one related to a specific necropolitical regime (Mbembe

2003). Franco's dictatorship (1939–1975) built part of its political legitimacy on the harsh discrimination between the bodies of the winners and the losers of the war. In the early years of his rule, Franco exerted great effort to research and document all crimes committed by the "reds"—and not the crimes committed by his own supporters—in a major judicial procedure called the Causa General that reached all municipalities in the country. In parallel to this huge postwar effort to identify civilian victims, the circumstances of their deaths, and the name of alleged perpetrators, nationwide instructions and forensic protocols were used to conduct official exhumations of Civil War heroes and martyrs. A complete funerary ritual was developed to honor the martyrs in a way that would fit with the mainstream National Catholic political ideology of the time, which considered the war as a crusade against evil. These rituals were established with the support of the Catholic Church (Casanova 2001; Box 2010). While all this happened, the mass graves containing the bodies of Republican sympathizers were abandoned and radically excluded from legislation and state funerary practice, and became an integral part of a topography of terror, a space of death expressing the regime's blood pedagogy (Taussig 1987; Preston 2012). An unambiguous lesson for all potential dissidents to learn.

Starting in the late 1950s, more than thirty thousand Civil War bodies were exhumed from across the country and reburied in the Valley of the Fallen, a controversial monument drenched in Francoist iconography and meaning, which continues to house the dictator's tomb and that of the founder of the Spanish Fascist Party. An unknown number of Republicans were removed from mass graves and brought to this monument without their families' knowledge (Ferrándiz 2011). Meanwhile, other Republican mass graves were exhumed clandestinely during Francoism, and after Franco's death, groups of relatives and neighbors unearthed many more graves, using their own resources and work tools. There has not yet been systematic research on these early exhumations of civilian Republicans, although they seem to have been more numerous and extensive that previously thought.

In the twenty-first century, a new wave of exhumations started. These more recent exhumations are characterized by the participation of technical teams, the presence of the media and the public visibility provided by the advent of the digital information age, and the influence of the contemporary international human rights regime. Times have changed drastically between the moment of the executions—the black and white Spain—and the contemporary reappearance of the bodies—the digital Spain. Children of the twenty-first century, these exceptional bodies, retrieved in extremis from the shadows and interstices of history, must now face late modernity on a planetary scale, a globalized modernity that many authors define in terms of interconnection, interdependence, collapse of time and space, cosmopolitanism, deterritorialization, acceleration, vertigo, simulation or saturation of experience (Harvey 1989; Watts 1992; Castells 1996).

Their public revelation is therefore determined by a radical spatial and temporal disjunction between the conditions of life and death in the war and postwar period, and a society profoundly transformed by globalizing processes and successive technological revolutions (Lyotard 1984). The same transformation and acceleration or chronic emergency of human experience that affects the inhabitants of this late modern age affects the dead bodies of the past irrupting into this same social fabric. Thus, the executed bodies make a dramatic and spectacular reappearance in the information and knowledge society, deeply conditioned in their appearance and diffusion—not just within the scope of a nation-state but also, simultaneously, in a transnational context—through the viewing and dissemination capabilities of digital devices, and through proliferation in the media and social networks, particularly after 2005.

An integral event in this most recent wave of exhumations, the excavation in Villanueva de la Vera is exceptional due to the combination of three factors. First, it is directly related to important attempts to connect Spanish contemporary exhumations with international human rights law. Second, the crimes committed in this case were crimes perpetrated against women. Finally, and as in many other instances, the investigation failed to locate any human remains or traces of former graves. Yet Villanueva de la Vera is also an emblematic case that illustrates Spain's contemporary mass grave exhumation drive, which started in the year 2000 and has involved more than three hundred excavations and the recovery of over five thousand bodies (Etxeberria 2012). In regard to the first factor above, this case's relationship to comparative transitional justice is important because of the striking lack of legal coverage over exhumations conducted in Spain, which in most cases take place in a sort of judicial limbo with only limited institutional involvement. The second factor relates to the emergence of neo-Republican political cultures in the last decade and the important role that the execution and mistreatment of women has acquired as a crucial symbol of Franco's repressive brutality. The third factor allows me to step away from the bones and the forensic and body-centered regime of truth increasingly attached to them—which, during the past decade, has received the lion's share of public, academic, and media attention—and focus specifically on the process of searching for mass graves and on the dignifying and mourning strategies employed by associations, relatives, and activists in local contexts (Ferrándiz 2013).

Justice Unleashed, Soon Back to the Leash

The search and excavation of the two close-by sites where, according to local oral memory, the bodies of the five women had been buried started in the midst of judicial and media turmoil caused by a controversial ruling that Judge Baltasar Garzón had issued on October 16, 2008, only two weeks before the exhumation procedures began. Garzón, famous for his involvement in the arrest of former Chilean president Augusto Pinochet in London on October 16, 1998 (Golob 2002), had declared himself legally competent to investigate the crimes of Francoism within the framework of international law, arguing for the use of the concept of crimes against humanity, especially forced disappearances, until the cases were fully solved. That pronouncement brought considerable media attention to the site where the five women were allegedly killed. Had any bones been found, they would have been the first ones to be recovered under this kind of international human rights umbrella. They thus could have become the first potential criminal evidence against the longstanding impunity of Francoism. In fact, at this time the stakes were high in Spain: in a follow-up to Garzón's ruling, the search in Las Albarizas began barely one day after the Spanish Central Criminal Court (Audiencia Nacional) had granted authorization to dig in this specific site, to exhume the grave believed to hold the remains of Federico García Lorca and others, and to investigate the huge cemetery located in the Valley of the Fallen.

Until Garzón attempted to apply international human rights law to the Spanish case, most registered cases requesting that judges treat the human remains contained in mass graves as criminal evidence were dismissed, as this would exceed the statute of limitations of twenty years established by the Spanish penal law. Furthermore, if the lapse of time between when crimes were committed and the present was not enough, potential crimes were also rendered null in the 1977 Amnesty Law. For a few weeks in October 2008, many in the memorial movement believed that things would finally turn around and that Garzón's intervention could crack open this judicial lockup. Yet none of this would ever happen.

Figure 4.1 Representatives of Associations for the Recovery of Historical Memory talk to the media in front of the National Audience in Madrid before turning in to Judge Baltasar Garzón lists with the names of tens of thousands of disappeared during the Civil War and the era of Francoism, September 22, 2008. Photo by the author.

To better understand this judicial thriller, let's step back a few months, if only briefly. The process was set in motion on December 2006, when a number of civil associations filed suits before Garzón's office at the Spanish Central Criminal Court, requesting that he assert his competence for judicial inquiry and use it to investigate alleged crimes of illegal detention. The claimants' chief argument was that throughout the Civil War and the postwar period "a systematic and pre-devised plan to liquidate political opponents" had been carried out "by means of countless acts of murder, torture, banishment and through forced disappearances, which occurred in several parts of the country."[1] Similar suits were subsequently brought by other associations and by private citizens. The decision to proceed before Garzón was not accidental: indeed, the idea was to capitalize on his media visibility and on the international reputation that he had earned during that the "Pinochet affair," in the hope that the civil actions might make some impact on the Spanish public, even if such actions were eventually dismissed. The civil associations' discontent arose as a result of a widespread sense of dissatisfaction with what they viewed as piecemeal government intervention and with the little progress they thought was being made toward their goals, which were expressed in debates on what was to become Act 52/2007, or the Historical Memory Act,[2] passed by Parliament on December 27, 2007. I will return to these debates in more detail later in the chapter.

When Garzón decided to pursue the case, it was havoc. Images of Franco and his generals appeared on front pages of newspapers. Some media outlets hailed the news, others denounced it. Experts and talk show guests yelled at one another in tense disputes. Garzón himself was acclaimed by some while reviled by others. Conservative political parties and the media cried foul play and accused Garzón of reopening old wounds that had been sealed through acts of reconciliation during the transition to democracy. The judicial system knew better. In a few weeks, Garzón was forced to recognize his lack of jurisdiction in hearing the case. In a far-fetched operation of judicial closure whose description is beyond the scope of this chapter, Garzón quickly found himself impeached by the Supreme Court on three different counts, which led to rumors that he was the victim of an ad hominem partisan campaign. Although he was finally absolved in the Francoism case on February 27, 2012, the Supreme Court ruling foreclosed any further legal inquiry into Civil War and postwar crimes. In the meantime, Garzón had already been convicted in a parallel case regarding his questionable methods in a judicial investigation of corruption, which removed the judge from office for eleven years, thus possibly ending his professional career in Spain. There were other aftereffects that would follow Garzón's 2008 controversial ruling. In 2009, the two main political parties in the country jointly pushed for the reform of a crucial 1985 article in the main laws that defined the jurisdiction of Spanish tribunals as universal. This article had transformed Spain into a champion of universal jurisdiction, making, for example, the Pinochet case possible. Not anymore. This amendment was a major blow to the ability of the Spanish judicial system to assume cases of human rights violations worldwide.

Terror on Women

The Villanueva de la Vera case illustrates how the Francoist topography of repression is experienced today in regional and local contexts and how this topography continues to maintain some of its former terrorizing efficacy. Besides the media attention that was brought to this particular search for bodies by its almost accidental intersection with Garzón's high-profile judicial inquiry, the fact that the investigation referred to the armed paramilitary's execution of five defenseless countryside women carried great emotional resonance for those historical memory associations and activists committed to promoting exhumations in contemporary Spain. The cold-blooded assassination of peasant women is, within the political logic of these associations, proof of the remarkable cruelty, senselessness, and distinctly inhumane nature of the Nationalist repression. Far from spontaneous or scattered, violence toward women was adopted and encouraged by top military commanders from the early days of the war. The nightly radio speeches of Gonzalo Queipo de Llano—one of the main rebels—in Unión Radio Sevilla in the early months of the military coup explicitly encouraged the use of repression and, more specifically, sexual violence on Republican women. In one of his most famous broadcasts, on July 24, 1936, he asserted that "our courageous soldiers have proved to the *Red* cowards what it means to be a real man. Likewise, to their women. This is completely justified as these communist and anarchist women defend free love. Now at least they will know what a true man is, as opposed to those militia fags. They will not get away, no matter how much they scream and kick." Violence against women involved mistreatment, rapes, tortures, executions, public humiliation, and imprisonment both during and after the war (Vinyes 2002; Espinosa 2003; Díaz-Balart 2009; Preston 2012).

Even in the region, gendered repressive killing of women was not an extraordinary matter. In the same hot terror days of 1936, six women were killed in the neighboring village of Losar (Chaves 1995), at least four in Oropesa (Toledo), and three more in the nearby municipality of Candeleda, who were exhumed in 2002 (Ferrándiz 2013). In other regions of the country, there have been some other important investigations, whereby women's mass graves have been dug up. For example, in 2008, in Andalusia, where Queipo de Llano was based, fifteen women were exhumed in a mass grave in the village of Grazalema (Cádiz). In 2012, the exhumation of seventeen more women in the Sevillian town of Gerena, who were to be reburied in their hometown of Guillena, became a relevant media event in the memorialist movement and is credited as the cornerstone of an emerging gender-based memory culture in the Andalusian region (Fernández Albeniz and Sosa Campos 2012). As a spin-off of this last exhumation, in May 2013 a group of women dressed in black mourning attire ironically offered a wreath in memory of all repressed women on top of Queipo's tomb in Seville's Macarena Basilica, in the very town where Queipo aired his infamous inflammatory broadcast. Later, the women danced flamenco over a wooden replica of his tombstone.

In the contemporary social movement to recuperate historical memory, exhumations linked to the mistreatment and execution of women are associated with the political and symbolic capital of the emblematic post war execution of thirteen young female, left-wing militants, known as the Thirteen Roses, which happened after Madrid fell to the rebels in 1939. This execution has become iconic to the Republican Left in Spain, and has been taken up by investigative journalists, writers, artists, and filmmakers.[3] Every August 5, a commemorative ceremony takes place in the Almudena Cemetery in Madrid by the wall where the thirteen women were shot in 1939.

On-the-Ground Mass Grave Activism

As is often the case in Spain, in Villanueva, a memory association called Our Memory (Nuestra Memoria) played a pivotal role throughout the exhumation process. The main memory entrepreneur in this context was Lucio García Tornero. In this text, his story exemplifies the experience of many local activists across the country, who for a number of years had timidly, at times secretly and often fearfully, cherished the hope of recovering their relatives. The new social legitimacy created by the media exposure of exhumations in other parts of the country since 2000 and reinforced by particular institutional memory policies made it possible for people like Lucio to come out of the closet and move forward with exhumation projects. Lucio had plenty of reasons to become engaged in the invariably complex and often frustrating tasks involved in initiating and carrying out the project of unearthing the past, including securing the necessary permits and agreements for conducting exhumations, talking landowners into cooperating with these investigations, negotiating with public authorities, applying for possible funding, recruiting a reliable technical team, dealing with the media, and, more important, managing the profound effects that an event of this kind causes in the region, in one's native community, and in one's own family, particularly in the rural areas.

It was believed that one of the two women's graves being searched for in Las Albarizas contained the remains of Lucio's grandmother and those of his mother's two sisters, one of whom was pregnant and had a fifteen-month-old baby when she was killed. On the male side, Lucio's mother's brother, cousin, and brother-in-law were believed to be buried in a similar grave in another location, which was scheduled to be explored later in the year. First, Lucio wanted the women to be unearthed. He said, "My mother's lifelong dream is being fulfilled" through his memory awareness efforts and the search for the bodies. Throughout his mother's life, she had deeply and silently resented that a significant part of her family spent decades "dumped off like dogs in the countryside."

Since he was very young, Lucio had been eager to know more about the crimes that affected his family and his village so deeply. During Francoism, he told me, it was extremely difficult to discuss these public secrets (Taussig 1999), especially outside family quarters, but at times also within them. Fear and distrust were predominant in social relations during the dictatorship. Many of the surviving victims had to live for decades next door to their family's killers, who more often than not had also confiscated at least part—if not the majority—of their properties (Álvaro Dueñas 2009). "In the past, people hardly ever spoke about it," he said. However, thanks to a semiclandestine fellowship that arose among victims' relatives living in his village after Franco's death in 1975, Lucio had been able to gather details regarding the tragic events related to the Civil War and its aftermath in a more systematic way, while also focusing his attention on the location of the unmarked graves.

When I met him, he knew nothing about the exhumations conducted by individual families in different parts of the country since the late seventies. But he remembered perfectly the local aftereffects of 1981's failed military coup: "At the time of the coup, I was seized with pessimism. People wouldn't talk anymore, it was impossible, they were even more scared than they had been under Franco and feared a backlash." Around 1988, as alarm over regression to a dictatorship receded, Lucio took up the issue again with renewed eagerness. This was also due to his collaboration as informant with historian Julián Chaves, who was working on his doctoral research on the repression experienced in the province of Cáceres (1995). But it was only when exhumations in other parts of the country started to appear in the media and in public debate after 2000 and when he realized that the Socialist government was passing a memory act that would give some legitimacy to the exhumations and the memory of those defeated in the war that he believed it was feasible to actually search for the corpses and rebury them in a dignified manner.

After Lucio got involved in both national and local "associations for the recovery of historical memory," preparations began for the disinterment. In the period 2006–2011, the Socialist government of Rodríguez Zapatero established a line of funding for "activities related to victims of Civil War and Francoism," which included money for exhumations.[4] The local association Nuestra Memoria had applied for such funds, and could pay for preliminary search tasks—including the use of a georadar and the hiring of a bulldozer. In this case, the archaeological and forensic team never came to Villanueva since the unmarked graves were never found. Consequently, the remaining money was used to carry out searches for other graves that were still pending in the region. For Lucio the difficulties were plenty. Even though he had devoted a number of years to investigating the matter, Lucio had never managed to find documents concerning any of the killings. This is not unusual for the hot terror killings in the early months of the war, which often went unreported. Knowledge of what had allegedly happened to the five women from Villanueva was embedded in the oral stories that circulated at first within familial contexts, then among victims' relatives, and subsequently in more public environments in the village and the region, as the excavation drew near and the news of the event began to spread.

"They were hunted like doves," a woman commented to me, thus attesting to the common sense of injustice that such extrajudicial killings incited in both relatives and onlookers. Many nodded in silence or elaborated on the metaphor. A photocopied text written by Lucio was distributed among those attending the exhumation in Villanueva de la Vera. It included the names of the five women killed, their age, profession, and marital status, and a list of their descendants. The text also described how the women were purportedly placed in the two neighbouring unmarked graves that were being unearthed. It also read:

> The circumstances of their deaths have been reconstructed on the basis of accounts given by relatives and neighbors that now belong to the historical memory that the village preserves regarding the events that took place between July and September 1936. In the beginning of September, several defenseless women were taken from their homes by well-known Falangists living in the village. They were kept in custody at the Town Hall, which at the time had been transformed into a prison. They had their heads shaved; they were demeaningly forced to mop up the streets, and finally they were taken to Las Albarizas, where they were forced to collect beans and then shot by the gunmen who held them prisoners.

Figure 4.2 Bulldozer at work in the search for the five women buried at Villanueva de la Vera, Spain, October 30, 2008. Note the presence of media on both sides of the ditch. Photo by the author.

Had the "Garzón effect" been absent, the search for bodies would have remained a primarily local operation. Some relatives actually wanted to maintain the event's low profile. But Lucio and some members of the main nationwide association, Asociación para la Recuperación de la Memoria Histórica (ARMH), considered publicity and public exposure to be a crucial part of the dignifying process. The country and the world *had to know*. This disagreement regarding privacy and exposure created some tension among relatives. Since the search for the burial sites began, several professional filming teams had been present, including some from television networks (two of which were foreign) and two teams of documentary filmmakers. The program *Esquina Viva*, broadcast by the radio station Canal Extremadura, decided to report the event; regional and national newspaper and news agency reporters also showed up at different stages of the disinterment.[5] As the excavation proceeded, all those present paid keen attention whenever a bone fragment seemed to emerge from the removed earth. But not one appeared. No sensational material was recovered. Instead, only tree roots that had been torn apart by the bulldozer were unearthed. Once these artifacts were reviewed and discarded by the archaeologist in charge, they were passed from hand to hand, until someone tossed them away in the debris. To the media, the goal was not just finding the remains of the five women but a discovery that would positively link the Spanish case to transnational justice processes. Exploration work concluded at 5 P.M. Much to the dismay of those present, what was unearthed was a deep, twenty-inch layer of hardened earth situated on top of a water table. It was impossible for any human remains to have survived for such a long time under such harsh conditions. Later in the day and in the following days the search continued, but the media was mostly gone.

When the bulldozer stopped for the day, Marcos Rodríguez Peña, a local member of Foro por la Memoria (Forum for Memory, or Foro), another key national association, suggested that I visit another grave site located in the neighboring municipality of Madrigal de la Vera. Since 2000, there has been an explosion of associations related to the "recovery of historical memory" in Spain. Some of them are national in character—such as ARMH or Foro—while others maintain regional, provincial, or local profiles. Still others act as ad hoc groups of relatives associated with a particular or single grave. Some of them are well established, and some of them short-lived. Some of them collaborate with or include stable research and exhumations teams (ARMH, Foro), while some maintain more provisional arrangements with technical teams. Some of them maintain a distinguishable political ideology (especially Foro), while some of them maintain diverse sensibilities (Del Río 2005). The availability of economic aid for memory recovery activities from the Ministry of the Presidency between 2006 and 2011 contributed greatly to the proliferation of these groups—a proliferation that later receded. Overall, in hindsight, it is difficult to find a town or a village that has not had any "memory recovery" activity during this period. At times such activity has resulted in fullfledged, highly publicized exhumations and reburials, and at times in only informal conversations and information exchange. This is the context in which a myriad local activists like Lucio or Marcos operate. Through their advocacy, their lives constantly intersect with sites linked to killings, other victims' relatives, oral narratives and hearsay concerning Civil War repression, and a wide range of evidence—from documents extracted from national or municipal archives to private letters, photographs, or personal objects that reappear within the context of a particular memory research project.

The case of Madrigal, which Marcos had recently discovered, was different from that of Villanueva. The suspected grave had not yet been investigated by local activists or professional teams, no information was available on who might be buried there, and no relatives had yet requested that the area be explored. However, like many such places on the extensive map of Francoist repression, the grave was still recognizable in the contemporary landscape. In the lower part of a crop field that stretched across a hillside there was an oval-shaped, grass-covered area of untilled land. According to local testimony, it had been left untouched for decades. This was due to a certain permanence of its terrifying power throughout the previous decades, and a wariness about re-moving dangerous bones, but also—as contemporary research demonstrates—to a widespread and semiclandestine geography of resistance (Pile 1997) that was established and maintained by relatives, sympathizers, and neighbors and that expressed a sense of respect for the unduly dead and improperly buried (Ferrándiz 2008). Fieldwork across the country is bringing to light other un-tilled spots, almost imperceptible marks in neighboring trees or in plaster, in-formal tombstones in forests, or curved paths made to avoid a grave's location in addition to other latent funerary marks.

"Someone related to the victims should thank the property owner for hav-ing kept the area untouched all these years," said Marcos while on the spot. He went on to tell me the following piecemeal story, gathered in his home village—a story paradigmatic of thousands of similar stories being dusted off in the last decade. One night, while passing through the area, a shepherd heard his dogs barking anxiously, and then, in the distance, a voice shouting for mercy: "'Please don't kill me, I have four children!' . . . I'm not sure how many he said," recalled Marcos in an imperfect act of ventriloquism. The memory of that desperate plea and the howling of dogs continues to be the clearest indication that people had been executed in this area. Marcos did not know whose remains might be found in the alleged grave. In his conversations with people in the village, only one person had accepted the possibility that his grandfather might be among those buried in that spot. The villager's father had told him so on several occasions before he died, but he was unsure and not cooperative. "He's the only one so far," said Marco. "The people you talk to in the street won't say a word, as of today. We just need someone to speak out and say 'My grandfather is buried there and I want him out.'" Then they could move on, as in Villanueva.

It was almost nightfall when I returned to Las Albarizas. New develop-ments concerning the exhumation were being discussed in the country house owned by relatives of one of the missing women, Úrsula, where the few people remaining at the grave site had taken refuge from the fitful rain. The dispirited tone that pervaded conversations when I left the place two hours before had given way to renewed enthusiasm. "Little wonder," they said. The bulldozer had missed the graves by inches. Apparently an old shepherd had come over to the excavation site and suggested, on the basis of rumors he had been hearing all his life, that one of the graves, the one holding Úrsula and Bernarda, might actually be only a few feet away from the area under exploration. The people in the house had gone back to the site where the grave was supposedly located in order to discuss with the archaeologists whether this new location could in fact contain a grave, the extent to which it was consistent with the testimonies that had been gathered during the previous months, and the likelihood of finding it reasonably well preserved. Lucio had walked around the place a number of times holding a pendulum in his hand—an old peasant technique to trace water wells, equivalent to a dowsing rod—trying to draw a message of hope from the less-than-promising spot. Although the site was as close to the shallow water table as the rest of the meadow, spirits were high again.

As they began breaking the news to me, Charo, the current owner of the plot, arrived. She had been vey cooperative with Lucio and others regarding the search for the graves, which involved turning her plot upside down. She had chosen that particular moment to reveal to the murdered women's relatives that the person who had sold her the land twenty-eight years before had recommended that she not dig up the earth beneath four oak shoots if she did not want to come across human remains dating from the Civil War. Once again, as in Madrigal, plowing had apparently respected a presumed grave location. The new potential location was right across from the excavated area and the place indicated by the shepherd, but it doubled the number of exploration options for the following day, as the team would need to look for two close-by graves.

Around ten of us went down to the spot where the bulldozer had been digging. A drizzling rain fell steadily on the meadow in Las Albarizas. Some of the technicians, relatives, and activists were still getting late-hour calls on their mobile phones, as they had throughout the day, from people asking for aid in locating and unearthing human remains buried in other parts of the region or from journalists who needed eleventh hour data to complete an article. Charo, in near darkness, recalled the conversation she had had with the former landowner, as well as the information she had gathered about the

Figure 4.3 Nightly body-to-body grave search, after revelations displaced its presumed location by a few meters. Photo by the author.

killing: " 'Maybe you're thinking of ploughing and sowing this small patch of lowland,' he told me, 'and that might be a problem. . . .' He told me to be very careful. He said I shouldn't be surprised if the tractor unburied the bodies of some women. Then my father and some others told me the whole story. . . how they'd been shot and so on. . . . So I said to myself, 'Oh God, this is a weird place I've bought. . . .' But then I thought, 'if indeed those poor women are buried here, let them rest in peace.' " One of Úrsula's granddaughters interrupted, "My grandmother was holding a handful of vegetables in her hand. . . . They shot them all in the back. . . . They spent the whole day humiliating the women." Her words lingered in the night, as many grasped for words.

A few weeks later, Lucio told me a more elaborate version of the story, with a new cast of characters. By then, his information had been completed and enriched by the testimonies given by the descendants of some of the people connected with the events and who had remained silent until deciding to speak to him. The exhumation attempt had created quite a fuss in the village—where versions and counterversions were often made to confront one another in homes, bars, and other private and public spaces—but it had also encouraged people to break their silence. After the killing, the gunmen had asked some peasants and builders who were in the area to bury the corpses. The foreman for a crew working to build a tobacco drying place nearby told them that one of the women seemed to be alive. In response, they ordered, "Hit her with the hoe head." The master builder refused to do so. Two of the gunmen then killed her off themselves. A few days after the exhumation, the builder's son told Lucio that his father "was never quite the same again, he hid a machete underneath his pillow while he slept, he became ill and soon died."

The following day, after having successively experienced hope and despair, the archaeological team dismissed the possibility that someone might be buried in the meadow. Not a single trace of human remains had been found. Some of the victims' relatives had assisted with their own mattocks in the excavation of other possible locations nearby, but this proved equally unsuccessful. Yet in Lucio's view, the mere act of undertaking the excavation had made it possible, at least for a few hours, to publicly circulate the memory of these crimes. This meant reaching beyond familial and local contexts. Now many people in Spain, and even abroad, have learned about the tragedy of these five women, as an example of generalized repression. There was a Central Criminal Court document expressly urging an investigation into the events. Yet everything indicated that the remains of the women had been swallowed by the earth.

Institutional Involvement in Contemporary Exhumations

In the last decade, "memory recovery" work can be traced by following the ebb and flow of innumerable associations, exhumations, reburials, and different kinds of commemorative acts, some of which have received extensive media exposure in Spain and abroad. It has contributed to an increase in a more or less politically militant awareness of historical injustice and impunity among the families and comrades of the Republican rearguard victims who lie in mass graves. One main element behind this awareness raising is the belief that these graves—which were shamefully abandoned not just during the dictatorship, which was expected, but also during more than thirty years of democracy—were a form of infrahuman burial that needed to be dealt with if the country really wanted to confront the dirty secrets of the past. In general

terms, the social movement and its repertoire of claims and actions have managed to elicit a sense of solidarity in the political Left, whereas right-wing
parties and sympathizers have claimed foul, circulating in the public domain
a discourse that hails Spain's transition to democracy—including the 1977
Amnesty Law—and laments the unnecessary vindictiveness of opening up
"old wounds" after social peace was supposedly achieved in the late 1970s and
early 1980s. Amid political controversy, the steady work of associations and
the accumulation of shocking media reports have exerted pressure on local,
regional, and national authorities. Particularly where left-wing parties—
mostly socialist—have had institutional responsibilities, they have been expected to provide institutional umbrellas for exhumations and all activities
related to them, to draw up legislation, and to set up funding and logistical
support. Yet the scale and details of the intricate process of local, regional, and
national memory politics is complex and well beyond the scope of this chapter. I will just give a brief overview.

Elsewhere I have exposed the limits and sluggishness of the Spanish institutional exhumation model, a sort of human rights outsourcing scheme that
has generated at least as many difficulties on the ground as it has solved (Ferrándiz 2013). Many of the problems are linked to the fact that, for many years,
exhumations preceded the legislation that gradually—though insufficiently—
has come to frame them. In this sense, most have taken place in a sort of legal
and legislative limbo, as no existing regulation protects either mass graves or
exhumed bones. To give but one crucial example, in their quest against the
impunity of Francoism, some associations have consistently informed local
authorities about the discovery of Civil War bones that exhibit signs of violence whenever such graves have been found and unearthed, thus trying to
drag the exhumations into criminal cases. As noted earlier, the statute of limitations for an alleged crime is twenty years in Spanish law, and Civil War
killings at least triple that span. In addition, the 1977 Amnesty Law and later
judicial rulings like Garzón's 2012 acquittal by the Supreme Court have
blocked any further judicial prosecution of the crimes of Francoism. Thus, in
most cases, judges have interpreted recovered bones as being outside their
jurisdiction. Some Autonomous Communities (Catalonia in 2009, Andalusia
in 2009, and Navarra in 2011) have progressively legislated on such excavations by approving technical protocols and, in some cases, establishing uneven
public policies to support or assist them (Etxeberria 2012). But this has been
done either belatedly or, in some cases, such as in most communities gov-
erned by the right-wing Partido Popular, not at all.

Here I focus only on legislation directly concerning exhumations passed at the national level. As noted earlier, between 2006 and 2011 the central government established a line of funding for "memory recovery" activities, amounting to more than 25 million euros. This initiative was linked to the design of a memory law. After bitter political debates in Parliament and the media, the Socialist government led by José Luis Rodríguez Zapatero (2004–2011) finally passed Act 52/2007, or the Historical Memory Law, which is considered grossly unsatisfactory by most associations. Associations and relatives particularly resented that the kangaroo military trials that led tens of thousands to the shooting squads and the mass graves after 1937 (Consejos de Guerra) were described by the law as *illegitimate* but not *illegal*. The law also fell short of expectations with regard to exhumations. The law pledged that the state would "facilitate" the tasks of "locating and identifying persons who violently disappeared during the Civil War or subsequent political repression and whose whereabouts is unknown" (Art. 11). It also states that "the competent public authorities will authorize prospection tasks" and that "exhumations shall be submitted for administrative authorization by the competent authority" (art. 13). In article 12, the government guaranteed the drafting of a "multidisciplinary protocol of scientific action." Although funding was provided, exhumations, identifications, and the overall management of the executed bodies was transferred to the associations and groups of relatives and, ultimately, to the technical teams collaborating with them. The disappointment with the elaboration of this law led many activists and relatives to file reports on forced disappearances in Garzón's office at the National Court, leading to the developments described at the beginning of the chapter and the importance of the attempts to conduct exhumations in Villanueva.

The national Protocol of Action on Exhumations was not published in Spain's Official State Bulletin until the end of September 2011,[6] when Rodríguez Zapatero's second government was about to lose the upcoming general elections, almost four years after the passing of the Historical Memory Law, six years after the implementation of the funding scheme, and eleven years after the inaugural Priaranza del Bierzo 2000 excavation, and after more than 280 exhumations had been conducted throughout the country. In those parts of Spain where no regional protocols had been drawn up, for more than a decade there were neither official guidelines regarding technical methodologies to be used in exhumations nor clear regulations on the scientific and funerary management of the bodies recovered (Etxeberria 2012; Montero 2010). It was the archaeological and forensic teams themselves who, since 2000, have

developed and fine-tuned excavation, laboratory, and identification procedures, basing their practice on international documents such as the Minnesota Protocol and on an action plan published by forensic doctor Francisco
Etxeberria (2004), a crucial actor in the technical organization of the excavations and associated laboratory and identification tasks. Yet for more than a
decade, and in the absence of mandatory protocols, some exhumations have
been conducted with questionable procedures. In the 2011 document, where
the administrative aspect of funerary management is concerned, section E
describes the "final destination of the bodies." The differentiating factor is the
identification of the cadavers. In the first type, "the families receive them and
conduct the ceremony they wish." In the second, "they are buried in the cemetery of the municipality where the mass grave is located." The protocol concludes that "for the transfer of mortal remains and their reburial or cremation,
a permit is required from the Autonomous Community and competent local
authority." Until 2011, state indolence with regard to the management of exhumed bodies gave rise to bizarre situations and, in practice, to self-
management by relatives, associations, and some specialized technical teams.
After that, the new bureaucratic and technical demands established in the
protocols have made the diggings and reburials even more difficult to perform, especially in the absence of official funding after 2012.

"Dumped Off Like Dogs": Dignifying
Graves and Memories of Past Crimes

Dignifying the bodies that are perceived as having been thrown or buried like
dogs on roadsides; in pits, wells, or ditches; and off cliffs is a crucial part of a
dynamic political culture that can be interpreted differently depending on the
profile of the historical memory groups charged with conducting particular
exhumations and on how such work has been incorporated into a growing
repertoire of memorialist actions during the past decade. In this context, improper, insufficient burial or offensive burials; burials used as a form of punishment; all the animal-like burials carried out after deaths that resulted from
a coordinated, repressive strategy designed to exclude those killed from the
community of the dead through the absence of funerary rites and mourning
practices; and burials where bodies were piled up, undifferentiated, "thrown"
in a disorderly manner are still entangled in the violence that put an end to
individuals' lives. In fact, it is important to highlight that the necropolitical

journey of the bodies now exhumed actually began with the arrests, tortures, executions, and burials of persons in mass graves seventy years ago. All these techniques are to be understood as instruments of political terror. Many of these individuals were executed for their left-wing ideals, both real or attributed, whether they were militants or people with softer political profiles. From this point of view, the process of exhumation and reburial of mortal remains reverts a systematic form of repression and discipline and intentionally offensive placement of cadavers in unnamed graves beneath an ideological umbrella that theorized and treated the "reds"—those who experienced insurgent and subsequently Francoist violence—as "infrahumans" (Rodrigo 2008:62). Taking into account this historical perspective regarding exhumed and recuperated remains is essential for a contemporary interpretation of excavations capable of providing understanding of the civil, political, and religious rituals they trigger (Ferrándiz 2013).

Differing opinions regarding how to revert the systematic violence waged on persons and cadavers during the war and Francoism continue to exist in contemporary Spain. In the early twenty-first century, some associations, such as the one that continually cares for and watches over a mass grave in Oviedo where at least thirteen hundred bodies are buried, believe the most appropriate homage to those killed is to preserve the burial ground in a way that keeps it intact and unexcavated. This strategy seeks to keep the site alive through yearly commemorations, thus accentuating the didactic potential of the atrocity committed and the very disorder and inhumanity that the burial represents. From this perspective, to dig up the grave without judicial accountability would amount to erasing a key chapter in the history of the Franco regime's cruel repression. This point of view was eventually displaced by the body-centric turn in the memory-recovery field, as exhumations accumulated and executed skeletons and human remains took center stage in public debates. Other associative groups, in contrast, have since 2000 decided to revert Francoist necropolitics through the exhumation and open exposure of the cadaveric remains, the attention paid to victims' wounds and their personal objects wherever possible, and the meaningful reburial of remains, thus triggering the complex and delicate postmortem journey that Verdery calls "the political [life] of dead bodies" (1999).

Concerning reburial, there is no agreement as to what an honorable funerary treatment actually means, or as to the most appropriate death and political rituals to achieve this. When I asked Lucio what his mother meant when she used this expression, he replied, "she felt that they were not in the cemetery like 'the people,' that she was not allowed to mourn for them, that they were there without any funeral honors." The lack of preestablished guiding principles regarding "proper" commemoration and reinhumation of bodies exhumed in Civil War mass graves together with the transformation in funerary practices and the state's lax, inconsistent attitude regarding such practices, has sparked a process of largely self-managed funerary "neoritualization." Initially it was improvised on the spot and varied widely from place to place. However, funerary neoritualization has become more stable and self-conscious with the passing of years and as associations and practices have consolidated previously unstructured patterns in reburial rituals.

In the simplest of terms, there seems to be two dominant sensibilities regarding exhumation practices, which are represented by the two dominant associative groups: the ARMH and Foro. In both cases, the Civil War reburial rituals of Francoism, the only formal historical precedents of commemorative practice, are obviously alien and politically offensive to members of associative groups. A second consideration is that, although on the local level some politicians—mayors, council members, even senators—have officially attended commemorative reburial ceremonies, there has been a noteworthy reluctance from key political authorities during both conservative or socialist governments to get formally involved in these events or to define these rituals as "state" funerals. Third, it is important to take into account the thorny relationship of associations with religious ceremonies and Christian burials (*cristiana sepultura*) that dominate the country's funerary culture and that are often the preferred reinhumation ritual for exhumed bodies by many relatives. ARMH does not encourage religious rituals but respects the relative's choice, whereas Foro is overtly opposed to them and fights them actively, bringing overly political ceremonies to the very Catholic cemeteries. Religious intervention in the reburials would, by this logic, be totally counterproductive—even a betrayal of those who have been exhumed—in light of the church's involvement in more than a few of the *paseos*—the promenades that often ended in the extrajudicial execution of Republicans. In fact, the church's ideological narration of the Civil War, its embrace of Francoism as a part of a larger crusade, its current refusal to support the exhumation process—which church spokespersons have described repeatedly as divisive—and its continued support for and promotion of the beatification of martyrs who were victims of Republican repression are only a few examples of why Catholic rituals are under scrutiny and often eschewed.

Overall, since 2005, there has been a growing trend in the repertoire of secular funerals, especially with regard to their political content, that seeks to establish continuity with the Second Republic (1931–1939)—a desire often expressed in the ubiquity and preeminence of the Republican tricolor flag and other associated emblems. The slippery concept of "dignifying," like the other facets of similar dynamic processes, is also being transformed, enriched, and diversified by time and social practice. For some it is a necessary act of emotional closure, for others a call for further political action, while for others it is both. Also, while the Republic grows as a necessary referent, there are considerable differences among dignifying actions in, say, Andalusia, the Basque Country, or Catalonia that are associated with different necropolitical constructions of victimhood during the war and Francoism and that are framed within different political imagined communities. This can be easily seen in the language in which they are performed, or in the flags or flag ensembles that translate the historical experience of those exhumed into the present. Globally and locally, the expanding repertoire of dignifying practices includes the naming all the disappeared (*todos los nombres* projects); narrating and recording of victims' stories; excavating, identifying, and reburying those found in mass graves; commemorating events and persons, erecting monuments, and establishing commemorative cycles; promoting research projects; drawing up mass grave maps (*mapas de fosas*); or working through mourning through the search for a particular mass grave, even when such a search fails, as was the case in Villanueva.

Villanueva is an example of the tensions between different approaches to reburial and dignification. In view of the absence of bodies, the symbolic closure of the search consisted in an act of tribute initially planned as a private ceremony, but which eventually brought together a significant number of people. Exceptional as it was, it shows the versatility of funerary arrangements made in conjunction with contemporary exhumations of Spain's mass graves. It was organized by members of the Spanish chapter of Psychologists Without Borders (Psicólogos sin Fronteras). Psychologists have been present at many exhumations conducted by the ARHM, Foro, and other associative groups where they have offered to accompany relatives with psychosocial support. Usually, psychologists are present at commemorative events, but they do not design such homages. In the case of Villanueva, however, the psychologist Guillermo Fouce, who was also the coordinator of the emotional wrap-up of the body search, suggested that in view of the futility of the extended search attempt to exhume, the effort might best conclude through creation of an ad hoc mourning structure. Although the rationale behind these closure ceremonies is

Figure 4.4 Lucio García Tornero addresses friends and relatives during the closure ceremony. The three stones under a Republican flag stand for the missing women. Photo courtesy of Lucio García Tornero.

increasingly under fire in certain critical academic quarters that are wary of the rising power of transitional justice and its hegemonic paradigms to colonize historical suffering, and the fear that such actions might reflect a poor understanding of the complexity of social trauma, it certainly makes sense to many of the social actors involved on the ground (Bevernage and Colaert 2014).

The relatives in Villanueva chose two places as the symbolic locations of the mass graves of the disappeared women. They placed stones on these, two in one case and three in the other with each stone symbolizing one of the five women, and decorated them with flowers. The only material object recovered during the search for the mass graves was a Republican coin, which was placed beneath one of the stones. The ceremony at each site differed slightly, each one expressing the divergences between the relatives regarding the proper tone for the ceremonies. A more private homage was conducted at the site commemorating the lives of Úrsula Sánchez and Bernarda García. Two round stones and bouquets of flowers were placed and then buried with spadefuls of earth. At the place chosen to mark the grave of Lucio's three relatives, the ceremony was more public and political. A Republican flag was used and the flowers offered were arranged on it. Relatives, including Lucio, told the story of the women who had been murdered at this particular site and talked about the importance of the search process and the public resurfacing of the forgotten women. He also recited two poems. Although the women's bones had not been found, said Lucio in his speech, their memory had been saved from oblivion and was bound to become a guide for future personal and political action.

Notwithstanding disputes, the two types of sensibilities—different associations and clusters of relatives—are each influenced by the other, each in its own way; they are also nourished by new commemorative, dignifying elements from elsewhere in the world. As the category of "disappeared" has become consolidated and more widespread as a way of referring to the people shot, especially after Garzón's 2008 judicial mise-en-scène, a more political usage has evolved, for instance, of the first portraits and photographs of the people executed, which relatives have retrieved and taken with them to share with those present at the exhumations (Ferrándiz and Baer 2008; Ferrándiz 2010). In this growing interweaving of acts to dignify those defeated in the Spanish Civil War with forms of tribute, remembrance, and reparation that are now part of a transnational repertoire, a growing number of associations and relatives define the fundamental and inexorable objective of this process as the public recognition of the fact that these deaths were part of a systematic plan of extermination, making them, according to international human rights law, crimes against humanity. I indicated at the beginning how Villanueva de la Vera was on the verge of reaching this point of contact. But this aspect of the many-sided contemporary dignifying processes, an angle we might call a "transnational dignifying route" that is closely connected to the global expansion of human rights discourse and practice, has already expanded beyond the particular circumstances of this specific case where families and technical teams attempted to exhume five missing women from the province of Cáceres.

Notes

This essay was written with support from Spain's Ministerio de Economía y Competitividad (project MINECO CSO2012-32709), and is based on a case study formerly published in Spanish (Ferrándiz 2009).

1. See Garzón's ruling of October 16, 2008, p. 3.

2. See http://www.boe.es/boe/dias/2007/12/27/pdfs/A53410-53416.pdf, accessed on May 10, 2013.

3. See Ferrándiz (2013) for an analysis of *Soliloquio de grillos*, a play based on Candeleda's grave containing three executed women.

4. In the period 2006–2011, the Socialist government assigned around 25 million euros to these activities, which included, besides exhumations (30 percent of the total budget), testimony gathering projects (13 percent), archival research (11 percent), documentaries (9 percent), exhibitions (7 percent), publications (7 percent), etc. After the huge Socialist defeat in the November 2011 general elections, the landslide-winning right-wing party (Partido Popular) vowed to continue funding only exhumations—at a rate of 2.5 million a year—but the expense soon disappeared from the government's budget.

5. The television networks included the Franco-German network ARTE, a Canadian network, Canal Extremadura TV, and regional television. The nationwide public television network mentioned it in its afternoon programs. *Periódico de Extremadura, Hoy, Público*, and Agencia EFE were among the newspapers and news agencies that provided on-site news coverage. In the following days, several Spanish dailies including *El Mundo, ABC, La Razón,* and *El País* published stories about the event; *El Mundo* ran an entire page.

6. The *Protocolo de actuación en exhumaciones de víctimas de la Guerra Civil y la dictadura*, published in the Official State Bulletin of September 27, 2011, can be consulted at http://www.boe.es/boe/dias/2011/09/27/pdfs/BOE-A-2011-15206.pdf, accessed on May 10, 2013.

Bibliography

Álvaro Dueñas, Manuel. 2009. Control político y represión económica. In *La gran represión: Los años de plomo del franquismo*, ed. Mirta Díaz-Balart, 235–282. Madrid: Flor del viento.

Bevernage, Berber and Lore Colaert. 2014. History from the Grave? Politics of Time in Spanish Mass Grave Exhumations. *Memory Studies* 7(4): 440-456.

Box, Zira. 2010. *España: Año cero*. Madrid: Alianza.

Casanova, Julián, 1999. Rebelión y revolución. In *Víctimas de la Guerra Civil*, ed. Santos Juliá, 57–177. Madrid: Temas de Hoy.

———. 2001. *La iglesia de Franco*. Madrid: Temas de Hoy.

Castells, Manuel. 1996. *The Rise of the Network Society*. Vol. 1 of *The Information Age: Economy, Society and Culture*. Oxford: Blackwell.

Chaves, Julián. 1995. *La represión en la provincial de Cáceres durante la Guerra Civil (1936-1939)*. Cáceres: Universidad de Extremadura.

Del Río, Ángel. 2005. Los alcances del movimiento social de recuperación de la memoria histórica: Apuntes de la experiencia andaluza. In *Las políticas de la memoria en los sistemas democráticos: Poder, cultura y mercado*, ed. Susana Narotzky and José María Valcuende, 133–153. Seville: ASANA-FAAEE.

Díaz-Balart, Mirta. 2009. Las mecánicas de la infamia. In *La gran represión: Los años de plomo del franquismo*, ed. Mirta Díaz-Balart, 133–234. Madrid: Flor del viento.

Espinosa, Francisco. 2003. *La columna de la muerte*. Barcelona: Crítica.

Etxeberria, Francisco. 2004. Panorama organizativo sobre antropología y patología forense en España: Algunas propuestas para el estudio de fosas con restos humanos de la Guerra Civil española de 1936. In *La memoria de los olvidados*, ed. Emilio Silva, Asunción Esteban, Javier Castán, and Salvador Pancho, 183–219. Valladolid: Ámbito.

———. 2012. Exhumaciones contemporáneas en España: Las fosas comunes de la Guerra Civil. *Boletin Galego de Medicina Legal e Forense* 18: 13–28.

Fernández Albendiz, Carmen and Lucía Sosa Campos. 2012. *Memoria de Guillena: Tierra de rosas silenciadas*. Seville: Aconcagua.

Ferrándiz, Francisco. 2008. Cries and Whispers: Exhuming and Narrating Defeat in Spain Today. *Journal of Spanish Cultural Studies* 9(2): 177–192.

———. 2009. Fosas comunes, paisajes del terror. *Revista de Dialectología y Tradiciones Populares* 64: 61–94.

———. 2010. De las fosas comunes a los derechos humanos: El descubrimiento de las desapariciones forzadas en la España contemporánea. *Revista de Antropología Social* 19: 161–189.

———. 2011. Guerras sin fin: Guía para descifrar el Valle de los Caídos en la España contemporánea. *Política y Sociedad* 48(3): 481–500.

———. 2013. Exhuming the Defeated: Civil War Mass Graves in 21st-Century Spain. *American Ethnologist* 40(1): 38–54.

Ferrándiz, Francisco and Alejandro Baer. 2008. Digital Memory: The Visual Recording of Mass Grave Exhumations in Contemporary Spain. *Forum Qualitative Sozialforschung/ Forum: Qualitative Social Research* 9(3): Art. 35.

Garzón, Baltasar. 2008. *Auto, Diligencias previas (proc. abreviado) 399/2006V* (16–10–2008). Madrid: Juzgado Central de Instrucción n 5, Audiencia Nacional.

Golob, Stephanie. 2002. "Forced to Be Free": Globalized Justice, Pacted Democracy, and the Pinochet Case. *Democratization* 9(2): 21–42.

Harvey, David. 1989. *The Condition of Postmodernity*. Cambridge: Blackwell.

Lyotard, Jean-François. 1984. *The Postmodern Condition: A Report on Knowledge*. Minneapolis: University of Minnesota Press.

Mbembe, Achille. 2003. Necropolitics. *Public Culture* 15(1): 11–40.

Montero, Juan. 2010. Exhumando el legado material de la represión franquista: De la percepción social a la encrucijada jurídica y patrimonial. In *Recorriendo la Memoria/ Touring Memory*, ed. Jaime Almansa, 67–82. Oxford: Archeopress.

Pile, Steven. 1997. Introduction: Opposition, Political Identities and Spaces of Resistance. In *Geographies of Resistance*, ed. Steven Pile and Michael Keith, 2–32. London: Routledge.

Preston, Paul. 2012. *The Spanish Holocaust: Inquisition and Extermination in Twentieth-Century Spain*. London: Harper Press.

Rodrigo, Javier. 2008. *Hasta la raíz: Violencia durante la Guerra Civil y la dictadura franquista*. Madrid: Alianza.

Taussig, Michael. 1987. *Shamanism, Colonialism and the Wild Man: A Study in Terror and Healing*. Chicago: University of Chicago Press.

———. 1999. *Defacement: Public Secrecy and the Labor of the Negative*. Stanford: Stanford University Press.

Verdery, Katherine. 1999. *The Political Lives of Dead Bodies*. New York: Columbia University Press.

Vinyes, Ricard. 2002. *Irredentas: Las presas políticas y sus hijos en las cárceles franquistas*. Madrid: Temas de Hoy.

Watts, Michael. 1992. Capitalisms, Crisis and Cultures I. Notes Towards a Totality of Fragments. In *Reworking Modernity: Capitalisms and Symbolic Discontent*, ed. Allan Pred and Michael Watts, 1–19. New Brunswick, NJ: Rutgers University Press.

Chapter 5

The Quandaries of Partial and Commingled Remains

Srebrenica's Missing and Korean War Casualties Compared

Sarah Wagner

In the aftermath of war, the acts of excavating graves and exhuming bodies are often cast as a grim yet incontrovertible means of truth telling. The veracity of mortal remains seems axiomatic: as forensic anthropologists and archaeologists are wont to say, bones don't lie, and graves tell stories.[1] In the related discourse of transitional justice and redress, forensic science intervenes to give voice to the silenced, cutting through the layers of postconflict political contestations to reveal and fix facts (Sanford 2003; Wagner 2008; Rosenblatt 2010; Ferrándiz 2013; Aronson 2011). But science is never apart from politics, and postwar circumstances are rarely so neat or amenable to tamping down truth. More often than not, the conditions of postconflict societies and states are messy and chaotic. There is perhaps no better emblem of the lingering, disordering effects of violent conflict than the partial bodies of missing persons whose remains emerge from temporary, unmarked, and illicit graves in the aftermath of war. They invite weighty questions: what happens when the story is incomplete, when bones returned are too fragmented or too sparse to piece together a full account of past loss or a narrative of future care?

In embodying both presence and absence—that which is found and that which remains lost—partial remains illustrate both the legacy of violence and the necessarily insufficient nature of repair. In destruction's wake, communities of mourners (Rosenblatt 2010:949) and their advocates, state officials, and forensic personnel are left to grapple with the phenomenon of missing persons and unidentified remains, some of which may be highly fragmented, severely degraded, and impossibly incomplete. Thus, beyond dealing with mass casualties, these communities and actors face the conundrum of partial remains—that is, the dilemmas of practice and knowledge that arise when fragmented bodies are recovered and returned to surviving families in pieces and in stages. This chapter examines this process and its complications, illustrating how partial remains compel improvisations in the social and scientific care for the dead. It explores two cases in which forensic experts faced enormous challenges in identifying partial remains, endeavors that in turn compounded and complicated the grief experienced by surviving families as they attempted to care for their missing loved ones: remains recovered from the secondary mass graves of the July 1995 Srebrenica genocide in Bosnia and Herzegovina and remains of U.S. service members killed in the Korean War and later turned over by the North Korean government to U.S. officials in the early 1990s. Although situated in very different contexts—from the conflicts themselves to the circumstances of recovery and identification—these two instances reveal both the extraordinary successes of the scientific efforts to reattach names to unrecognizable remains and return them to surviving families and the ethical dilemmas raised by evolving forensic practice, including advances in forensic genetics. Significant lapses in time and the incomplete condition of the remains themselves introduce especially perplexing questions for the forensic personnel and families that redefine notions of scientific resolution and ritual ministrations for the dead. The story of these partial remains reminds us of the dynamic interplay between scientific knowledge and social meaning, defying facile claims of "closure" at the same time as they expose the necessarily improvisational side of caring for the dead whose bodies have undergone repeated dislocation and disruption.

Fundamental Forensic Tenets of
Partial, Commingled Remains

The problems presented by the Srebrenica and Korean War cases examined in this chapter derive not only from the partial and degraded conditions of the skeletal remains but also from the commingled state in which they were recovered. As a social action, commingling demonstrates a fundamental lack of care: in times of war, bodies of the enemy dead are stripped of humanity, devoid of their sacredness—viewed literally as refuse to be disposed of or, as Sophocles warns, carrion left "unwept, unsepulchred, a welcome store for the birds . . . to feast on at will."[2] But from the medico-legal perspective, as a scientific object, commingled remains complicate set boundaries about what is known and what can be known. To begin with, commingled remains are not just "mixed up" in the same way a single skeleton haphazardly jumbled on an examination table with dirt and debris can be regarded as "mixed up." What is lost is not merely the anatomical order and organization of the body but also, critically and specifically, the wholeness and separateness of the individual. In resolving commingling in large assemblages of remains, forensic scientists are not simply "unmixing" the remains and restoring anatomical order; they are seeking to rebuild individuals, trying to address loss of life and identity, alongside loss of physical, corporeal integrity.[3]

Furthermore, as a scientific object, commingled remains resulting from mass fatality incidents raise specific, compelling issues surrounding forensic practice itself—that is, the intent of the identification efforts and the ties between exhumation as an archaeological endeavor and identification as an anthropological one. Parameters must be set: does identification mean identifying all victims (e.g., some biological element of each person is identified) or identifying all the recovered remains? In postwar Bosnia and Herzegovina, as with the U.S. government's attempts discussed here, identification efforts aimed to reassociate an individual name with each skeletal element recovered, no matter how partial, fragmented, or degraded. For reasons that will be outlined below, this has not always been possible, but the objective driving efforts is consistent: the responsible institutions have sought to identify and return all possible remains to surviving relatives. In both instances these efforts have encountered formidable obstacles regarding the extent to which recovered remains have been commingled. Commingling adds an element of uncertainty beyond that of a nameless set of complete or partial remains, which nevertheless are associated with one individual decedent. Where does one set of remains begin and the other end? How to distinguish and disassociate them? The work begins with a fundamental presumption: "In a mass fatality context, the overarching tenet regarding commingling is that human remains with no anatomical/physical connection must be considered to be commingled. This principle also applies to remains that are spatially associated but present no valid anatomical connection. From the perspective of the forensic investigator, resolving commingling, and ultimately decedent identification, requires careful management of both the human remains and the data generated during the recovery and postmortem examination" (Kontanis and Sledzik 2008:317). Provenience—the position of the artifact (here mortal remains) charted in time and space—informs the forensic anthropological examination in important ways, helping to parse out individual skeletal remains based on the "story" told by the grave (Tuller 2012:165).

Adhering to this tenet is especially critical in cases of mass graves from armed conflicts where disarticulation and commingling are always a real, pressing possibility given the illicit nature of the sites and the criminal intent behind their creation: "Not only are bodies initially commingled, as they are deposited in the grave, but the conditions of the bodies prior to burial, decomposition processes, taphonomic conditions within the grave,[4] and the intentional destruction and/or tampering of the bodies by those who buried them contribute to the eventual disarticulation and mixing of elements, more so when an initial (primary) mass grave is disturbed and bodies are moved to a (secondary) mass grave" (Tuller, Hofmeister, and Daley 2008:7). Thus, intent to identify in good faith and according to standardized scientific protocol must nevertheless confront countervailing intent—criminal, malfeasant, or simply negligent.

Just as underlying scientific presumptions about corporeal integrity, and its violation and resolution, inform forensic efforts to isolate and identify individual sets of remains from larger commingled assemblages, the social value placed on integrity depends on the community that has experienced the loss of life—namely, the surviving mourners. While the examples of Srebrenica and the Korean War casualties prioritize return of remains for sanctified burial (including, in the latter case, burial of cremated remains), not every culture requires a complete body, or a complete set of remains, to undertake ritual care for the deceased. Rather, the point here is that the dilemmas raised by commingled remains within these two communities, one shaped by Islamic practice, the other dominated by Judeo-Christian tradition, reflect the sociocultural values attached to notions of corporeal integrity and, especially with the Korean War cases, the primacy of the individual and therefore individual identity.[5]

Srebrenica's Secondary Mass Graves

Within the world of forensic science, Srebrenica, Bosnia and Herzegovina, is known for its mass graves, in particular its secondary mass graves filled with commingled, partial sets of skeletal remains. Srebrenica had been a UN "safe area," an enclave that housed at its height some fifty thousand Bosniak (Bosnian Muslim) refugees throughout much of the three-and-a-half-year war begun with the disintegration of former Yugoslavia in the early 1990s. In July 1995 the Army of the Republika Srpska (Vojska Republike Srpske or VRS), led by Bosnian Serb general Ratko Mladić, overran the enclave, expelling twenty-five thousand women and children, and killing over eight thousand men and boys.[6] In an effort to hide traces of the war crimes, several weeks later VRS forces returned to primary gravesites, and with heavy machinery, including backhoes and dump trucks, they dug up, transported, and reburied the victims' remains in secondary mass graves. The manner of disinterment caused severe skeletal disarticulation, and remains became highly commingled in the process with individual victims' skeletal remains scattered into two or more subsequent, secondary grave sites (Komar 2003; Stover and Peress 1998).

In the immediate postwar years, recovering and identifying missing persons, including the Srebrenica missing, were chief among the goals of repair and reconstruction. But the Srebrenica graves, with their trenches of commingled, partial bodies, presented a formidable obstacle, overcome only after significant political, financial, and technological intervention gave rise to a DNA-based identification system. Over the past nineteen years, the forensic efforts, assisted by the International Criminal Tribunal for the former Yugoslavia and the International Commission on Missing Persons (ICMP) and its associated facility of the Podrinje Identification Project, the local Federal Commission for Missing Persons, which was eventually subsumed into the Missing Persons Institute of Bosnia and Herzegovina (Wagner 2010:35–41),[7] have succeeded in identifying over 6,922 Srebrenica missing.[8] The number, however, belies the complicated nature of this work. Many of those identified were individuals whose remains had been exhumed from multiple secondary mass graves; piecing them back together has required significant resources and time. It also necessitated improvisations of forensic work beyond, and in some instances because of, the success of the DNA technology.

As the case of Srebrenica's secondary mass graves has repeatedly underscored, recovering partial remains is at its core an incomplete process. From the very beginning, the VRS's intentional jumbling of bodies made identifying the missing a frustratingly disjointed endeavor. Scattered across eastern Bosnia, the secondary mass graves were often linked to a common site of execution and primary burial location; in some instances, they were directly linked to one another (Congram and Tuller 2013; Vennemeyer 2012).[9] Knowledge of these connections introduced a troubling question for the forensic specialists in the early years of the

DNA-based identification program: given the potential for future related exhumations, how much of a body constituted enough to complete an identification and therefore a resolved case? How partial was partial, how complete was complete? Related questions arose surrounding communication with families of the missing—namely, the conundrum of how knowledge was to be imparted. Local and international experts deliberated about when to present evidence of identification to families. Should they do so after all possibilities of recovery had been exhausted or as soon as any part of the skeleton was identified? A final set of questions addressed the issue of reburial. The nature of the ongoing excavation and exhumation activities meant that the fragmented bodies of the secondary mass graves would be recovered piecemeal. Should they also be returned piecemeal or amassed over time to allow for as complete a burial as possible? With already recovered and reburied cases, should newly discovered remains necessitate reexhumation for osteological analysis?

This final issue points to one of the most problematic developments within the identification efforts of recent years, as DNA testing has uncovered past mistakes—highly infrequent but painful ones nevertheless. Partial bodies returned to families and subsequently reburied have turned out to contain skeletal elements that do not belong to the same individual. Incomplete or erroneous forensic work, including osteological examinations, may have mistakenly reassociated bones with a set of skeletal remains identified primarily through DNA testing of samples cut from long bones (e.g., the femur or humerus).[10] A subsequent exhumation (at another secondary mass grave) reveals the error, when DNA testing provides evidence that recovered remains appear to duplicate some elements among those already buried. For example, a set of remains identified through DNA-led evidence was originally buried with a left tibia that had been reassociated through osteological examination (e.g., pair matching, articulation, or taphonomic analysis), but a later exhumation from an associated secondary mass grave yields a second left tibia, reassociated this time through DNA matching. The original left tibia is, in all likelihood, an erroneously associated skeletal element. The finding in turn requires that forensic staff reexhume and reexamine the originally buried set of remains. The body—buried, dug up, ripped apart, and then reburied by the perpetrators—undergoes a different though connected series of disruptions, once again buried, dug up, and reburied by the forensic personnel.

For the Srebrenica families, the social reckoning of partial bodies and the inherently messy, complicated process of reconstituting individual identity have encompassed a careful negotiation of scientific practice and religious doctrine. When the DNA-based program began to identify more and more partial remains, the Islamic Community (Islamska zajednica) of Bosnia and Herzegovina was asked for its guidance. Its clerics crafted a theological response to the question of what merited enough of a body for burial, drawing from Sharia law to argue that even one bone could be accorded the funeral rites of the Muslim tradition (Wagner 2008:215–218).

Despite this imprimatur of the sacred, families nevertheless fretted about the possibilities of future excavations and future recovered bones. Partial remains complicated the already fragmented process of ministering to bodies that had been so violated in death and in posthumous disposition. Under normal conditions, funerary rituals work to contain and transform the contaminating presence of the corpse; they also tend the spirits of the bereaved. Émile Durkheim notes that ceremonies of mourning have the effect of "bringing individuals together, putting them into closer contact, making them participate in the same state of the soul. . . . The group feels its strength gradually return; it begins to hope and to live again. Mourning is left behind, thanks to mourning itself" (2001:299). Just so is the atmosphere of the annual July 11 commemoration of the Srebrenica genocide: tens of thousands of people, the overwhelming majority Bosniaks, convene in the open spaces of the Srebrenica-Potočari Memorial and Cemetery to witness the sanctified burial of victims whose remains have been identified over the previous year. Typically, there are four or five hundred coffins being interred in individual plots within the collective cemetery. But set against the interrupted and revived anguish of families for whom skeletal remains return in fragments over time, Durkheim's words underscore the aberration of ritual at hand. How many times should one bury the same person?

To be sure, the identification of partial remains does not always mean additional bones will be recovered. But the incomplete, interrupted nature of the process shades the ritual reckoning of death and forces on the families and forensic specialists alike improvisations of practice. One of the primary and most burdensome improvisations relates to the passage of time. Contrary to social and religious prescriptions of how to care for the dead, many of the Srebrenica families have decided to hold off on burying partial remains with the hope that imminent excavations will unearth more bones. This is true for some two hundred cases of the already identified. But there are competing clocks: relatives, especially parents, fear their own time will run out before subsequent recoveries, and they will not live to partake in the postponed burial. Distance further frustrates the matter as many families left Bosnia in the wake of the genocide, their movement echoing the violent dispersal of victims' bodies. Material considerations constrain their ability to tend the dead, especially when remains are returned in stages. Families weigh costs of travel and time against the probability of future recoveries, the grim calculations born from the phenomenon of Srebrenica's mass graves. For the surviving relatives, then, rather than being left behind, mourning lingers and resurges with the unsettling news of additional recoveries.

With the DNA technology's success in identifying partial remains exhumed from the secondary mass graves and, in those rare instances, revealing past errors of reassociation, the forensic specialists acknowledged the anxiety produced by the piecemeal recovery process. Designing a consent form that anticipated the unpredictable course of recovery and identification efforts, case managers at the Podrinje Identification Project began presenting families with options of what to do in the face of possible additional remains.[11] Among other required information, the form poses the following questions to the representative of the missing person (the primary contact among the surviving relatives):

- Do you wish to be notified about new DNA test results?
- If yes, do you wish to be notified (a) of every new DNA test result, or (b) when the mortal remains are relatively complete?
- Do you want the additional remains to be buried (a) along with those already buried remains, or (b) in the collective ossuary at the Srebrenica-Potočari Memorial and Cemetery?
- Do you wish to be present for the reexhumation/reassociation/burial?
- Do you want the remains that have been found to date to be buried in the originally planned burial site?[12]

The consent form structures future communication between the families and the forensic specialists. On one level, it sets the ethical parameters of decision making whereby expert and layperson agree to the terms under which information will flow and be acted on. It becomes the road map for the discomfiting possibilities that lie ahead. On another, it negotiates the prickly terrain of authority over the dead, extending the possibility of collective rather than individual responsibility for future ceremonial mourning. From its earliest conception, the memorial center's cemetery was to offer shelter to every victim of the genocide: a white tombstone would be erected regardless of whether remains were ever recovered and identified. Though at present a rose bed, the collective ossuary will house the remains that forensic experts cannot reassociate with individual skeletons, as well as serve as a resting place for partial remains in instances when surviving kin decide against disturbing the gravesite of already buried bones.

Improvisation in forensic practice and social ritual converge on the occasion of reexhumations, prompted by the recovery and identification of additional remains. These are carried out collectively: since July 2006, on eight separate occasions forensic specialists working on the Srebrenica identifications have reexhumed 336 cases.[13] Currently, there are several hundred additional cases for which reexhumation will be necessary. While close family members may choose to attend (which the majority of them do), it is a juridical and scientific procedure with representatives of the local court, the Missing Persons Institute, pathologists, anthropologists, and technical support workers all present to oversee and carry out the painstaking task of disinterring coffins to examine and reassociate newly recovered remains with the already buried bones.

Though sanctioned and witnessed (both in a religious and scientific manner), the reexhumations nevertheless underscore the imprint violence made on the lives of the Srebrenica survivors. In his essay on the collective representation of death, Robert Hertz concludes that "mourning is in its origins the necessary participation of the survivors in the mortuary state of their relative; it lasts as long as the state itself" (2009:145). For the families of the Srebrenica missing, in particular those who must care for bodies torn asunder and recovered in fragments, the disjointed, often suspended, mortuary state of their deceased protracts and intensifies their mourning. Grief is interrupted, and ritual extemporized. These improvisations help navigate the impasses of Srebrenica's partial bodies and partial knowledge, providing families with some source of comfort against the possibilities of indefinite absence. At the same time, they testify to the unpredictable, uncertain work of forensic truth telling in a society where illicit graves still abound and bones still elude.

Korean War Missing: The K208 Cases

On the second floor of Building 220 on Pearl Harbor Naval Station there is a large examination room dedicated to the U.S. military's most challenging forensic task: the "K208" cases, so named for the 208 boxes containing remains of missing U.S. service members turned over to U.S. officials by the government of the Democratic People's Republic of Korea (DPRK) between 1990 and 1994. Thousands of bones cover the room's tables and counter space, from osseous flakes that fill petri dishes, the residue of postmortem degradation, to long, solid femora that could only have belonged to a robust young man cut down in the second or third decade of his life. The room's order—its carefully arranged sections, separated by provenience and mitochondrial DNA (mtDNA) sequencing—belies the utter chaos that characterizes the K208 cases. Despite what North Korean officials initially intimated and U.S. forensic scientists at first believed, the 208 boxes did not represent 208 individual sets of skeletal remains; rather, as the story slowly unfolded and evidence gradually emerged, the boxes contained the skeletal remains of upward of 600 U.S. service members killed during the war, with a minimum number of one individual per box, sometimes many more (Jin et al. 2014:409); indeed, among all of the K208 accession boxes, the average number of mtDNA sequences represented in one box is 4.3.[14] How these bones became so commingled is subject of debate within the Central Identification Laboratory (CIL) of the Joint POW/MIA Accounting Command (JPAC), the U.S. government's forensic facility responsible for recovering and identifying unaccounted-for U.S. service members from past conflicts.[15]

Understanding the complexities of the identification procedures developed to resolve the K208 cases depends first on contextualizing U.S. casualties in the Korean War and governmental responses, on the Korean peninsula as in the United States, which extend well into present-day foreign policy debates. The Korean War has not ended, either as a political reality or a social experience. In this volume, Heonik Kwon traces the contours of a war comprising so many different and entangled sites of conflicts—between international powers, between postcolonial states, and among neighboring villages—through the memory of surviving families and their care for the dead. Paying particular attention to the untold, often agonizing, stories of the Korean War among families of the missing, he notes how the conflict's specter looms large and how its "human dramas exist and are still unfolding in Korea." So too, related stories of missing U.S. service members and their unrecognized remains persist, gradually rising to the fore through the work of forensic identification and surviving families' engagement in that process.

Overshadowed by the alternately triumphant and contentious narratives of World War II and the Vietnam War, the "Forgotten War," as it is known in the United States, was hardly unremarkable in its scale of human destruction: an estimated 2.5 million civilians died and hundreds of thousands of lives were lost in battle among North Korean, South Korean, Chinese, British, and U.S. forces.[16] In addition to the 33,651 killed in action, some 7,900 U.S. service members are still missing from the conflict, and JPAC is charged with recovering and identifying those yet unaccounted-for individuals. But as the K208 cases illustrate, these forensic efforts have met with significant obstacles, proceeding in fits and starts, dependent on the often mercurial political dynamics between the DPRK and United States. While the U.S. government works closely with South Korea on recovering war dead,[17] the majority of missing U.S. service members are thought to have died in North Korea, in major battles or in prisoner-of-war (POW) camps.[18] Access to potential burial sites, however, is tied to broader geopolitical concerns, and, consequently, remains of U.S. dead repatriated from North Korea have come not as much from U.S.-led excavations (as is the case with Vietnam-era and World War II missing), but through unilateral turnovers received directly from the North Korean government. With such accessions, remains are acquired without American forensic personnel involved in their original excavation or procurement. In this regard, unilateral turnovers present a particular dilemma of knowledge, as uncertainty surrounding the remains' posthumous state and whereabouts during their forty years of rest in North Korea bedevils the scientific work of identification back in the United States.

Uncertainty shades the K208 cases in a manner different than in Srebrenica. The secondary mass graves of Srebrenica presented forensic scientists with a relatively closed set of unknowns: graves had to be found and correlated with execution and detention sites, and remains had to be exhumed and matched to members of a known population of missing persons. Authorities knew generally how the remains came to be partial and commingled. Furthermore, the forensic work has been carried out and explicitly documented not by former combatant forces but by legally authorized local and international officials. Thus, while VRS forces purposefully sought to hide traces of the crimes by destroying remains, principles of transparency and accountability have dictated how the responsible forensic personnel excavate, exhume, reassociate, and identify remains in postwar Bosnia. The K208 boxes, on the other hand, raise multiple, interconnected uncertainties. To begin with, the cause or origin of the commingling is unknown: the remains came to the CIL in stages, through a series of unilateral turnovers that took place from 1990 to 1994, with the bulk of the boxes arriving in 1993; although the North Korean officials provided the provenience (i.e., location) of recovery at the village level, there was no means to verify its accuracy or guarantee control over the evidentiary chain of custody tying those remains to a specific place or incident of recovery (Jin et al. 2014:420). Rather, puzzling taphonomic evidence suggested that the remains might have been stored for several years above ground (rather than recently exhumed) before the North Korean government decided to repatriate them.[19] Furthermore, the very *incomplete* state of the remains presented an enormous black box, complicating every aspect of the scientific enterprise of establishing what is knowable and unknowable about the remains and individual identity. Were associated remains still in North Korea? Were they among the boxes but too small or degraded to be reassociated? Persistent uncertainties undercut U.S. scientific autonomy, a fact that became increasingly obvious with subsequent excavations, osteological analyses, and, most conclusively, DNA testing, which helped reveal the problematic conditions of the incomplete remains with their incomplete posthumous record.

The plot twists in the story of the K208 cases are many, but running throughout is the thread of trust in expert knowledge, performed and legitimized by officials from two former combatant states. Within the broader political discourse, forensics becomes a proxy stage on which each state projects both its ideologically distinct narrative about the past conflict and its current geopolitical positioning. Joint recovery operations thus are begun and suspended because of larger political points of contention between the two states: for example, the Bush administration indefinitely suspended operations in North Korea in 2005, citing security concerns and the status of the DPRK as a "State Sponsor of Terrorism" (Dyhouse 2012). In late 2011, the U.S. and North Korean governments signed an agreement to resume recovery efforts and plans were drawn up for joint recovery operations in 2012. These were once again halted, however, after the North Korean government launched a ballistic missile on April 13, 2012. Families of the missing track these false starts, lamenting lost opportunities and decrying political obstructionism, their criticism aimed at U.S. administrations and the North Korean state.

While foreign policy and diplomatic wrangling have dictated the terms of engagement between the two states on the MIA issue over the past two decades, contestations around knowledge and scientific practice have simultaneously shaped the recovery and identification processes on the ground and in the lab. DNA testing had begun to uncover isolated discrepancies in the early years after the K208 turnovers, but the first signs that something more widespread was amiss with the K208 cases—that they were not each one individual from the location named by the North Koreans—arose when a joint U.S.-DPRK operation excavated a site of a supposed infantry fighting position

in October 2000. Remains recovered appeared to have been placed there recently, and osteological analysis of taphonomy and trauma patterns suggested
that they might not even be associated with an infantry ground loss.[20] Once
the remains were received at the CIL and samples were sent to the Armed
Forces DNA Identification Laboratory, mtDNA sequencing established that
some of the remains belonged to individuals already identified several years
earlier through dental evidence—namely, individuals received as part of the
K208 unilateral turnovers. This discovery ushered in a period of review and
reorientation toward the K208 cases, as the disconcerting truth about commingling within the boxes became clearer and CIL scientists recognized the
possibility that their North Korean counterparts might still have additional
remains, including portions of remains of individuals who had already been
identified by the CIL and returned to surviving families.

Far from an evidentiary "silver bullet," DNA testing raised as many questions as it answered with the K208 cases, not only in what might be possible
in terms of accounting for the missing but also regarding disposition of the
remains. The CIL began aggressively sampling the K208 cases in 2000, and the
mitochondrial sequences that came back from the DNA lab over the next
several years helped to define more sharply the locations of loss and pools of
missing associated with the proveniences provided by the North Koreans,
reassociate previously disarticulated and commingled skeletal elements, and
identify some 101 individuals as of December 2013 (Jin et al. 2014:408). But
one look at the massive Excel spreadsheet created by CIL scientists to track
and order the chaotic, jumbled contexts of K208 boxes makes its limitations
clear. On the one hand, the results are limited by the probabilistic nature of
genetic profiling, particularly mtDNA sequencing, which is less exclusive than
autosomal (nuclear) testing. Rather than constituting a "truth machine"
(Lynch 2008; Aronson and Cole 2009; Kreimer 2005) understood by the lay
public and its *CSI*-fueled imaginaries to fix facts, the DNA results yielded
inherently partial data. With a relatively rare mitochondrial sequence, and
provided a family reference sample existed with AFDIL, the mtDNA analysis
might well produce a probative match.[21] But probative matches did not translate directly to reassociating additional remains, some of which might be too
small or too degraded to yield a viable sample for DNA extraction and analysis. Furthermore, mtDNA testing in some instances uncovered duplicative
elements, as in the Srebrenica cases. Thus, while on an empirical level, the
genetic evidence generated a wealth of critical (albeit partial) data, it also
raised significant ethical dilemmas about scientific protocol for the already

identified and buried remains and subsequent decisions about disposition that the family would have to face.

In a manner different from that in the Srebrenica cases, which are largely driven by DNA analysis, the CIL has adopted a more balanced approach to untangling the commingled remains of the K208 cases, whereby DNA evidence is firmly nested in a larger process of knowledge production. The balance struck between the powerful, though limited, probative value of the mtDNA testing and other anthropological methods of analysis, including osteology and dental and radiographic evidence, is apparent in the lab's standard operating proce-dure—namely, the addendum created specifically to address the K208 cases as representative of commingled human remains: the guidelines set out the steps of "segregation" whereby subsets of remains, for example, sharing the same mtDNA sequence, are removed from the larger assemblage of commingled re-mains; and "consolidation," by which discrete individual sets of remains are isolated from a subset.[22] In each of these stages of disaggregating and reassoci-ating remains, the usefulness of mtDNA testing is understood strictly in rela-tion to other lines of evidence, especially data gleaned from anthropological analysis—from pair matching and articulation to taphonomy, osteometric sort-ing, the biological profile generated, and trauma analysis.[23] Genetic profiles join and must converge with those different results to move a set of remains closer toward reestablishing (even if only partially) its corporeal integrity.

However balanced an approach JPAC has developed to segregating sub-groups and consolidating individual sets of remains, K208 nevertheless poses a cluster of related problematics, ethical and social: (1) what constitutes "identification"—not only in a forensic but also a social context—when a skel-eton has been so disarticulated and thus its elements so commingled? Is it the first or second or fifth time that DNA evidence conclusively matches a bone to a missing individual? Within the context of the K208 remains, what becomes the threshold to act on the evidence assembled and inform the surviving family (specifically the primary next of kin)? (2) In the case of already identified and buried remains, when additional elements are subsequently associated, point-ing toward the presence of duplicative elements among the already buried, what obligation does the surviving family have to the larger community of the missing and their mourners? That is to say, do they have a duty, beyond caring for their own identified relative, to assist other families by allowing their loved one's grave to be disinterred and the remains to be reexamined? (3) How best to address the existential crisis of partial data produced by genetic evidence and by the possibility of future recoveries, unilateral turnovers, and newly associated skeletal elements? This final question circles back toward the original conundrum posed by partial, commingled remains and the need to determine the intent behind identification—that is, all remains or all individuals? Here, however, the issue concerns the intent of families regarding how, when, and what to bury, and their sense of connection to the wider community of mourners. While the CIL, along with the larger MIA accounting community, has sought to craft ethically sound, compassionate guidelines for how best to engage surviving families in these perplexing circumstances, there are no easy answers, especially as each identification emerging from the K208 has undergone its own unique journey from recovery to examination, sampling, reassociation, and eventual recognition.

That this journey has stretched across so many decades is confusing, and in some cases, troubling for surviving families. With the very rare exception, parents of the Korean War dead have gone to their own graves without the much-desired return of their lost sons. The mantle of mourning passes down to the next generation of kin, who likewise struggle to understand the temporal gaps. In a 2012 letter published by the Coalition of Families of Korean and Cold War POW/MIAs, a family member laments time's cruel passage while rejoicing in the news of identification:

The long-awaited phone call came Sept. 26, 2011. A seemingly routine records update conversation changed dramatically when the question was asked, "Are you sitting down?" In an emotional mixture of shock, joy and relief, the surprising news that Sgt. 1st Class Rogers' remains had been identified was confirmed. In 61 years of fearing the worst, hearing the horror stories of trained Chinese killer attack dogs or American soldiers tied to posts and burned alive or POW's marched for miles over frozen ground to face an execution squad, at least a bullet to his head was swift. Sadly, by only three years, his mother did not live quite long enough see her boy come home, her "good kid" as she called him. At age 97, after 58 years of grieving, her prayers for a son's funeral unanswered, his mother barely missed his home-coming.

Could anyone have foreseen that learning of a loved one's death by probable execution was "good news"? How does a family describe the barrage of emotions? Over-whelming joy? Yes, that a lost soldier can be laid to rest next to his brother and sister and a father and mother who grieved for the remainder of their lives. Tremendous sadness? Yes, for a young life tragically extinguished by a bullet to the back of the brain. Extreme shock? Yes, for an event every family member prayed and desperately hoped for, but never really believed would happen. Disappointment? You bet, in the knowledge that remains retrieved in 2000 would not be identified until 2011, even though the lab obtained DNA samples from his mother & brother in 1999 (Coalition of Families of Korean and Cold War POW/MIAS 2012).

The range of emotions—joy, sadness, shock, disappointment—echoes sentiments in the newsletter's opening piece, which warns, "Time is an issue itself. Family members and eyewitnesses to many missing men's fates are aging." As with Srebrenica, the countermanding expectation is that science will defy time, both its degrading effects and its relentless metronome of mourning for missing remains and still unaccounted-for lives.

Conclusion

Placed side by side, the examples of Srebrenica's secondary mass graves and the K208 boxes challenge facile notions of swift and definitive resolutions in any forensic effort to recover and identify missing persons whose remains have been so disturbed. They deepen our understanding of the lingering effects of violent conflict, where sorrow spans decades and binds generations in degrees of grief and the enduring desire to care for and remember the missing. Thrown into relief are the myriad ethical dilemmas raised by such remains. Forensic scientists and surviving relatives are forced to untangle their own at times competing agendas, determining the appropriate balance between the demands of scientific protocol and the needs of a grieving community. Commingled remains especially highlight the complicated ties when mixed bones mean mixed needs and priorities, as relatives must sort out for themselves their obligations not only to their deceased but to other families of the missing, some of whom may depend on strangers' consent to recover the remains of their loved one.

For as much as they reveal the obstacles inherent in such incomplete and compromised remains, the examples of the Srebrenica and Korean War cases also illustrate the potential for innovation on both sides of the equation, social and scientific. Scientific improvisations in how to grapple with such partial and highly commingled remains have also led to improvisations in social care, in rites and rituals enacted by surviving families. In this sense, both communities (scientists and mourners) have developed systems for anticipating these painfully aberrant circumstances. Consent forms written to stave off heartache, collective ossuaries for the permanently unrecognizable bits of bone, ritualized reexhumations to assure against error all attest to the social and scientific attempts at normalizing the tragically abnormal. Embedded in those anticipatory strategies is the acknowledgment that time moves slowly and that recovery and identification are imperfect acts. But such resignation also breeds tempered hope—the hope for a return of corporeal integrity and human dignity before too long.

Notes

On the Srebrenica-related identification efforts, I am grateful to staff at the Podrinje Identification Project, especially Enver Mujagić and Nedim Duraković, and Matt Vennemeyer, Tom Parsons, and especially Adnan Rizvić at the International Commission on Missing Persons for their critical feedback at various stages of this work. An earlier version of text from the Srebrenica case study appeared in the chapter "The Social Complexities of Commingled Remains," in Bradley J. Adams and John E. Byrd, eds., *Commingled Human Remains: Methods in Recovery, Analysis, and Identification* (Oxford, UK: Academic Press, 2014). At JPAC's Central Identification Laboratory, special thanks likewise go to Drs. John Byrd, Jennie Jin, and Laurel Freas for their assistance with the Korean War cases. Research for this study was supported by the National Institutes of Health (RO1 HG0057020).

1. Forensic anthropologist Clyde Snow has popularized this saying (Sanford 2003:47), often elaborating that "they don't forget" and "they make good witnesses." See Joyce and Stover's biography of Snow, *Witnesses from the Grave* (1991), and, as another example, Maples's memoir *Dead Men Do Tell Tales* (1995).

2. From R. C. Jebb's translation of Sophocles's *Antigone* (Cambridge: Cambridge University Press, 1891). In this volume, see Kwon's discussion in Chapter 3 of Antigone's dilemma between the duties of kinship and the dictates of the state.

3. I am grateful to Laurel Freas for this insight.

4. *Taphonomy* refers to the conditions and processes (such as burial, decay, and preservation) by which organisms become fossilized.

5. For example, Robben traces the nineteenth-century Catholic belief in the spiritual force of the soul after death and its power over the world of the living in shaping the "Argentine political obsession with corpses and their spirits" during the late twentieth-century "dirty war" (2000:98–103, quote on 100). On the U.S. military's efforts to commemorate war dead through individuated identifications, see Wagner (2013).

6. For a full account of the wartime enclave, its fall in July 1995, and the crimes that followed, see Rohde (1997); Honig and Both (1997); Matton (2005); Wagner (2008:21–57); Nettelfield and Wagner (2014:8–16).

7. Since 1999, the Podrinje Identification Project has existed as the primary facility dedicated specifically to the Srebrenica cases. Until 2010, it operated as part of ICMP,

itself tasked with assisting the governments in the former Yugoslavia to account for forty thousand people missing as a result of the conflicts of the 1990s, including over eight thousand men and boys missing from Srebrenica. In 2010, the project was removed from ICMP and transferred to local control, specifically the Tuzla Canton-run Commemorative Center (Komemorativni centar). See ICMP, news release, "Podrinje Identification Project: Successful Partnership Between ICMP, MPI and Tuzla," April 27, 2010, http://www.ic-mp.org/press-releases/podrinje-identification-project-to-mpi/, accessed on June 27, 2013. Other international organizations integral to the recovery and identification process of the Srebrenica missing, especially in the immediate postwar years, include the Ludwig Boltzmann Institute of Human Rights, Physicians for Human Rights, and the International Committee of the Red Cross.

8. This is the total number as of September 29, 2014. For updated figures on reference samples collected and remains identified, see the ICMP's online inquiry which provides statistics for missing persons in Bosnia and Herzegovina per municipality of disappearance: http://www.ic-mp.org/fdmsweb/index.php?w=per_municipality&x=search&l=en.

9. Matt Vennemeyer (2012) has examined connections between execution sites and mass graves, using DNA to help map the five major "mass grave assemblages" (Branjevo Farm; Kozluk; Petkovci Dam; Lazete; and the Kravica Warehouse).

10. See Komar (2003) on inaccuracies and errors generated in osteological analysis of Bosnian cases.

11. On the transfer of control of the project to local authorities, mentioned earlier, see ICMP, "Podrinje Identification Project," accessed on February 5, 2013.

12. JKP Komemorativni Centar Tuzla, "Saglasnost za ukop, odnosno reekshumaciju sahranjenih posmrtnih ostataka radi reasocijacije" (Agreement regarding burial, specifically the reexhumation of buried mortal remains for the purpose of reassociation), on file with the author.

13. Reexhumations took place in July 2006, May 2011, April 2012, May 2012, December 2012, April 2014, July 2014, and October 2014.

14. Although relatively rare, there are a number of single-box cases within the K208 group, i.e., just one individual is represented in a box. Notably, these single-box cases are much more common for POW camp accessions, while the "battlefield clean-ups" are significantly more commingled; when soldiers died in a POW camp, often their fellow service members buried them, resulting in relatively intact individual sets of remains. In a battlefield situation, however, it is more likely to have multiple bodies commingled from the onset.

15. Established in 2003, JPAC is part of the U.S. government's long-standing efforts to account for service members missing and killed in action, a tradition that dates back to the Civil War (Faust 2008). JPAC emerges specifically from the Vietnam War, with its antecedents being the Joint Casualty Resolution Center, itself the successor institution for the wartime casualty processing organization Joint Personnel Recovery Center, which operated in-theater, with mortuary facilities in Saigon. In 1973, at the war's end, U.S. Army mortuary operations were relocated to Thailand, and three years later the laboratory was transferred to Hawaii and reopened as the CILHI. In 1992, the Joint Task Force–

Full Accounting was established as a finite entity with a finite mandate; nine years later, in 2003, it and CILHI merged to become JPAC, which included the CIL.

16. The war pitted the DPRK and People's Republic of China, supported by the Soviet Union, against the U.S.-led United Nations forces. Other nations involved included Australia, Belgium, Canada, Colombia, Denmark, Ethiopia, France, Great Britain, Greece, Holland (Netherlands), India, Italy, Luxembourg, New Zealand, Norway, Philippines, South Africa, Sweden, Thailand, and Turkey.

17. The South Korean government established its own Ministry of National Defense Agency for Killed in Action Recovery and Identification, which signed a memorandum of understanding with JPAC in 2008 to support joint investigations and operations in South Korea. In May 2012, JPAC hosted a repatriation ceremony for remains of Korean War unknowns determined to not be U.S. service members; the UN flag-draped coffins were returned to Seoul, where the ministry's scientists continued to try to identify the remains. For use of DNA analysis on resolving South Korean MIA cases, see Lee et al. (2010).

18. According to the Defense POW/Missing Personnel Office, "[o]f more than 7,950 men lost and unrecovered from the Korean War, about 5,500 were lost in North Korea, and most of these men were part of well defined, geographical populations." DPMO fact sheet, "Major Remains Concentration in North Korea," http://www.dtic.mil/dpmo/korea/maps/, accessed on February 5, 2013.

19. A forensic geneticist at the Armed Forces DNA Identification Laboratory, Suni Edson, notes that DNA testing also supported this conclusion: "The hypothesis was that the K208 were most likely stored in less-than-optimal conditions (i.e., room temperature); therefore, the mtDNA present would be more degraded and tend to produce partial or no sequence data" (2007).

20. See also Jin et al. (2014:411).

21. Once samples are cut from remains at the CIL, they are sent to the Armed Forces DNA Identification Laboratory for DNA extraction and analysis. JPAC employs mtDNA testing because it is long-lasting, is abundant, and does not change much from generation to generation. See JPAC's web page, "Family Reference Samples," http://www.jpac.pacom.mil/index.php?page=frs&size=100&ind=3, accessed on May 3, 2013.

22. JPAC Laboratory Manual, part 3, SOP 3.3, annex B, "Segregation and Analysis of Commingled Human Remains (CHR)," B4.3.2.

23. Ibid., B4.3.3.

Bibliography

Aronson, Jay. 2011. The Strengths and Limitations of South Africa's Search for Apartheid-Era Missing Persons. *International Journal of Transitional Justice* 5(2): 262–281.

Aronson, Jay D. and Simon A. Cole. 2009. Science and the Death Penalty: DNA, Innocence, and the Debate over Capital Punishment in the United States. *Law and Social Inquiry* 34(3): 603–633.

Coalition of Families of Korean and Cold War POW/MIAS. 2012. Newsletter, winter. http://coalitionoffamilies.org/newsletters/Coalition%20Newsletter-Winter%202012. pdf (accessed September 27, 2014).

Congram, Derek and Hugh Tuller. 2013. Spatial Analysis and Modeling of Missing Person Burial Locations in Multiple Armed Conflict Contexts. Presentation at the Annual Meeting of the American Academy of Forensic Sciences, February 18–23, Washington, DC.

Durkheim, Émile. 2001. *The Elementary Forms of Religious Life.* Trans. Carol Cosman. New York: Oxford University Press.

Dyhouse, Tim. 2012. U.S. Will Resume MIA Searches in North Korea. *VFW Magazine* February, 8. http://digitaledition.qwinc.com/publication/?i=95290&p=10 (accessed March 4, 2014).

Edson, Suni. 2007. Identifying Missing U.S. Servicemembers from the Korean War—Do Storage Conditions Affect the Success Rate of mtDNA Testing? www.promega.com, March. http://www.bioplein.nl/attachments/File/Humane_Sporen/ProfilesInDNA_1001_14.pdf (accessed March 4, 2014).

Faust, Drew Gilpin. 2008. *This Republic of Suffering: Death and the American Civil War.* New York: Knopf.

Ferrándiz, Francisco. 2013. Exhuming the Defeated: Civil War Mass Graves in 21st-Century Spain. *American Ethnologist* 40(1): 38–54.

Hertz, Robert. 2009. A Contribution to a Study of the Collective Representation of Death. In *Saints, Heroes, Myths, and Rites: Classical Durkheimian Studies of Religion and Society,* ed. and trans. Alexander Riley, Sarah Daynes, and Cyril Isnart, 109–180. Boulder, CO: Paradigm,

Honig, Jan Willem and Norbert Both. 1997. *Srebrenica: Record of a War Crime.* New York: Penguin Books.

Jin, Jennie, Ashley L. Burch, Carrie LeGarde and Elizabeth Okrutney. 2014. The Korea 208: A Large-Scale Commingling Case of American Remains from the Korean War. In *Commingled Human Remains: Methods in Recovery, Analysis, and Identification,* ed. Bradley J. Adams and John E. Byrd, 407–424. Oxford, UK: Academic Press.

Joyce, Christopher and Eric Stover. 1991. *Witnesses from the Grave: The Stories Bones Tell.* Boston: Little, Brown.

Komar, Debra A. 2003. Lesson from Srebrenica: The Contributions and Limitations of Physical Anthropology in Identifying Victims of War Crimes. *Journal of Forensic Sciences* 48(4): 713–716.

Kontanis, Elias and Paul Sledzik. 2008. Resolving Commingling Issues During the Medicolegal Investigations of Mass Fatality Incidents. In *Recovery, Analysis, and Identification of Commingled Human Remains.* ed. Bradley J. Adams and John E. Byrd, 317–336. Totowa, NJ: Humana.

Kreimer, Seth F. 2005. Truth Machines and Consequences: The Light and Dark Sides of Accuracy in Criminal Justice. *New York University Annual Survey of American Law* 60: 655–674.

Lee, Hwan Young, Na Young Kim, Myung Jin Park, et al. 2010. DNA Typing for the Identification of Old Skeletal Remains from Korean War Victims. *Journal of Forensic Sciences* 55(6): 1422–1429.

Lynch, Michael. 2008. *Truth Machine: The Contentious History of DNA Fingerprinting.* Chicago: University of Chicago Press.

Maples, William R. and Michael Browning.1995. *Dead Men Do Tell Tales: The Strange and Fascinating Cases of a Forensic Anthropologist.* New York: Random House.

Matton, Sylvie. 2005. *Srebrenica: Un génocide annoncé* (Srebrenica: A genocide foretold). Paris: Flammarion.

Nettelfield, Lara J. and Sarah E. Wagner. 2014. *Srebrenica in the Aftermath of Genocide.* New York: Cambridge University Press.

Robben, Antonius C. G. M. 2000. State Terror in the Netherworld: Disappearance and Reburial in Argentina. In *Death Squad: The Anthropology of State Terror*, ed. Jeffery A. Sluka, 91–113. Philadelphia: University of Pennsylvania Press.

Rohde, David.1997. *Endgame: The Betrayal and Fall of Srebrenica, Europe's Worst Massacre Since World War II.* New York: Farrar, Straus and Giroux.

Rosenblatt, Adam. 2010. International Forensic Investigations and the Human Rights of the Dead. *Human Rights Quarterly* 32(4): 921–950.

Sanford, Victoria. 2003. *Buried Secrets: Truth and Human Rights in Guatelama.* New York: Palgrave Macmillan.

Stover, Eric and Gilles Peress. 1998. *The Graves: Srebrenica and Vukovar.* Zurich: Scalo.

Tuller, Hugh, Ute Hofmeister, and Sharna Daley. 2008. Spatial Analysis of Mass Graves Mapping Data to Assist in the Reassociation of Disarticulated and Commingled Remains. In *Recovery, Analysis, and Identification of Commingled Human Remains*, ed. Bradley J. Adams and John E. Byrd, 7–29. Totowa, NJ: Humana.

Tuller, Hugh. 2012. Mass Graves and Human Rights: Latest Developments, Methods, and Lessons Learned. In *A Companion to Forensic Anthropology*, ed. Dennis Dirkmaat, 157–174. Malden, MA: Wiley-Blackwell.

Vennemeyer, Matt. 2012. An Analysis of Linkages Between Robbed Primary Graves and Secondary Graves Related to Srebrenica Missing. Presentation at the Alpe-Adria-Pannonia International Meeting on Forensic Medicine, May 31–June 2, Sarajevo.

Wagner, Sarah. 2008. *To Know Where He Lies: DNA Technology and the Search for Srebrenica's Missing.* Berkeley: University of California Press.

———. 2010. Identifying Srebrenica's Missing: The "Shaky Balance" of Universalism and Particularism. In *Transitional Justice: Global Mechanisms and Local Realities after Genocide and Mass Violence*, ed. Alex Hinton, 25–48. New Brunswick, NJ: Rutgers University Press.

———. 2013. The Making and Unmaking of an Unknown Soldier. *Social Studies of Science* 43(5): 631–656.

9/11: Absence, Sediment, and Memory

Francesc Torres

There is no place for the past to take place except right now.
—Robert Duncan

1

At 08:46 A.M. on 11 September 2001, I was in New York, three hundred meters from the World Trade Center. Until then, I had never been in a situation remotely similar to a lethal act of air-borne aggression on a civilian population, a mode of war that appeared with the twentieth century and which has accompanied us since then in all its savagery. A few days after the attack, contemplating the devastation of Ground Zero and recalling that indelible moment, I thought: this must have been how the catastrophe in Guernica began, that market day in 1937; one moment you were in the world and the next you were in hell.

2

In his book *A History of Bombing,* Sven Lindqvist maintains that all the forms of mass, industrialized death that targeted Europe during the last century's two world wars, particularly in the second, had already been used long before in the colonies of European powers in Africa and the Middle East. In fact, the Germans used chemical weapons—gas—to annihilate the whole Herero population in southwestern Africa in the decade of the eighties in the nineteenth century; Belgium's King Leopold II used forced labor to kill ten million Congolese in twenty years, also in the nineteenth century; Spain attacked the holy city of Xauén in Morocco with white phosphor bombs in 1925, using airplanes lent by France and flown by American mercenary pilots; the English bombed Iraqi villages to observe the psychological effect of air attacks on the civil population in the same decade of the last century; the Italians did the same in Abyssinia a decade later. The victims' physical traits and skin color, as Joseph Conrad would say, meant that these cases were never considered war crimes or genocides. Even in Europe, more than sixty years had to pass from the end of World War II for the Germans to finally feel on relatively secure moral grounds to raise the issue of the criminality of Allied carpet bombings of their cities (see W. G. Sebald, *On the Natural History of Destruction*). The Japanese silence regarding Hiroshima and Nagasaki as war crimes, however, is remarkable, while Washington's Smithsonian Air and Space Museum exhibits with complete moral comfort the B-29 bomber *Enola Gay*, which carried out the Hiroshima mission on 6 August 1945. The attack on the World Trade Center was unquestionably an act of terrorism, but we have to invert our perspective to realize that every air bombing on civil populations, since airplanes first appeared, have been more acts of terrorism than acts of war.

3

In the year 2004, I photographed the exhumation of a mass grave from the Spanish Civil War in Villamayor de los Montes, in the province of Burgos, for two reasons. The most obvious was to contribute as much as I could to revealing a crucial aspect of the war's legacy, that is, the abandonment of the bodies of Republicans persecuted and murdered by paramilitary groups in areas taken over by the rebels under Franco. That repression continued after the war ended, well into the decade of the fifties in the last century. Almost eighty years after the end of the war in Spain, there

continue to be tens of thousands of bodies abandoned all over
Spanish territory as testimony of a pathological apathy, affecting
practically the entire Spanish political class, though particularly the
country's two main parties, which have been swapping power for
the last three decades: the People's Party (Partido Popular, rightist)
and the Spanish Socialist Workers' Party (Partido Socialista Obrero
Español, PSOE, center-left). The second reason for photographing
the Burgos exhumation was of a more personal nature. A long time
ago now, I discovered that the event with the most decisive
influence on my life, making me who I am and what I am
politically, ideologically, culturally, and emotionally, was a war that
had taken place almost a decade before I was born. Since then, the
absolute impossibility of a physical connection with those years I
had not experienced became a genuine obsession. It seemed unfair
to be denied an active or testimonial role in an event of which I was
a direct outcome. Reducing this gulf between my history and
History, even symbolically, was what took me to Villamayor de los
Montes.

4

In 2006, thanks to a friend who works in urban development for
New York's City Hall, I learned of the existence of an extraordinary
place that practically nobody knew anything about, except for those
involved: a very small group of people. It was Hangar 17 in the cargo
area of the city's John F. Kennedy Airport. This obscure site housed
the objects from Ground Zero of the World Trade Center that were
identified as historically and testimonially relevant for preservation.
This was carried out as the cleaning went along, literally from the
first day of the clean-up; in other words, somebody was immediately
aware that a significant part of the story of September 11, 2001, was
already deposited in the huge mountain of debris that the two towers
became when they collapsed, and that it was absolutely necessary for
millions of tons of debris to be filtered in order to select what could
help narrate and help people remember that terrible day, both for the
generation of citizens who lived through it as well as for future
generations. This meant creating an archaeology of the present, a
radical contradiction in terms unless it was carried out from a

perspective whose vanishing point is a hypothetical future, perceiving the present as the past in a prodigious intellectual feat. It was a work of enormous merit by the Port Authority of New York and New Jersey, owner of the World Trade Center, so what the Authority decided to conserve ended up temporarily in an empty aviation hangar it had jurisdiction over. The only things missing were the remains of the airplanes used in the attack, parts of which were withheld as forensic evidence and the rest returned to the airline owners.

5

Hangar 17 was closed to the public. After a process that was shorter and less complex than expected, I was allowed to visit the area without cameras. The impression I got was unforgettable. There was

A bicycle rack from the vicinity of the World Trade Center. Some months after this rack was brought to Hangar 17, a messenger contacted the Port Authority to reclaim his bicycle. The rider came to JFK International Airport to get it, but seeing its condition, pulled a key from his pocket and took the lock, leaving the bicycle behind. Photo by the author.

room in the hangar for a whole jumbo passenger airplane with space left over, and it was filled with thousands of tons of all kinds of objects: gigantic structural parts of the towers, fire service vehicles, police vehicles, ambulances, PATH train wagons (the line connecting the south of Manhattan with Jersey City, passing below the Hudson River), even bicycles padlocked to urban furniture, objects from stores in the underground shopping area, huge balls that looked like volcanic magma—to which I will return later—clothes, personal belongings. . . . The place was extraordinary, extremely moving and unique in the sense that it showed the layout of a museum that was never to be. Everything had entered in a planned way and been ordered into categories. The most complicated objects from a conservation point of view were kept under museum environmental conditions; as humidity and temperature could not be controlled in the whole hangar area, generic grouping allowed the creation of independent zones, sometimes simple plastic tents, in which the necessary environmental control could be achieved. However, the objects remained, shall we say, in a clinically pure state as historical sediment before being categorized and incorporated into a politically acceptable and culturally assimilated historical narrative. In other words, they had been taken away from Ground Zero but they had not yet arrived at the (symbolic) Ground Two of the future Memorial Museum, the area of memory, of historical narrative, of supreme ideological balance, and of political consensus on how that event should be remembered. The objects were, therefore, in suspended animation between two planes, in a fascinating Ground One that hardly anybody knew about. They conserved all the gray dust that became one of the symbols of the attack, the dirt and marks of impact or fire. The vehicles' glove compartments and receptacles still had their contents untouched. Uniforms, tools, bottles of serum, and so on. It was clear that the purity of this accidental and temporary museum project could not be comparable to anything that would come after and, consequently, had to be documented—container and content—as the testimonial monument and narrative device it actually was, even though it was lost somewhere in an airport, or maybe precisely because of that. This desire spurred on by need ended up becoming a long-term photographic project.

Objects brought into the Hangar 17 collection were tagged and catalogued. The majority of these objects were structural elements of the buildings, which often showed extreme damage from pressure or heat. Much of the large steel had to be cut into smaller pieces for transport to the hangar. Photo by the author.

Though most of the vehicles at Hangar 17 came from first responders, this taxi, an emblem of daily life in New York, was also preserved. The tags hanging from the frame indicate its Port Authority inventory number and mark its selection for inclusion in the permanent collection of the Memorial Museum. Photo by the author.

The collapse of the twin towers created a series of iconic objects, transformed by force and fire from their daily uses into artifacts that tell a story. At Hangar 17, tented enclosures were built for artifacts of various kinds that, in the view of curators and conservators, needed the added protection of humidity control and stillness. Perhaps the most dramatic example of this transformation could be found inside the vehicle tent, where trucks and cars, normally left outside in all conditions, were given shelter. Photo by the author.

The truck belonging to FDNY Squad 270. No members of this company died on 9/11. Photo by the author.

Formed during the collapse of the towers, and then months of exposure to high-heat fires, this object has come to be known as the composite. Weighting between twelve and fifteen tons, it holds the compressed remnants of four stories of one of the towers, though which one is unlikely to ever be known. It is just over four feet high. Photo by the author.

In spite of the extreme heat that forged this composite and its outdoor exposure at the World Trade Center site, bits of carbonized paper remain on its surface. In effect, these are ashes of the original paper, which remain intact, though they would disintegrate at a touch. Photo by the author.

6

From 2006 to 2009, I spent a lot of time alone in Hangar 17, making an inventory of its contents with a digital camera before starting the definitive photographic session with a medium-format analogue panoramic camera. Every one and a half minutes, the sound of an airplane taking off or landing filled the space and reminded me of the tragic irony that those remains were preserved in a commercial aviation hangar, when the attack on the Twin Towers was perpetrated with passenger airplanes suddenly converted into lethal weapons, into bombs that were already carrying a significant percentage of the victims who were to be caused. Among the objects, some had particular emotional power, such as, for example, the rocks that looked like volcanic magma mentioned above. One of them in particular, which measured approximately 250 centimeters wide by150 centimeters high by 150 centimeters deep, made shivers run down my spine. The first time one sees it, one doesn't realize what it actually is unless someone explains, then one notices four slightly different colored layers. It turns to be a chunk of four compacted floors from the North Tower. The energy generated when the tower collapsed must have been comparable to atomic fusion. Its nooks and crannies contain black areas that originally were blocks of incinerated office paper whose edges were open and could be separated. On the small sheets of carbon that fell off, you could still read what had been written on them. This object was the center of a bitter controversy involving some victims' relatives when they found out that the Memorial Museum had decided to include it in the permanent collection when it was inaugurated, in May of 2014. The objection consisted of assuming that inside the magma, there could be organic matter of human origin and that, consequently, it was an insult to expose it to the public when the proper thing would be to bury it, literally, in a cemetery as if it were a corpse.

In this debate, still unresolved, two aspects come to light. The first one demonstrates the victims' relatives' sense of ownership over the historical event, that is, given their suffering for the loss of loved ones, nobody has the right to do or say anything without their consent. Although it is perfectly understandable for them to defend their rights over the commemoration of lost relatives, let's imagine

for a moment that the relatives of U.S. casualties in Iraq and
Afghanistan were equally obstinate in the absolute control over the
government's handling of soldiers killed in action. It would make
such a process unmanageable. The second aspect is more complex.
Unlike other cases of mass violent death during this century and the
last, 9/11 did not leave visual, iconographic traces of the victims as
such. As in the case of aviation accidents, for example, there are
images taken by the forensic services, by the police, and by the secret
services, but they will never be seen out of respect for the dead and
consideration for their relatives.

It is out of the question to suggest any sort of direct specular
relationship between these genuinely vetoed photographic files and
Hangar 17 as a repository of evidence that is not just forensic but also
historical, but I believe it is legitimate, nonetheless, to think that there
has existed a subtle relationship between the two while the objects were

Though the hijacked American Airlines Flight 11 was intentionally crashed
into the north tower, there is no certainty about the origins of this slipper,
which was found in the rubble. Because this type of courtesy slipper was only
distributed on international flights, perhaps one of the flight crew had been
carrying it. Alternatively, it may have been one of a pair kept in a World Trade
Center office. Photo by the author.

kept in the limbo of the hangar. The photo and video images taken on the day of the attack, showing the final plunge of those who refused to die in the flames, stopped appearing on television and in newspapers on the third day after the attack. It is a decent, perfectly comprehensible reaction but I think it generates a complex problem: by eliminating visual traces of the victims, the September 11 attack becomes a black hole that has swallowed its dead and denies both relatives and the general public closure in the process of grief, whose starting point is the sight of the victim's lifeless body, even though in many cases, nearly all, it would have been atrocious. I quote, despite the obvious differences between the two events, the Argentinean senator Norma Morandini in an article published in the newspaper *El País* on 23 December 2012, where she tells how her brothers were murdered during the dictatorship by being thrown into the River Plate from a military airplane in flight. However, she never found out what happened until very recently, through the press: "It is very hard and very difficult to transmit what the word 'missing' means. It is a ghost. But to say it is a ghost is to say nothing. It is a presence that is not there. You have not seen them die and nobody gives you their condolences, there is no funeral or grave. You never think of them as dead, which is very different to hoping that they will appear alive." I would suggest that the first silent testimony of any act of violence is the victim's body. Without the emotional impact of its sight, the tragedy becomes an abstraction, an enigma that will never be fully resolved either for the relatives or, in the case I describe, for the people of the country. The historian Keith Lowe, in his book *Inferno: The Fiery Destruction of Hamburg, 1943*, describing the mourning for the victims of that terrible episode, says the following: "If mourning the city was difficult, then mourning the people who had died here was often impossible. The bodies had been removed so hastily that there was often nothing left to mourn—no proof that those people had died at all."

7

A fascinating, extremely illustrative chapter showing the complexity of managing the consequences of September 11 has to do with preserving the 9,000 human remains recovered from Ground Zero. From the beginning of the operation to clean the ruins of the World

The Warner Bros. Studio Store was one of more than sixty shops at the Mall at the World Trade Center. Located on a concourse one story below street level, the mall held 427,000 square feet of retail space and was the third-largest-grossing shopping center in the United State. Photo by the author.

Trade Center, all remains found were kept in refrigerated trailers in front the New York's Bellevue Hospital under the responsibility of the Office of the Chief Medical Examiner (OCME). Identifications are still being made, though not very often, but this uninterrupted work has led to significant developments in forensic technology, a direct result of a problem whose magnitude was unprecedented, with the possible exception of the work carried out to identify remains in the Balkans. As the current situation has always been considered temporary by the OCME, the remains are planned to be taken to Ground Zero when construction of the whole complex is finished.

The arrangement inside the area has changed according to the changes in the project that have taken place during construction. The decision at this time is to conserve the remains in an area located in the granite bedrock inside the museum, behind the large wall of the Eastern Chamber, between where the towers stood. This wall will bear a quote from Virgil's *Aeneid*, with letters forged from recycled steel from the World Trade Center, which says: "No day shall erase you from the memory of time." This area will remain under the jurisdiction of the OCME, and the museum staff will have no role in its administration. The quote by Virgil will indicate the existence of the repository, no more. It will not be part of the museum or of a visit to it. Neither the OCME nor the museum refers to the repository as anything other than a temporary solution that allows the conservation and identification process to continue. It is not defined as a grave or cemetery as this would imply a permanency that contradicts the OCME's mission to identify and return the identified remains to the victims' families. A small group of relatives opposes this temporary solution and demands that the remains be permanently deposited in the Memorial Plaza, which would require a radical change in the design of the memorial itself. The matter is not fully resolved.[1]

8

Without doubt, the objects in Hangar 17 have an aura that gives them a unique voice. In no way can they stand as a substitute for the absent bodies or even simply act as a metaphor for them, but the huge vacuum created by the "disappearance," literal in many cases, of the victims' bodies inevitably permeates all those vestiges that I photographed over three years. One object perfectly exemplifies and illustrates what I am saying: among the vehicles preserved, only one did not belong to the medical, security, or fire services. It was a taxicab. A Ford Crown Victoria, the model that has represented the quintessence of a New York taxi for over a decade. Anyone who has lived in the city or has visited it has gotten into a Crown Vic. Seeing it for the first time in the room of vehicles caused an impact. The vehicle, which has been selected for the permanent exhibition at the Memorial Museum, has its roof flattened down to the seats and the front pillars of the cabin have been sawed through, making it clear that someone trapped inside had to be rescued, alive, I think, as no mark can be seen of the type 1-K or 2-K (one killed, two killed) sprayed onto the hoods of other vehicles by the rescue teams. I felt that we were all inside that empty taxi, both the living and the dead, after the machinery of destruction had, once more, done its work.

Remnants of a sculpture made by Alexander Calder, which was installed in the World Trade Center complex in 1971. Known as the "Bent Propeller," the work was bright red and stood twenty-five feet tall. The recovery of these pieces raised hopes that the sculpture might be restored, but no other pieces were found. Photo by the author.

9

The emotional connection we have with history, not just recent history, is provided to us by the images and objects that have remained as sediment of its different episodes. The power of images needs no apologies, but they are reflections in a mirror as distant as the very facts they project. The objects, however, have a tangibility that is unique; they are time capsules that contain "the decisive moment" of a photograph as defined by Henri Cartier-Bresson, but their tangible reality takes us directly to the Big Bang moment of the historical event. The body of the victim of an act of violence has the same power of temporal retroactivation. That was clear, for example, in the exhumation of the mass grave from the Spanish Civil War that I photographed in Villamayor de los Montes, Burgos, mentioned above. The grave, once open, seemed like a splinter of frozen time, a "decisive moment" if ever there was one, which could be read like a book. That was what the victims' relatives saw. Their reunion with loved ones through their remains and both the sight of them and of the setting and circumstances of their death is what gave closure to a traumatic event in families' lives, seventy years after it happened.

The use of a camera in cases like the ones I mention goes beyond mere documentation and enters the territory of preservation and rebellion against oblivion or against historical falsification for political and ideological interests. Although photography has never been immune to self-serving instrumentalization, it still has its ability to bear independent witness and to show the truth. The pictures taken by the Nazis themselves in concentration camps ended up condemning them. It is interesting that, in Spanish, in the case of analogue photos, the process of developing a photo is called "revealing" (*revelado*). "Revealing" film is a performative action that in the case of the Villamayor grave, announces the subsequent revelation that generates a "positive" image of the process of excavation and

During the recovery at the site, some ironworkers would cut religious or other symbols out of pieces of steel from the World Trade Center and give them as keepsakes to family members or other visitors. Photo by the author.

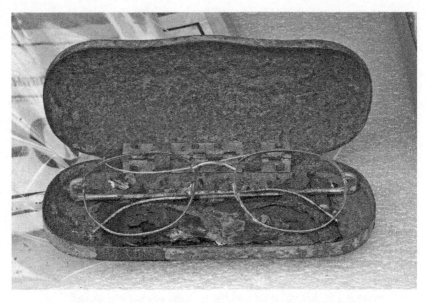

Articles of clothing and personal belongings were taken out of a dumpster that had been filled with construction rubble and brought to Hangar 17. As the dumpster was slowly emptied, conservators found tattered clothing mixed in with rebar and concrete. No owners have been identified for any of these objects. Photo by the author.

exhumation in the same place where the tragedy occurred. This metaphoric aspect is diffused by the immediacy of digital photography, but it still has the common, definitive denominator of any kind of photographic technology, which is the literal use of light to set, reveal, uncover, and show a truth maybe so far unknown or kept hidden. In a metaphorical sense, we are once more linked with Kant's concept of light as a symbol of reason.

10

In managing traumatic events that indiscriminately befall civil populations and which have a special historical importance for the affected communities—in mourning the victims and their memory, in their narrative for coming generations—it is essential not to resort to filtering or editing the tangible and intangible sediment of the event (images, documents, objects, and subjective narratives by affected persons) and so disabling their power for evocation and catharsis with the pretext of not hurting people's feelings, upsetting them, or simply offending visitors to memorial institutions. I think it is exactly the other way around, without ever ignoring objectivity and respect. The healing function of bereavement and memory only takes place at the end of a process of unveiling and revelation. History itself only speaks if it is known. Would the memory of the Holocaust be possible without images of its victims, without its preserved objects, without the sites of the Shoah turned into spaces of memory? If it does not exist in the present, the past has no future.

Note

1. Source: National September 11 Memorial and Museum, New York.

PART II

EXHUMATIONS AS MEMORY

Chapter 6

Buried Silences of the Greek Civil War

Katerina Stefatos and Iosif Kovras

The Greek Paradox

Several societies in the Balkans and southern Europe have invested in the symbolic capital inherent in mass graves. The public exhumations and reburials of World War II victims of atrocities carried out by the Croat military units of Ustasha were powerful symbols of Serbian nationalism in the former Yugoslavia (Denich 1994:382). More recently, the effort to exhume, identify, and bury the remains of the approximately thirty thousand persons who went missing during the war in Bosnia (1992–1995) has become a way to deal with the violent past, as the process provides some form of closure (Wagner 2010). The Cypriot case is more puzzling. During the two major stages of violence on the island (1963–1967 and 1974), approximately two thousand persons went missing from the Greek and Turkish Cypriot communities (Sant Cassia 2005; Kovras and Loizides 2011). The unresolved problem of the missing became the symbol of the impossibility of peaceful coexistence between the two communities (Sant Cassia 2006). Since the early 2000s, however, despite the absence of a political settlement and the de facto partition of the island for almost four decades, the bicommunal Committee on Missing Persons has been successful in exhuming, identifying, and returning the remains to the relatives. The committee has paved the way for the emergence of other pro-reconciliation grassroots actors that transcend the divide (Kovras 2013). Finally, the exhumations of the *desaparecidos* (disappeared) of the Spanish Civil

War (1936–1939) led to the crumbling of the "pact of silence" that dominated Spanish politics since the consolidation of democracy in the late 1970s (Ferrándiz 2006).[1]

Since the early 1990s a consensus has been reached by policymakers and academics that dealing with the traumatic past not only constitutes a moral imperative but is the best way to move forward and consolidate peace and democracy.[2] Stock phrases like "revealing is healing" or "dealing with the past" now dominate public debates. The considerably revised international normative context—that reserves a privileged position for the discourse of human rights—partly explains the growing demand for truth and for justice as a form of catharsis. Similarly, the recovery of "forensic" truth from mass graves gradually has become synonymous with the effort of societies to face their violent past.[3] This trend is also found in the relentless demand by international media for powerful images of suffering, such as bereaved relatives at the exhumation sites (Ferrándiz and Baer 2008).

Irrespective of the reasons why societies decide to "unearth" violent chapters of their past, exhumations of common graves and the identification of victims of violence have become central policies in the agenda of peace building. There is a tendency in the literature to focus on "success stories" where exhumations have been implemented, including but not limited to notable cases in Latin America and the former Yugoslavia. Little attention has been paid to why certain countries resist this trend.

Greece is especially interesting as it seems to conflate two trends: although an official policy of exhumations of the victims of the Civil War has never been implemented, over the past three decades, several unofficial exhumations have been carried out on the island of Lesvos. The violent legacy of the Greek Civil War left thousands dead, and many more were refugees; an unknown number had been executed and buried in common graves.[4] With the exception of Lesvos, the overall Greek experience contravenes both the relevant experience of neighboring countries discussed above and the hypotheses of the literature. For one thing, Greece's transition to democracy was a textbook case that satisfied all the requirements of transitional justice, including the trials of the coupists and the establishment of policies of lustration (Sotiropoulos 2010). In addition, in almost any part of Greece, the living memory of clandestine executions and disappearances foregrounds the demand for truth. Finally, one of the biggest mass graves in Europe, located in the region of Florina in northern Greece, contains an estimated seven hundred persons.[5] Given this, one might have expected Greek society to be the first to "unearth" the divisive past; yet Spain, whose Amnesty Law forbade a comprehensive dealing with past atrocities (Aguilar 2002), led the way by exhuming the desaparecidos, albeit tardily.[6]

Why do certain societies defer the recovery of the bodies of those executed in a traumatic period? Why do the relatives of some victims remain reluctant (or ineffective) in their demand for truth? To address these questions, we examine the interesting experience of the Greek island of Lesvos. It contravenes the national experience of silence because exhumations were carried out from the 1980s to the 2000s. In what follows, we discuss the role of bones in the Greek Orthodox tradition specifically, as well as the symbolic value of remains in post-traumatic societies more generally. We consider why policies of exhumations were never implemented in Greece, before focusing on the instructive case of Lesvos and its choice of a different path. In the concluding section, we offer a number of insights that can be drawn from the Greek experience.

The Symbolic and Analytical Value of Bones

It seems that in contemporary nation-states, the dead take on a vibrant political life because "the dead body is a mark of [a] good political symbol: it has legitimating effects not because everyone agrees on its meaning but because it compels interest despite divergent views of what it means" (Verdery 1999:31). Benedict Anderson in his *Imagined Communities* captures the symbolic capital of the dead body in the culture of nationalism, by referring to the "Tomb of the Unknown Soldier" (1991:9).

It is precisely because dead bodies are such powerful political symbols that the study of exhumations (and nonexhumations) can be a useful analytical tool for understanding how different post-traumatic societies deal with their violent past. As the human community is composed of both living and dead (Verdery 1999:108), the decision to unearth, identify, and bury properly the dead body that was previously buried in a common grave signifies a major political decision that changes the way we look at our past. As Kieran McEvoy and Heather Conway aptly remark, "The question who 'owns' the dead is not simply a question of the exclusive exercise of authority over the remains, but is inextricably linked to the notion of who 'owns' the past" (2004:545).

These moral tensions between the past and the present are even more acute in postconflict societies where the moral duty to honor the dead may be at odds with the need to look forward and consolidate peace and democracy (Lederach 1998:177). Hence, studying the "politics of (non)exhumations" can tell us a great deal about how societies deal with their traumatic past. Victoria Sanford notes: "Mass graves of massacre victims . . . were hidden in that they were silenced, but survivors, witnesses and most community members know the locations of these graves" (2003:17). The study of clandestine graves is analytically important because it provides insight into the social construction of silence as well as the local dynamics of "resistance" to this hegemonic silence.

Although in most cultures the recovery of human remains is critical in the mourning process of the relatives, there are exceptions. For example, in his fascinating study of the families of the missing in Timor, Simon Robins (2013) shows that access to the remains is not essential to confirm the fate of the disappeared, as contact with spirits can remove ambiguity by using a substitute body to perform the ritual. Yet the Greek Orthodox tradition reserves a sacred position for human remains. Exhumation of remains is seen as a "rite of passage," a necessary stage for the deceased to enter paradise (Danforth 1982:50–62). The condition and color of the bones serve as indications that the soul of the dead has entered paradise and that the person had a "good soul" (*kalopsychos*) (Danforth 1982:50–62). In fact, the whole burial ritual is based on the premise that (impure) flesh should decompose naturally in order to leave bones untouched; the central role of bones partly explains why cremations are prohibited in the Greek Orthodox tradition.[7] Apart from its relation to the deceased, though, the process of exhumations signifies a rite of passage for the family as well. The exhumation of the body indicates the end of a period of mourning—especially for female relatives—and their reincorporation into the human community (Danforth 1982: 50–62).

Human remains are also central in the Greek national identity, which is founded on a linear view of history, from ancient to contemporary Greece. The bones link *time* and *space*, two important ingredients of Greek nationalism. For example, the bodies of the Greek Cypriot persons who went missing in 1974 in the northern part of the island, currently under the control of the Turkish Cypriot community, demark the (imaginary) borders of the Greek (Cypriot) community. As Paul Sant Cassia shows, the role of the dead body and human remains is also central in Greek literature and poetry (2005:102). Ilias Venezis, in his famous book *Aioliki Gi* (Aeolian Earth), describes the experience of a group of recently displaced Asia Minor Greeks and their decision to carry the remains of their ancestors to their new land. Perhaps the starkest illustration of the sanctity of bones in the Greek tradition is the national anthem. Based on the poem "Hymn to Liberty," written by Dionysios Solomos, the anthem glorifies the bravery of the ancestors in securing liberty (ibid.). The most renowned verses go: "From the sacred bones, of the Hellenes arisen, and strengthened by your antique bravery, hail, o hail, Liberty!" This makes the topic of exhumation an extremely interesting one in the Greek case.

The Greek Civil War and the Case of Lesvos

The Greek Civil War was fought between the Greek Democratic Army (DSE), officially formed in December 1946 under the auspices of the Communist Party, and the National (governmental) Army.[8] The war was the outcome of a highly polarized, socially and politically unstable period, closely connected to the brutal German, Italian, and Bulgarian occupation (1941–1944). The Communist defeat, following the last act of the Civil War drama played out at the end of August 1949 in the mountains of northwestern Greece, led the country into a long period of turmoil and instability. The end of the Civil War resulted in widespread persecution, repression, abuse, banishment, and incarceration of leftist citizens; the Greek Communist Party remained outlawed until 1974 and its members and sympathizers were treated as social and political pariahs.

The Greek Civil War, considered one of the first episodes of the Cold War, had disastrous socioeconomic and political effects that were to formulate the everyday lives of the population. The Civil War (and the preceding Axis occupation) left a painful legacy, including famine, destruction and evacuation of villages, political refugees and the deportation of thousands of Greeks, tens of thousands of dead on both sides, and the victimization of women, children, and the elderly.[9] The sociopolitical consequences and traumatic—both personal and collective—memories of the Civil War defined the Greek political culture and local political identities until the fall of the military dictatorship (1967–1974) and the transition to multiparty democracy.

Concurrently, the country remained divided between two opposing poles, the communists or leftists and their supporters and the "nationally minded" (εθνικόφρωνες, ethnikofrones) citizens.[10] These sociopolitical divisions were not as evident or as rigid in Lesvos as in other areas, for instance, in northern Greece or the Peloponnese. This can be attributed to two factors: the democratic tradition of the island and the fact that it had not witnessed mass executions of and atrocities against the local population by either side during the Civil War.

Even so, Lesvos was a communist stronghold, and the climate of fear, po-larization, and persecution, primarily against leftist citizens, was intense, forc-ing partisans to flee to the mountains. Besides the gendarmerie, the perpetrators of violence were paramilitaries and rightist bands that targeted well-known members of the Communist Party and leftists, as well as their families, relatives, and members of the local communities.[11] By the end of summer 1946, a significant number of guerrillas had fled to the mountains of the island and three main armed groups were created, one situated in the northwest, another in the area of Agiasos, a village built on the inland slopes of Mount Olympus at an altitude of 967 meters, and the third in Gera in the south of the island. Six main battles took place in Lesvos between the govern-mental and gendarmerie forces and the Democratic Army of Lesvos (DSL),[12] a branch of the DSE, including one deadly ambush; sixty-eight guerrilla fight-ers of the DSL were killed or executed during the battles, more than 60 per-cent of its total manpower; fourteen leftists or communist sympathizers (including three women) were executed or murdered by paramilitaries; twenty-two, primarily political detainees, were executed or died away from the island during exile due to hardships and lack of medical treatment.[13]

Despite this opposition, the violent activity of the DSL in Lesvos was ac-tually quite restrained. In other regions, especially in Macedonia and the Pe-loponnese, it committed a number of atrocities against local communities. But the survival of the DSL depended exclusively on voluntary contributions, in-cluding food, medicine, and tolerance and cover, from the locals rather than the central mechanism of the DSE, which was based in the inaccessible region of Macedonia. This partly explains why the DSL did not direct its violent ac-tion against the larger population in Lesvos; simply stated, to survive, it needed to gain the support of locals. Some crimes were committed against individual locals, but these were guided by personal motivations and interests (for example, crimes of honor and revenge), causing distress to the relatives of the victims, of course, but not decimating whole populations as elsewhere.[14] One can reasonably expect the aftermath of the Civil War to be quite different in Lesvos, given this relative restraint.

Reconciliation Through Silence

Over the past few decades, exhumations have become a key policy tool to bring about reconciliation in deeply divided societies, a tool deployed by major international organizations such as the UN. Yet Greece remains resistant to this norm. The Greek policies of national reconciliation in the period following the consolidation of democracy (1974) did not include exhumations.

The coming to power of the Socialist Party in 1981 signified a turn in the national discourse about the past by taking measures of symbolic and economic repair to the "defeated."[15] Yet because these moves were guided by electoral considerations, they were shortsighted and failed to establish a comprehensive policy of reconciliation. The formation of a coalition government composed of the main parties of the Left and the Right in 1989 finally shaped a national policy of reconciliation in Greece.[16] The coalition government passed the law on the "official rehabilitation of the defeated of the Civil War" and also provided financial benefits and pensions to the disabled participants of the defeated side (Close 2004:265). Paradoxically, the most essential aspect of the policy of reconciliation was the unprecedented decision of the government to literally burn millions of personal files of leftists from past decades (Close 2004:265). Interestingly, the parties representing the defeated perceived the "burning of the past"—and subsequently silence—as a prerequisite of reconciliation.

It seems, then, that at the political level, a subtle agreement was reached to silence certain inconvenient aspects of the violent past, precluding the possibility of truth-recovery processes such as exhuming mass graves.[17] The strategy of silence is frequently used by political elites in an effort to eschew the past and address more effectively critical political objectives like democratic consolidation, economic reconstruction, and reconciliation. Yet it remains puzzling why the relatives and descendants of those buried in common graves did not initiate a bottom-up pressure group to demand the rectification of the injustice done to their relatives. As democratic consolidation and accession to the European Community and European Union offered new institutional tools, one might have expected the emergence of a grassroots truth-seeking actor demanding the recovery of the inappropriately buried of the Civil War. A grassroots actor similar to the Spanish NGOs that promotes policies of exhumations has yet to emerge in Greece.[18]

To understand why unearthing individual victims of the Civil War was never included in the agenda of the political parties or civil society, consider the case of Florina. As noted above, one of the biggest mass graves in Europe, containing approximately seven hundred members of the DSE, is found in this region of northern Greece. The mass grave, often called the *lakka* (the pit) by the locals, is in a plot just a kilometer outside Florina; it often goes unnoticed, as the only visible object is a stone plate.

Figure 6.1 Image from the plain where the mass grave in Florina is located. The photo was taken before 2009, when the Greek Communist Party bought the plain; since then the marble has been replaced. Photo: Courtesy of Prof. Vlasis Vlasidis.

The most significant factor that constrains both local politicians (representing the defeated) and civil society from exhuming the grave is the prospect of facing inconvenient truths. More specifically, although the personal details of those buried in the grave remain unknown, there are rumors that a sizeable number of the fallen were Slav-Macedonian youths violently recruited from the neighboring region of Naousa.[19] The prospect of verifying in a scientific way that violence was a strategy DSE used to recruit fighters has the potential to delegitimize the master narrative of the defeated, namely that they fought for a noble cause and their members were idealists. Meanwhile, civil society remains reluctant to open the grave because identification of Slav-Macedonians remains among the victims could potentially lead to a new confrontational chapter in the "Macedonian conflict."[20] Hence, the politicization of the mass grave in Florina and its relationship to one of the most sensitive issues of Greek foreign policy, the Macedonian problem, prevents the possibility of opening it. Exhumations are like a "Pandora's box"; once you start "digging" up the past you can never be sure what you will find.

Civil War Exhumations: The "Paradox" of Lesvos

Whereas Florina is typical, Lesvos is an outlier case; it is the only known place where victims of the Civil War have been exhumed over past decades. Lesvos is situated in a privileged location, connecting the Aegean with the Black Sea; it has been a cultural crossroad for East and West and an important commercial center for sea trade and the industrial production of local goods.[21] Self-sufficient economically, with a rich cultural tradition in arts and literature (including some of the most influential Greek poets, writers, painters, and educators), and having integrated the traditions of the post-1922 Asia Minor refugees, Lesvos provides an ideal setting for critical political thinking and democratic, participatory political culture.

Combining the local intelligentsia with the craftsmen, merchants, and rural workers, the island's unique sociopolitical conditions enabled the formation of a strong leftist tradition. At the same time, the island also has a rich religious tradition and important Orthodox monuments, and the Greek Orthodox faith and religious beliefs seem to peacefully coexist with the leftist and communist political beliefs. A typical example is Mantamados, a village in the northeast of the island, known as "Little Moscow" due to the high electoral percentages of the Communist Party. Meanwhile, the village patron saint, St. Taxiarchis (Archangel), is highly respected among the local population, leftists included.[22]

Lesvos is also known as the "red island" because of its strong communist and leftist traditions. Within its local culture of tolerance, during the Civil War those on the right were tolerant of the guerrillas and as noted above, the fighters of the DSL did not commit atrocities against the local population as a form of retaliation. The mutual tolerance is reflected in the fact that the last two DSL guerrillas to drop their arms, Giorgos Skoufos and Kostas Achlioptas, left the mountains of Lesvos in 1955, more than five years after the official termination of the Civil War.[23] The two guerrillas managed to survive thanks to the sympathetic attitude of the local communities.[24]

Within this tolerant setting and following an unofficial bottom-up reconciliation process, the exhumations in Lesvos can be roughly placed into three periods: the first attempts took place in absolute secrecy from the early 1950s until the early 1960s; the second and most visible wave occurred in the 1980s during the democratic consolidation; finally, in 2009, there was renewed interest in exhumations. Because of the clandestine nature of the first exhumations, information about them is limited, coming from either oral testimonies or material traces uncovered in subsequent exhumations. We therefore focus on the second and third periods, identifying six cases of successful or attempted exhumations initiated and undertaken in most cases by former comrades, relatives, and (mostly leftist) local administration representatives. Of these six cases we elaborate on the sixth, unfinished exhumation as an exemplary case, which we believe best demonstrates both the local specificities of Lesvos and the political complexities of silencing and resistance to strategies of silence in the wider framework of negotiating Civil War legacies in Greece.

On August 1, 1982, the former comrades of Dimitris Pitaoulis, the captain of the DSL, attempted to exhume his remains in the Agiasos pine forest (*Megali Limni*) where he was accidentally killed when his gun went off on December 10, 1947.[25] During the exhumation his comrades realized that the makeshift grave had already been excavated and some of the bones were missing, probably due to a previous secret exhumation by his relatives (Skoufos 2009:197). The remains were transferred by Pitaoulis's comrades to his hometown, Agiasos, to the offices of the Partisan Basis Organization, where they are still kept. A few months later, on December 5, 1982, at the outskirts of the town of Mytilene in Kratigos, another exhumation took place on the site where seven DSL fighters were executed on April 29, 1947. On July 24, 1983, in Lambous Mylous, six guerrilla fighters killed during the Seitan-Ntere battle (February 21, 1948) by governmental forces and whose bodies were thrown along the roadside were exhumed by relatives, former comrades, Communist Party representatives in Lesvos, and locals.[26]

A few months later, on October 9, 1983, in Aghia Paraskevi, another exhumation took place, this time of five guerrilla fighters; among them were three well-known DSL captains. The DSL captains and fighters were killed by the gendarmerie and governmental forces in October 1950 during the last civil war battle in Lesvos. Their corpses were left to decay in several villages and then buried in a field outside the village. Two years later, in 1985, the mayor of Eressos, Giorgos Karakousis, with the support of the Communist Party, attempted to exhume the body of Manolis Philipou, also known as Karakostas. A native of Eressos, Karakostas was killed along with four others during a battle in the spring of 1947. Their bodies were displayed in the village square and then buried in a common grave in the cemetery. No remains were found, however, in the area indicated as the site of execution.

On New Year's Eve 1948, eight months before the official end of the Greek Civil War, thirteen guerrilla fighters of the Democratic Army of Lesvos were

Figure 6.2 The exhumation of six guerrilla fighters in Lambous Mylous (July 24, 1983). Photo: Personal Archive of Panagiotis Koutskoudis, used with kind permission.

ambushed by a supporter of governmental and paramilitary forces in the Ip-peios area, a woman refugee from Asia Minor, Eleni Iordanoglou (or Zoulfie Hanoum), known also as "Tserkeza," who settled on the island after the forced displacement of the Greek-Orthodox population from Asia Minor in the af-termath of the Greek-Turkish war, in 1922. She was closely connected to the local authorities, including the gendarmerie (especially the commander, Pa-nagiotis Skourtis), but reportedly also had ties with General Nikolaos Plastiras who had served as the prime minister on several occasions.[27] She offered to feed the guerrilla group. They decided to accept her invitation, despite their initial hesitation and suspicions, mostly because they had not eaten or drunk water for days. They explored the area before entering and they made her taste beforehand the food and beverages she offered: *vasilopita*, the traditional Greek pie cut for good luck on the final day of the year (on New Year's Eve); *melomakarona* (*foinikia* in the dialect of Lesvos), soft Christmas cookies; and wine. She left the hut (*dami*), lit her cigarette, and ignited the hut, which was surrounded by ammunition. The thirteen fighters were buried in the ruins; six of them died on the spot; the remaining seven, however, managed to escape,

Figure 6.3 Photo taken at the exhumation of and memorial for five guerrilla fighters and DSL captains in Aghia Paraskevi (October 9, 1983): family and relatives mourning, red carnations on the remains. Photo: Personal Archive of Panagiotis Koutskoudis, used with kind permission.

severely wounded. The bodies of the six guerrillas were informally buried by the authorities in a ditch near the village cemetery.

Almost sixty years after the guerrillas' death, in the summer of 2009, the local authorities, along with the local representatives of the Greek Communist Party and the relatives of the victims, decided to exhume their bodies, to properly bury them, and to have a political memorial.

The exhumation process, however, proved to be more complex than expected. First, it was conducted without formal approval by the state. Second, the bones that were found belonged to a female suicide,[28] not to the guerrilla fighters. Thus, local claims that relatives of the killed guerrillas secretly removed their bones in the midst of state terrorism in 1952 were confirmed. In fact, it was revealed that the bones of one of the guerrillas had been kept in secrecy for years at a relative's house.[29]

The locals recall that at the time, these six corpses were moved over a period of days in a carriage from village to village, until they started to smell and had to be buried in a common grave. They say that in another instance, the dead bodies of guerrillas were exposed in an open pit, with an inscription

Figure 6.4 Photo from a memorial service for the six guerrilla fighters who were killed in the "Tserkeza" ambush that took place in 1989. Photo: Personal Archive of Panagiotis Koutskoudis, used with kind permission.

reading, "come and throw a rock on the bones of the anathemas."[30] Most of the dead were displayed in central parts of the village, usually in the village square, and were moved from village to village for derision and vilification by the local population before being buried in makeshift mass graves, even in land-fills.[31] This was the case with two guerrilla fighters who were killed in the spring of 1949 and buried in a dump; but when people secretly left flowers on this "burial site," the authorities had to bury them elsewhere (Kalogeras and Koutskoudis 2002:49).

Within the Greek Orthodox religious tradition, the bodies of the dead and the rituals of burial and mourning have important symbolic connotations. They help the family to honor their dead, to mourn, and to heal.[32] The relatives clean the corpse and dress the deceased in good clothes. Following death, the soul is understood to wander for forty days in the surroundings of the dead. For this reason, a candle at the family house should remain lit. The body is buried for at least three years for it to decompose. The decomposition process is crucial, since it is during this period that the person's sins are to be forgiven; if the bones turn white, the sins are forgiven and the deceased rests in peace and is admitted to paradise (Buck Sutton 2001).[33] The bones are then trans-ferred to the ossuary. During the decomposition period, the grave becomes a sacred place for close relatives and is visited often, cleaned religiously by the women of the family, and adorned with flowers, candles, personal belongings, and a photograph of the dead.[34]

If we shift the focus of attention to the link between Greek Orthodox doc-trine and the local traditions in Lesvos, the picture becomes even more fasci-nating. More specifically, one of the most striking features of the local identity is the harmonious blend of two seemingly contradictory identities: the reli-gious-orthodox with the leftist-communist. Lesvos is celebrated as a place of worship of two Orthodox saints (Rafael and Taxiarchis) whose reputation for (allegedly) causing miracles extends beyond Lesvos. Simultaneously, as al-ready discussed, it is also known as "Little Moscow," as it remains a stronghold of the Greek Left. Yet the vast majority of leftists in Lesvos have traditionally been religious. During the Nazi occupation in the 1940s, the leader of the only organized resistance group, the National Liberation Front, was the bishop of Lesvos, Dionysios. In his first speech after the liberation of the island, he stressed that "Christianity and Communism are two movements that run par-allel in their struggle for bringing about peace and justice in the world" (cited in Marantzidis 1997:60). This contradicts the national experience; throughout 1940s there was a clear rift between the communist-led National Liberation

Front and the Greek Orthodox Church, which became even more acute during the Civil War. Hence, the pivotal role of exhumations in Greek Orthodox doctrine coupled with the unique local blend of Orthodox faith with communism may partly account for the emergence of a pressing demand to unearth the remains of local victims of the Civil War. So, we next examine the conditions that enabled this outcome.

Why Did Exhumations Take Place in Lesvos?

The Lesvos exhumations extend over a period of sixty years, but three features remain constant: they are informal, local, and depoliticized. The elements overlap, making Lesvos a unique case. The first exhumations in the early 1950s and early 1960s were carried out by the relatives, wives, or other close family members in absolute secrecy, because of post–Civil War persecution, fear, and harassment.[35] Those occurring in the early 1980s, during the period of "national reconciliation," were more organized, but again quite informal, with no official endorsement by political parties or the government. They were typically initiated by the local communities: relatives, former guerrilla fighters, local representatives, including members of the Communist Party, and local residents. And as the most recent "unsuccessful" exhumation in the summer of 2009 indicates, all three factors remain salient today and are distinctive of the Lesvos context. In their informality, they are also indicative of the overall nature of reconciliation in Greece.

When we look at the almost sixty years of exhumations in Lesvos, we see that despite the ongoing silence about some aspects of the Civil War and the occasional manipulation or marginalization of past experiences, memories, and traumas, the case of Lesvos indicates that the past can be rewritten and memory re-created or retrieved (Verdery 1999:3) in more inclusive terms, through localized, depoliticized acts of resistance.

As has been noted, the exhumations in the early 1980s were initiated by the local communities, the relatives and former cadres, and, in some cases, by the local representatives and local cadres of the Communist Party, but were not directed by a central Communist Party order. However, it should be emphasized that in the "Tserkeza" exhumation, the initiative belonged to the village (Evergetoula) mayor, Mihalis Polypathellis, who was elected with the support of the right-wing party Nea Dimokratia (New Democracy). In fact, during the exhumation, the mayor told the local newspapers that beyond the event's historical dimension and significance, "the dead are dead and are at least entitled to be buried like everyone else. . . . We also believe that these incidents should be highlighted for many reasons" (*Empros* 2009b). Furthermore, besides the Communist-supported mayor of Agiasos, Hrysanthos Hatzipanayiotis, and the former guerrillas, among them the only living survivor, Thrasyvoulos Bousdos, a retired senior officer of the gendarmerie, Thanasis Siskas, was also present.[36] Additionally, the former DSL guerrilla fighter Giorgos Skoufos said during the memorial that the intention "is not to blame and seek the guilty, the [local political] opponents [or our covillagers] who were misled or feared. . . . They are forgotten and most importantly forgiven. But we will never forget and forgive the real culprits of this national tragedy, [namely] the British and American imperialists [and their collaborators]" (*Empros* 2009b). Despite this being an organized event, the context largely remains informal; the Prefectural Committee of the Communist Party was informed, but a license to proceed was not requested on a governmental level.

For the local communities, former comrades, and relatives, a proper burial and the rectification of a past injustice is the primary motive, while the Communist Party seeks the restoration of historical truth, regardless of how inconvenient that truth may turn out to be.[37] For the relatives, a proper burial according to Greek Orthodox Christian beliefs and traditions seems to be key as it can rectify past wrongs and help them to heal and come to terms with their traumatic memories. The localized and depoliticized processes of the Lesvos exhumation and the silence surrounding it should also be perceived as an instrument deployed by local communities and relatives to protect their children from traumatic truths, thus breaking the cycle of trauma and violence. To take a more concrete example, the father of two of our interviewees from the village of Eressos was executed during the Civil War for being a member of the DSE. Being a relative of a leftist was a major stigma. For this reason, his son could not find a job to support his family while he was prohibited from migrating to western Europe as his record was tainted by his father's activities. So for several years after the Civil War, even though younger, the female members of the family assumed the role of breadwinners. Thirty-five years after the conclusion of the war, the son became the mayor of the village. One of his first initiatives was to unearth the remains of victims of the DSE who were killed in the battle of Eressos (Aetos). The exhumation was unsuccessful, as it seems that information over the burial site was wrong. Still, even after several decades he believed that he had a moral obligation to address this issue, as his own father was executed in Athens but the body was never recovered.

Regardless of the specific motives, scope, and objectives, they are all inter-related, pointing to the importance of knowing the fate of the dead, to the symbolic capital of the bones, and to the political and historical meaning of the remains.[38] Humanitarian exhumations have the potential to bridge the gap between the often conflicting tensions between the individual right of the relatives to know the truth and the societal perception that silence is the best way to move forward.

Conclusion: Lessons from Greece

There are several important insights to be gleaned from the investigation of the understudied Greek Civil War. Although Greece's policy of reconciliation is based on silence, the outlier case of Lesvos shows that it is often an analytic mistake to equate the national level with local experience. The exhumations in Lesvos show that local communities can resist hegemonic silence. Victoria Sanford rightly asks, "How silent are silences?" (2003:7). It is frequently ar-gued that societies tend to "forget" or to deal with the past by forgetting. Yet the experience of Lesvos illustrates that people *do not forget*, they decide at times *to remain silent* and this is an instrumental—not a passive—decision.[39] Remaining silent does not necessarily indicate that local communities surren-der to this silence; in fact, in Lesvos exhumations were subtle acts of resis-tance. As James Scott argues, acts of resistance "require little or no coordination or planning; they often represent a form of individual self-help and typically avoid any direct confrontation with authority or with elite norms" (1985:29).

In Lesvos, the three waves of exhumations had a strong local identity. They were seen as a rectification of a past injustice, but they were depoliticized and definitely did not provoke a counterreaction. Political parties remain the cen-tral actors managing the political memory of the past; the only way to circum-vent this top-bottom approach is through bottom-up action, taking ownership of the situation. In fact, local ownership is of paramount importance in ex-plaining why exhumations took place in Lesvos but not in other parts of Greece.

The Greek experience can provide useful lessons to contemporary post-traumatic societies. Even more than six decades after the conclusion of the Civil War, both political parties representing the defeated and the civil society remain reluctant to proceed to exhumations. Unearthing and identifying dead bodies can lead to the forced acknowledgment of inconvenient truths about the past that have the potential to delegitimize well-entrenched, albeit false, views of the parties involved. For example, the Communist Party purports to be the heir of the DSE but abstains from implementing a policy of exhumations because the bodies could potentially reveal the truth about violently recruited soldiers. In addition, the decision by the defeated to open a mass grave could lead to a resumption of demand for exhumations by the relatives of the victims of "red terror," certainly an inconvenient aspect of the DSE (Kalyvas 2004).[40] Moreover, the remains constitute a corpus delicti, and the state is legally accountable for the fate of the buried in its territory. Unearthing the grave in Florina and identifying Slav-Macedonians among the dead could lead to a heated legal battle. Finally, Greek civil society remains reluctant to demand the acknowledgment of human rights abuses because it has not achieved a sufficient level of financial, structural, and ideological independence from the state.

In short, although in several neighboring countries exhumations have been central to the effort to address the violent past, for the time being, Greece remains resistant to these external human rights norms. But as the case of Lesvos indicates, even within a well-entrenched culture of silence, acts of resistance can emerge and challenge that silence.

Notes

1. The landmark law on the "Recovery of Historical Memory" (Law 53/2007) included provisions for the recovery of the bodies of those victims buried in mass graves and signified the symbolic break with the silence imposed during the transition to democracy (Aguilar 2008b).

2. This consensus is reflected in the literature of transitional justice, where the majority of scholars insist that retributive (trials, policies of vetting members of security services for past human rights record) and restorative (truth commissions) policies facilitate the consolidation of democracy and should be implemented during the transition from authoritarian regimes (Minow 2002; Sikkink and Walling 2007). For a more critical approach that challenges the view that dealing with the past is a sine qua non precondition for moving forward, see Snyder and Vinjamuri (2003). For a more critical position on the concept of transitional justice as a form of establishing the western "Liberal peace" project, see Newman, Roland, and Richmond (2009).

3. For a discussion of the legal framework covering the problem of enforced disappearances, see Scovazzi and Citroni (2007).

4. Interestingly, neither the National Army nor the veterans of the Greek Democratic Army have conducted systematic research to determine the precise number of those

disappeared or buried in common graves. This indicates a broader problem in the study of the Greek Civil War related to the absence of systematic research on local dynamics and the practice of violence. For some interesting exceptions, see Kalyvas (2002) and Van Boeschoten (1997).

5. Interview with MS, June 11, 2012.

6. Dealing with the traumatic past, although with a significant delay is a growing phenomenon in international politics; it is also known as post-transitional or delayed justice, a term coined by Aguilar 2008a. (See also Kovras 2014.)

7. Within the Christian Orthodox tradition, Panourgiá argues, "death is not considered the end of life, but rather the beginning of another dimension of life. . . . The dead person is automatically transformed into a possession of the religion and the Church" (1995:188).

8. The official commencement of the Civil War is still a contested issue within Greek academic and public debate. We employ 1946–1949 as the period, underlining, however, that the first conflicts between the different resistance groups occurred in 1943 and that the preceding periods, namely the occupation and resistance periods, are tightly connected to the outbreak, nature, and outcome of the Civil War. Among the prevailing approaches in relation to the Civil War period is the so-called theory of three rounds that recently reemerged in academic discussion of the Civil War. For more in relation to the three rounds theory, see Iatrides (2002) and Kalyvas and Marantzidis (2004); for a critique of this approach, see Panourgiá (2004, 2009).

9. For the historical context of the Greek Civil War, see Baerentzen, Iatrides, and Smith (1992); Close (1993); Kotaridis (1997); Mazower (2000); Nikolakopoulos, Rigos, and Psallidas(2002); Carabott and Sfikas (2004); Margaritis (2002). For more in relation to the persecution, incarceration, and terrorization of the leftists, including women and political refugees, see Panourgiá (2009); Voglis (2002); Vervenioti (2000); Voutyra et al. (2005).

10. In certain rural areas (on a microlevel), this friction and the Civil War's ideological framework have connotations in the everyday reality of the population; they define and affect social identities, political views, and social relations even today.

11. These bands were formed by the government in 1946 under the names Monades Asfaleias Ypaithrou (country security units) and Monades Asfaleias Dimosyntiritoi (municipal security units) (Voglis 2002:71).

12. For more details about the DSL, see Kalogeras and Koutskoudis (2002).

13. Elli Svorou, a twenty-five-year-old woman from Lesvos, was among the twenty-two political detainees who were executed (or died) during their incarceration. For more information in relation to the victims in (or from) Lesvos, see Kalogeras and Koutskoudis (2002:79–108).

14. Interview with GK, May 4, 2012.

15. The most significant laws were those enacted in 1982 officially recognizing the national resistance against the Nazi occupation (N.1285/1982); in 1983 a ministerial decree enabled thousands of political refugees to return to Greece. Yet this did not

include those of non-Greek descent, an exclusion mainly targeting the Greek Slavic speakers in northwest Greece.

16. The coalition government became known as the "government of national reconciliation," because it signified the symbolic end of the Civil War.

17. For an interesting analysis of the politics of memory, see Marantzidis and Antoniou (2004) and Van Boeschoten et al. (2008).

18. Perhaps the most vocal NGO in Spain is the Association for the Recovery of Historical Memory, which set the demand for exhumations at the top of its priorities.

19. Interview with MS, June 11, 2012, and GK, June 10, 2012.

20. On the Macedonian conflict, see Loizides (2007).

21. See Kizos and Koulouri (2006:331, 335).

22. For more on Mantamados and it being referenced as "Little Moscow," see Marantzidis (1997); for the relationship between religion and communism in Lesvos, see Marantzidis (1995).

23. See Kalogeras and Koutskoudis (2002).

24. To be sure, the enactment of Legislative Decree 3382 in 1955 conferring benefits on the "bandits" (referring to the guerrillas) who voluntarily surrendered should not be ignored; for more, see Skoufos (2009:19).

25. In this area, DSL fighters had dug out and built underground hideouts and shelters (*ambria*).

26. See Kalogeras and Koutskoudis (2002:40).

27. In 1945, 1950, and 1951–1952, primarily in the context of coalition governments.

28. According to oral testimonies, she was a villager from the area of Ippeios who allegedly committed suicide because of an illicit affair.

29. More information on the "Tserkeza" ambush and exhumation can be found in Apostolou (1999:55–57); Skoufos (2009:232–234); Kalogeras and Koutskoudis (2002:45–47); *Empros* (2009a, 2009b); *Neo Empros* (2009); also see the interviews with MP, June 9, 2012, and SB, April 26, 2012.

30. See the interview with MP, June 9, 2012.

31. Several cases can be found in Kalogeras and Koutskoudis (2002:44, 48).

32. See Panourgiá's (1995) anthropological study of death, pain, mourning and memory in Athens; in relation to the mourning rituals in Mani, see Seremetakis 1991.

33. See Panourgiá (1995:188–192, esp. 191–192); Panourgiá also argues that within Greek Orthodox religious beliefs, the undissolved body might also denote holiness (1995:191). Also see Danforth (1982).

34. Panourgiá (1995:189) describes the grave as a "home" within the cemetery, which is considered a "homeland."

35. See the interview with MP, June 9, 2012; also see Skoufos (2009); Kalogeras and Koutskoudis (2002).

36. See the interviews with MP, June 9, 2012, and SB, April 26, 2012; also see *Empros* (2009a, 2009b).

37. Interviews with DM and GM, June 12, 2012.

38. See Verdery (1999, esp. 33).

39. This point is also raised by Santos (2008) with regard to the Spanish experience.

40. For more about "white" and "red" terror, see Kalyvas (2000, 2002); Sakkas (2000); Sarafis (2002).

Bibliography

Aguilar, Paloma. 2002. *Memory and Amnesia: The Role of the Spanish Civil War in the Transition to Democracy*. London: Berghahn Books.

———. 2008a. Transitional or Post-Transitional Justice? Recent Developments in the Spanish Case. *South European Society and Politics* 13(4):417–433.

———. 2008b. *Políticas de la Memoria y Memorias de la Política*. Madrid: Alianza.

Anderson, Benedict. 1991. *Imagined Communities*. London: Verso.

Antoniou, Giorgos and Nikos Marantzidis. 2004. The Axis Occupation and Civil War: Changing Trends in Greek Historiography, 1941–2002. *Journal of Peace Research* 41(2):223–231.

Apostolou, E. Apostolos. 1999. *Skorpia apo tin Antistasi* [Scattered by the resistance]. Lesvos: Petra.

Baerentzen, Lars, John Iatrides, and Ole Smith, eds.1992. *Meletes gia ton Emfylio Polemo, 1945–1949* [Studies in the history of the Greek Civil War, 1945–1949]. Athens: Olkos.

Buck Sutton, Susan. 2001. Greece. In *Countries and Their Cultures*, vol. 2, ed. Melvin Ember and Carol R. Ember, 887–899. New York: Macmillan.

Carabott, Philip and Thanasis, D. Sfikas, eds. 2004. *The Greek Civil War. Essays on a Conflict of Exceptionalism and Silences*. Aldershot: Ashgate.

Close, David, ed. 1993. *The Greek Civil War: Studies of Polarization, 1943–1950*. London: Routledge.

———. 2004. The Road to Reconciliation? The Greek Civil War and the Politics of Memory in the 1980s. In *The Greek Civil War: Essays on a Conflict of Exceptionalism and Silences*, ed. Philip Carabott and Thanasis D. Sfikas, 257–278. Aldershot: Ashgate.

Danforth, Loring. 1982. *The Death Rituals of Rural Greece*. Princeton: Princeton University Press.

Denich, Bette. 1994. Dismembering Yugoslavia: Nationalist Ideologies and the Symbolic Revival of Genocide. *American Ethnologist* 21(2):367–390.

Empros. 2009a. O emfylios polemos . . . teleiwse [The Civil War . . . has ended]. July 27.

———. 2009b. To . . . "telos" tou emfyliou![The . . . "end" of the Civil War!]. July 1.

Ferrándiz, Francisco. 2006. The Return of Civil War Ghosts: The Ethnography of Exhumations in Contemporary Spain. *Anthropology Today* 22(3):7–12.

Ferrándiz, Francisco, and Alejandro Baer. 2008. Digital Memory: The Visual Recording of Mass Grave Exhumations in Contemporary Spain. *Forum, Qualitative Social Research* 9(3).

Iatrides, John. 2002. To Diethnes Plaisio tou Ellinikou Emfyliou Polemou [The international context of the Greek Civil War]. In *Emfylios Polemos: Apo ti Varkiza sto Grammo, Fevrouarios 1945–Avgoustos 1949* [The Civil War: From Varkiza to Grammos, February 1945–August 1949], ed. Ilias Nikolakopoulos, Alkis Rigos, and Grigoris Psalidas, 31–50. Athens: Themelio.

Kalogeras, Vasilis and Panagiotis Koutskoudis. 2002. *Dimokratikos Stratos Lesvou* [Democratic Army of Lesvos]. Lesvos: Neo Empros.

Kalyvas, Stathis. 2000. Red Terror: Leftist Violence During the Occupation. In *After the War Was Over: Reconstructing the Family, Nation and State in Greece, 1943–1960*, ed. Mark Mazower, 142–183. Princeton: Princeton University Press.

———. 2002. Morfes, diastaseis kai praktikes tis vias ston Emfylio (1943–1949): Mia proti prosegisi. [Types, dimensions and practices of violence during the Civil War (1943–1949): A first cut]. In *Emfylios Polemos: Apo ti Varkiza sto Grammo, Fevrouarios 1945–Avgoustos 1949* [The Civil War: From Varkiza to Grammos, February 1945–August 1949], ed. Ilias Nikolakopoulos, Alkis Rigos, and Grigoris Psalidas, 188–207. Athens: Themelio.

———. 2004. Kokkini Tromokratia: H via tis Aristeras stin Katohi [Red terror: Leftist violence during the occupation]. In *After the War Was Over: Reconstructing the Family, Nation, and State in Greece, 1944–1960*, ed. Mark Mazower, 161–204. Athens: Alexandreia.

Kalyvas, Stathis and Nikos Marantzidis. 2004. Nees taseis sti meleti tou emfyliou polemou [New trends in the study of the Civil War]. *Vivliodromio, TA NEA*, March 20–21:10–11.

Kizos, Thanasis and Maria Koulouri. 2006. Agricultural Landscape Dynamics in the Mediterranean: Lesvos (Greece) Case Study Using Evidence from the Last Three Centuries. *Environmental Science and Policy* 9(4):330–342.

Kotaridis, Nikos, ed. 1997. *To Emfylio Drama* [Civil War drama]. Conference proceedings. Athens: Dokimes 6.

Kovras, Iosif. 2014. *Truth Recovery and Transitional Justice: Deferring Human Rights Issues*. New York: Routledge.

———. 2013. Explaining Prolonged Silences in Transitional Justice: The Disappeared in Cyprus and Spain. *Comparative Political Studies*, 46(6): 730–756.

Kovras, Iosif and Neophytos Loizides. 2011. Delaying Truth Recovery for Missing Persons. *Nations and Nationalism* 17(3):520–539.

Lederach, John Paul.1998. Remember and Change. In *Transforming Violence: Linking Local and Global Peacemaking*, ed. Judy Zimmerman Herr and Robert Herr, 177–189. Waterloo, Ont.: Herald Press.

Loizides, Neophytos. 2007. "The Name Macedonia Is Our Soul": Elite Framing and Conflict (de)Escalation. Paper presented at the Annual Meeting of the International Studies Association, Chicago, 2 March 2007.

Marantzidis, Nikos. 1995. To thriskeutiko mesa sto politiko: Thriskeia kai politiki se mia agrotiki koinotita tis Lesvou [The religious within the political: religion and politics in a rural community of Lesvos]. *Nea Koinoniologia* [New Sociology] 20:36–44.

———. 1997. *Oi Mikres Moshes: Politiki kai eklogiki analisi tou kommounismou ston elladiko agrotiko horo* [The Little Moscows: Political and electoral analysis of communism in rural Greece]. Athens: Papazisis.

Margaritis, Giorgos. 2002. *I Istoria tou Ellinikou Emfyliou Polemou (1946–1949)* [History of the Greek Civil War (1946–1949)], 2 vols.. Athens: Vivliorama.

Mazower, Mark, ed. 2000. *After the War Was Over: Reconstructing the Family, Nation, and State in Greece, 1943–1960*. Princeton: Princeton University Press.

McEvoy, Kieran and Heather Conway. 2004. The Dead, the Law, and the Politics of the Past. *Journal of Law and Society* 31(4):539–562.

Minow, Martha. 2002. Breaking the Cycles of Hatred. In *Breaking the Cycles of Hatred: Memory, Law and Repair*, ed. Martha Minow, 16–75. Princeton: Princeton University Press.

Neo Empros. 2009. Gia tous pesontes tou DSL stin anatinaxi sto dami tis Tserkezas [For the fallen of the DSL at the "Tserkeza" explosion]. July 29.

Newman, Edward, Paris Roland, and Oliver Richmond. 2009. Introduction. In *New Perspectives on Liberal Peacebuilding*, ed. Edward Newman, Paris Roland, and Oliver Richmond, 3–25. Tokyo: United Nations University Press.

Nikolakopoulos, Ilias, Alkis Rigos, and Grigoris Psallidas, eds. 2002. *Emfylios Polemos: Apo ti Varkiza sto Grammo, Fevrouarios 1945–Avgoustos 1949* [The Civil War: From Varkiza to Grammos, February 1945–August 1949]. Athens: Themelio.

Panourgiá, Neni. 1995. *Fragments of Death, Fables of Identity: An Athenian Anthropography*. Madison: University of Wisconsin Press.

———. 2004. O Aghios Velouhiotis kai ta Tagmata Asfaleias [Saint Velouhiotis and the security battalions]. *Vivliodromio, TA NEA*, October 2 and 10.

———. 2009. *Dangerous Citizens. The Greek Left and the Terror of the State*. New York: Fordham University Press.

Robins, Simon. 2013. *Families of the Missing: A Test for Contemporary Approaches to Transitional Justice*. London: Routledge.

Sakkas, John. 2000. The Civil War in Evrytania. In *After the War Was Over: Reconstructing the Family, Nation, and State in Greece, 1943–1960*, ed. Mark Mazower, 184–209. Princeton: Princeton University Press.

Sanford, Victoria. 2003. *Buried Secrets: Truth and Human Rights in Guatemala*. New York: Palgrave Macmillan.

Sant Cassia, Paul. 2005. *Bodies of Evidence: Burial, Memory and the Recovery of Missing Persons in Cyprus*. Oxford: Berghahn Books.

———. 2006. Guarding Each Other's Dead, Mourning One's Own: The Problem of Missing Persons and Missing Pasts in Cyprus. *South European Society and Politics* 11(1):111–128.

Santos, Juliá. 2008. Amnistía como triunfo de la memoria [Amnesty as a triumph of memory]. *El País*, November 24.

Sarafis, Lee. 2002. I "Leuki tromokratia" Mohlos Synthlipsis tou Antistasiakou Fronima-tos ["White terror" the lever in smashing the resistance morale]. In *Emfylios Pole-mos: Apo ti Varkiza sto Grammo, Fevrouarios 1945–Avgoustos 1949* [The Civil War: From Varkiza to Grammos, February 1945–August 1949], ed. Ilias Nikolakopoulos, Alkis Rigos, and Grigoris Psalidas, 165–175. Athens: Themelio.

Scott, James C. 1985. *Weapons of the Weak: Everyday Forms of Peasant Resistance*. New Haven: Yale University Press.

Scovazzi, Tullio and Gabriela Citroni. 2007. *The Struggle Against Enforced Disappearance and the 2007 UN Convention*. Leiden: Martinus Nihoff.

Seremetakis, C. Nadia.1991. *The Last Word: Women, Death, and Divination in Inner Mani*. Chicago: University of Chicago Press.

Sikkink, Kathryn and Carrie Booth Walling. 2007. The Impact of Human Rights Trials in Latin America. *Journal of Peace Research* 44(4):427–445.

Skoufos, Giorgos. 2009. *Selides tou Agona* [Pages of the struggle]. Lesvos: Neo Empros.

Snyder, Jack and Leslie Vinjamuri,. 2003. Trials and Errors: Principle and Pragmatism in Strategies of International Justice. *International Security* 28(3):5–44.

Sotiropoulos, A. Dimitri. 2010. The Authoritarian Past and Contemporary Greek De-mocracy. *Southern European Society and Politics* 15(3):449–465.

Van Boeschoten, Riki. 1997. *Anapoda Hronia: Syllogiki Mnimi kai Istoria sto Ziaka Grevenon* [Troubled years: collective memory and history in Ziakas Grevenon]. Ath-ens: Plethron.

Van Boeschoten, Riki, Tasoula Vervenioti, Efi Voutyra, Vasilis Dalkavoukis, and Kon-stantina Bada, eds. 2008. *Mnimes kai Lithi tou Ellinikou Emfyliou Polemou* [Memo-ries and oblivion of the Greek Civil War]. Athens: Epikentro.

Verdery, Katherine. 1999. *The Political Lives of Dead Bodies*. New York: Columbia Uni-versity Press.

Vervenioti, Tasoula. 2000. Left-Wing Women Between Politics and Family. In *After the War Was Over: Reconstructing the Family, Nation, and State in Greece, 1943–1960*, ed. Mark Mazower, 105–121. Princeton: Princeton University Press.

Voglis, Polymeris. 2002. *Becoming a Subject: Political Prisoners During the Greek Civil War*. New York: Berghahn.

Voutyra, Efi, Vasilis Dalkavoukis, Nikos Marantzidis, and Maria Bontila, eds. 2005. "*To oplo para poda*": *Oi politikoi prosfyges tou ellinikou emfyliou polemou stin Anatoliki Europi* ["Ground arms": the political refugees of the Greek Civil War in Eastern Europe]. Thessaloniki: University of Macedonia Publications.

Wagner, Sarah. 2010. Identifying Srebrenica's Missing: The "Shaky Balance" of Univer-salism and Particularism. In *Transitional Justice: Global Mechanisms and Local Real-ities After Genocide and Mass Violence*, ed. Alexander Laban Hinton, 25–48. New Brunswick. NJ: Rutgers University Press.

Chapter 7

Death in Transition

The Truth Commission and the Politics
of Reburial in Postconflict Peru

Isaias Rojas-Perez

Following the advent of the democratic transition in late 2000, the question of clandestine mass graves containing the bodies of unknown victims of political violence became a problem in Peru. Since then, Peruvian legal institutions have been conducting a large project of forensic exhumation of mass graves scattered in former war-torn areas of rural Peru—a project they never attempted to realize during the twenty-year period of internal conflict (1980–2000). Until November 2012, these institutions had recovered the bodies of at least 2,220 victims of political violence, identified 1,238 of these victims, and returned 1,079 bodies to their relatives for "cristiana sepultura."[1] This chapter looks at the beginnings of this official project of recovering the remains of victims of political violence to explore the extent to which death can be grounds for reconciliation and reconstitution of the political community in the aftermath of protracted internal armed conflict. More specifically, it focuses on the Peruvian Truth and Reconciliation Commission's (CVR) involvement with the exhumation of mass graves and moral framing of these forensic and legal interventions within a broader project of political reburial of forgotten victims of violence. The chapter argues that the CVR's intervention introduces a subtle displacement of the problem of clandestine mass graves from one concerned primarily with the fate of the disappeared during the internal conflict to one concerned primarily with reburying the remains of unrecognized victims of violence. By means of this displacement from *unknown death* to *unacknowledged death*, the CVR situates tragic death, and Peruvians' response to it, as a foundational and moral condition of possibility of the post-conflict political community.

Three questions center the chapter's analysis of the CVR's engagement with forensic exhumations of clandestine mass graves and postconflict reburial of victims of political violence. The first asks how the CVR formulates the problem of responding to unaccounted and unacknowledged mass death as a moral ground for reconstituting the postconflict political community and how reburial emerges as a privileged mechanism for doing justice to the forgotten dead. The second asks how the question of wartime clandestine mass graves has become a legal and political problem in postconflict Peru in response to the Peruvian state's renewed recognition of its international obligations in regard to human rights as well as reception of global legal and humanitarian notions such as the "right to truth." The third interrogates the CVR's actual practice of reburial to consider the viability of official moral projects based on universal victimhood, as well as moral sentiments of compassion assumed to be a common human response to the experience of tragic death, within political cultures associated with nationalism and the modern nation-state that focus on the figure of the "internal enemy." While considering these questions, the chapter sustains the invisible presence of the disappeared throughout. Perhaps more clearly than any other, the figure of the *desaparecido* inhabits the temporality of the finished and unfinished past of the postconflict state.[2] As a suspected "terrorist," the disappeared person is a political transgressor whose death or disappearance needs to be forgotten. At the same time, he or she is a victim whose body needs to be recovered to complete the regenerative work of the law in the postconflict project of reconstituting the political community.

Justice to the Dead and the Political Community

On August 28, 2003, following two years of work, the Peruvian Truth and Reconciliation Commission presented its final report to then president Alejandro Toledo, in a solemn ceremony held at the presidential palace in Lima, the capital of Peru. In this highly anticipated act of state, the chairman of the CVR, philosopher Salomon Lerner, summarized his commission's findings before representatives of Peru's Spanish-speaking ruling elites, international organizations, and diplomatic community. Lerner began by announcing that the CVR had uncovered evidence of over sixty-nine thousand civilian and combatant deaths as a result of the twenty-year war between the Peruvian armed forces, the Peruvian Communist Party "Shining Path," and the Movimiento Revolucionario Tupac Amaru. Such a figure, the CVR concluded in its final report, meant that Peru had suffered more deaths during this twenty-year period than in all the wars fought since independence from colonial rule in 1821.[3] Indeed, as the CVR's new figures nearly doubled prior estimates of thirty-five thousand deaths and disappearances, Lerner was led to ask how so many deaths could have gone not only unaccounted for but also unnoticed, to the point that there was not even any remembrance of them. That such mass death should have gone unnoticed and unremembered demonstrated, as Lerner put it, that exclusion in Peru was so absolute that it was possible for tens of thousands of citizens to disappear without anyone in broader society even noticing. "In effect," he said, "we Peruvians used to say, in our previous worst-case scenarios, that political violence caused 35,000 casualties. What does it reveal about our political community to know now that 35,000 more people are missing, our brothers and sisters, and nobody missed them?"[4]

Since the CVR's new figures nearly doubled earlier estimates, Lerner asserted that the CVR's final report was exposing a double scandal: on the one hand, the vast scale of murder, disappearance, and torture, and on the other the "slackness, ineptitude and indifference of those who could have stopped this humanitarian catastrophe from happening, but just didn't" (Lerner 2003). Lerner suggested that this failure to take note of what was happening in the country expressed a larger moral failure in Peruvian mainstream society determined by the persistence of racism and social, cultural, and economic discrimination among Peruvians. The lethal effects of these racial, ethnic, social, and economic cleavages manifested themselves dramatically in the unequal distribution of suffering and mass death during the internal conflict. "Of every four victims of the violence," said Lerner, "three were peasants whose native tongue was Quechua—a large segment of the Peruvian population that has historically been neglected, and on occasions disparaged, by both State and urban society, but which does enjoy the benefits of the political community" (Lerner 2003).[5]

These figures constituted, then, in Lerner's words, "a mark of horror and dishonor for the Peruvian state and society." In this way, the truth about mass death that had gone unnoticed and unremembered opened up a time of "national shame." For Lerner, it was also a time of truth in which mainstream Peruvians had to learn to live with the truth of their betrayal and the shame and scandal of their neglect of and obliviousness to the fate of their fellow citizens. However, the revealed truth also opened up a possibility for Peruvians to remake their political community. In this sense, for Lerner it was also a time of justice, which demanded the need to "recognize and repair to the degree possible the suffering of the victims and to bring to justice the perpetrators of the acts of violence." Finally, it was also a time of reconciliation in which Peruvians had the opportunity to realize the promise of Peru's birth as a modern republic—that is, in Lerner's words, "a political community of human beings equal in dignity, in which the death of each citizen counts as our own misfortune; and in which, every human casualty resulting from either arbitrariness, or crime or abuse of power, sets into motion the wheels of justice to compensate for the loss and to punish the perpetrators" (Lerner 2003).

This formulation of transitional justice is noteworthy because it explicitly connects, in conceptual terms, the possibility of a democratic postconflict political community with the problem of (past) unjust death. As the notion of "national shame" suggests, for Lerner and the CVR, there is nothing heroic in the recent experience of violence that could serve as grounds for social solidarity and a cohesive national memory. Even worse, that Peruvians did not experience the internal war as a national tragedy revealed the absence of such social solidarity and national memory because of the persistence of entrenched racial, class, social, and cultural cleavages that make some persons more "killable" than others and their tragic mass deaths more negligible than others.[6] And yet as the ideas of "time for justice" and "time for reconciliation" suggest, for Lerner and the CVR, it is imperative for Peruvians to face up to such a shameful past and constitute a national memory of suffering and victimhood if they wish to emerge from this dramatic historical conjuncture with some renewed aspiration for a life together in a democratic society. In other words, speaking of (re)foundation of the political community in terms of instituting a (re)new(ed) moral economy, the CVR asks Peruvians to establish "a new relationship to time and memory, to mourning and obligations, to misfortune and the misfortunate" (Fassin and Rechtman 2009:276).

Their relations to the unknown and unacknowledged dead constitute the ultimate terrain where Peruvians can anchor this (re)new(ed) moral economy and open the way to becoming a political community composed of citizens equal in rights and dignity. Speaking the truth of this mass death, gone unnoticed and unremembered, was in itself a form of unmaking the historical distance that separates Peruvians as a result of the racial, class, and social cleavages that shape their society. But Peruvians also needed to recognize those deaths as their own as a crucial step to unmaking the moral distance that separates them and, by means of offering the dead proper burial, restore to the forgotten victims their dignity as members of the political community. Moreover, these unnoticed deaths needed to be submitted to the work of the law to unmake the legal distance that prevented those neglected Peruvians from enjoying their rights and the protection of the law. In other words, the possibility of a democratic political community is tied to the problem of how Peruvians are able to remake their relations with their dead by bringing the latter back into mainstream society as legal subjects (victims), cultural subjects (persons to be properly buried and mourned), and historical subjects (persons whose history is not to be forgotten).

The CVR thus fully articulates a renewed discourse of nation building that, inspired by the international languages of human rights and global humanitarianism, demands a *universal* reintegration of neglected victims of violence back into the political community as a response to human suffering. Since the central thrust of this project is to unmake the racial, ethnic, class, and cultural markers that made possible their exclusion from political community, the question of reburial of these victims acquires a crucial political and symbolic role. Along with the law, death and the moral sentiments of compassion assumed to be a common human response to the experience of tragic death appear in this formulation as a great equalizer. By burying their dead, humans express their distinctive humanness.

And yet as the experience of the CVR illustrates, this project of universal reburial seems to be unable to escape, or unmake, nationalism's political markers that distinguish between those who defended the nation and those who attacked it. Similarly to other truth commissions in the world, the CVR functioned within impoverished political conditions. In addition, as a state-appointed institution, it operated within previously established grammars and languages that presupposed the legitimacy of the state and the law as a source of order, and addressed previously constituted public spheres and political cultures. In what follows we will see how, owing to these conditioning contexts and grammars, the CVR's moral politics of reburial ended up by reintroducing an implicit moral and political qualification by means of which some victims are seen as more legitimate than others. This leads us to ask to what extent a project of postconflict reconciliation based on universal reburial can be carried out by state-appointed institutions. To hint at this question drawing from the Peruvian experience we need first to consider how it was that the CVR first became involved in the problem of clandestine mass graves.

Unknown Death as Legal Problem

The question of wartime clandestine mass graves emerged as a problem in Peru in the context of the democratic transition that followed the dramatic collapse of the Fujimori regime in late 2000. It emerged first as a legal problem associated with the search for the people disappeared by the Peruvian security forces during the counterinsurgency campaign of the 1980s and 1990s. In September 2001, the Fiscalía de la Nación–Ministerio Público took one of the first institutional moves to address this problem that had been pending since the beginning of the internal conflict in May 1980.[7] For the first time in two decades, the Fiscalía issued an ordinance instituting a sweeping set of rules and procedures that would, from that point on, govern the forensic investigation of clandestine graves in former war-torn areas of Peru.[8] The Fiscalía also ordered some important institutional rearrangements with the purpose of enhancing this kind of investigation. First, it decreed that two of its provincial branches would specialize in the investigation of human rights violations, forced disappearance, extrajudicial executions, and clandestine mass graves. Second, it ordered that prosecutors who worked in former war-torn areas should be trained in forensic techniques of investigation of clandestine graves. And finally, in order to guarantee the scientific character of the procedures and evidence collected in these investigations, the Fiscalía called for the participation of forensic archaeologists and anthropologists.

The Fiscalía justified these unprecedented bureaucratic moves as a response to media revelations about the existence of clandestine mass graves scattered throughout former war-torn areas of rural Peru.[9] Yet the sudden interest of the legal institution in the problem of political clandestine graves responded more to the broad shift in the Peruvian state's discursive practices of human rights that came with the democratic transition than to the public disclosure of their existence by the media. The caretaker civilian administration of Valentin Paniagua (November 2000–July 2001) took bold steps in the area of human rights as a means of gaining democratic legitimacy and establishing a clear-cut contrast with the authoritarian and corrupt regime of former president Alberto Fujimori. In mid-January 2001, in the first of these bold steps, the Paniagua regime signed the return of Peru to the contentious jurisdiction of the Inter-American Court of Human Rights, stating thus that the Peruvian state would abide by its international obligations on human rights and global democratic standards.[10] As a consequence, the new regime pledged to deal with past human rights violations in an utterly different way from its predecessor and, in March 2001, it signed friendly settlement agreements with the Inter-American Commission of Human Rights to investigate cases of human rights violations pending before the system since the 1980s—most of which pertained to cases of people disappeared by the Peruvian security forces during the counterinsurgency campaign.

More importantly perhaps, the new regime acquiesced to all the terms of the landmark sentence of the Inter-American Court of Human Rights in the *Barrios Altos v. Peru* case, which ruled that Peru's 1995 Amnesty Law was incompatible with the American Convention on Human Rights and, as such, was null and had no legal effects.[11] This acquiescence set the character and tone of the "postconflict" politics relating to Peru's recent past of violence in that the new regime pledged to address pending problems of human rights violations and state atrocities through the available legal languages and institutions. Since the Amnesty Law had no legal effects, all the legal obstacles that prevented the criminal investigation and prosecution of past human rights violations were removed, and the Peruvian legal institutions regained jurisdiction over a problem that Fujimori had attempted to bring to an end by legislation.[12]

Moreover, through its acquiescence, the Peruvian state established victim-oriented repertoires of action and thought articulated around novel legal notions such as the "right to truth." In the hearing on the *Barrios Altos* case before the Inter-American Court, the Peruvian representatives said that the new regime's strategy in the area of human rights consisted of "recognizing [international] responsibilities, but, above all, on proposing integrated procedures for attending to the victims based on three fundamental elements: the *right to truth*, the right to justice and the right to obtain fair reparation."[13] In Peru's recent history of violence, never before had a government made such a commitment to a victim-oriented perspective in which the truth about the past had such a central place. It seemed that the time had finally arrived for Peru to cast light on the fate of the disappeared through legal means, after so many years of official denial, oblivion, and silencing.

Accommodating the Right to Truth

This novel perspective showed that, with the democratic transition, the new regime was open to the languages of international human rights law and global humanitarianism—as expressed in the "right to truth"—in the official task of dealing with past state atrocities. The Peruvian state had previously been impervious to these languages, but now seemed receptive to these manifestations of global governance. However, the notion arrived on Peruvian soil with unmapped potentialities, as well as ambiguities. As Naqvi explains, the "right to truth" is an evolving concept that emerged first in international humanitarian law to respond to the specific problem of the forced disappearance of dissenters during internal wars and counterinsurgency campaigns. But then international human rights discursive practices started to expand the notion beyond the specific problem of forced disappearance, to address other forms of gross human rights violation. Even more, in further crucial shifts, given the presupposition that knowing has therapeutic effects, the "right to truth" came to be seen as a fundamental social and political mechanism to address traumatic legacies of violence and atrocity. In this perspective, the "right to truth" started to emerge as a right belonging to society at large rather than just to the victims of violence. In Naqvi's words, "the right to truth has emerged as a legal concept at the national, regional and international level, and relates to the obligation of the state to provide information to victims or their families or *even society as a whole* about the circumstances surrounding serious violations of human rights" (Naqvi 2006, emphasis added).

Because of these unmapped potentialities and ambiguities, the right to truth operated in the context of the political transition as a kind of "floating signifier" (Lévi-Strauss qtd. in Fassin and Rechtman 2009:276–277) that enabled a number of reconfigurations in the legal work dealing with past atrocities to which the Peruvian state committed itself after the recognition of its international human rights obligations. This chapter considers three of these. First, the notion of right to truth emerged on the premise that the truth about human rights violations is distinct from, and could not be subsumed by, the legal truth or evidence for trial (Naqvi 2006). This distinction between the truth of violence and legal truth enabled the possibility of disengaging the problem of punishing the perpetrators of gross human rights violations from the circumstances in which those crimes were committed. The legal obstacles that prevented criminal investigation as a consequence of the 1995 Amnesty Law may have been removed, but such removal did not necessarily guarantee that the perpetrators of atrocities in the name of the state would ineluctably be found, prosecuted, and punished in all the cases. What the legal institutions would definitely guarantee was to find out the truth about the circumstances of the crime as a means of opening the way for the potential healing of bereaved families.[14]

How the notion of right to truth started to reshape the ways in which legal institutions conceived of their work on past crimes against humanity became apparent to me in a conversation I had in February 2006 with the former chief prosecutor for human rights in Ayacucho, who articulated the new discursive regime in the following terms: "We are aware that most probably we won't be able to identify the perpetrators in all the cases under investigation. Consequently, we won't be able to prosecute them in every single case; but we want to say to the [victims'] relatives: 'Look, we could not make justice, but at least we have recovered the remains of your relatives. This is the way in which the state is trying to reach you.' We want to say: 'Look, we have sought the truth and the truth is that your relative was killed in these circumstances, this is the place in which he was buried, and now we are restoring him to you for proper burial.'"[15] In addition to the distinction between legal evidence and the truth of crime, this picture of the work of the law in contexts of human rights violations shows how the Peruvian legal institutions adopted the humanitarian notion that both truth and truth telling have therapeutic powers and considered that, while retributive justice could not perhaps be served in all cases, some form of restitution could be attained by both telling the victims' relatives the truth about what happened to their loved ones and officially returning their bodies for proper burial. Even if the law cannot bring the perpetrators of atrocity to trial, it can at least offer some form of restitution by finding out the truth about the crimes. Not surprisingly, convinced of the therapeutic value of the truth, the legal authorities encouraged survivors and relatives of victims to participate actively in the legal and forensic procedures dealing with human rights violations in the hope that this participation would not only guarantee fairness in their work of justice making but would also help the latter to gain certain closure to their suffering.[16]

The notion of right to truth enabled a second reconfiguration in the work of the law that was articulated around the tension between the rights of the victims and the rights of society. In June 2001, Paniagua's caretaker regime appointed a truth commission tasked with finding out the truth of the recent twenty-year period of violence and human rights violations in Peru. Appointing a truth commission was never part of Peru's international obligations on

human rights. However, coming to office on the heels of one of the most se-
cretive and corrupt regimes in contemporary Peruvian history, the reformers
considered that a truth commission would play a crucial role in a comprehensive political project aimed at cleansing the political center and reconstituting
the moral values of Peruvian society.[17] In the creation of the truth commission, the Peruvian case illustrates new developments in the evolution of transitional justice whereby the right to truth is asserted as a right that
simultaneously belongs to both the victims of past violence and atrocities and
to society at large. The supreme decree that instituted the truth commission
states this expanded notion of the right to truth in the following terms: "The
painful violence Peru experienced in the last two decades must be clarified,
not left to oblivion, and the state must guarantee *the right of society to know
the truth.*"[18]

The mandate asked the CVR to clarify "the process, facts and responsibilities of terrorist violence and human rights violations" that took place during
the "process of violence" that affected Peru from May 1980 to November 2000.
This truth had two components: first, the CVR had to analyze the political,
social, and cultural "conditions" as well as the "behaviors" of society and state
institutions that "contributed to the tragic episode of violence Peru went
through." In other words, by seeking an explanation for the origins and causes
of the recent episode of political violence, the mandate called on the CVR to
produce a social, historical, and political account of the internal conflict. Second, the mandate also asked the CVR to contribute, "when pertinent," to finding out the legal truth about crimes and human rights violations committed
by both "terrorist organizations and state officials" and to identify inasmuch
as possible "the presumed responsibilities" of these crimes. The mandate here
placed special emphasis on the question of the disappeared by asking the CVR
to seek "to *establish the whereabouts and situation of victims.*" The CVR was
also asked to draw up proposals for redressing and ennobling victims, and to
recommend institutional reforms "aimed at strengthening peace and concord
among Peruvians" and to promote "national reconciliation, the rule of justice
and the strengthening of the constitutional democratic regime."[19]

The distinction between legal truth and historical truth clearly reflected
the conceptual double bind by means of which the right to truth is intended
to respond to both the plight of victims and the presumed needs of society at
large for healing and reconciliation. While, in theory, the mandate reconciles
unproblematically this distinction between legal truth and historical truth, in
practice, the CVR had serious trouble in doing so. As a full discussion of these

problems is beyond the scope of this chapter, suffice it to say that initially the commissioners interpreted their mandate in terms of finding broader historical, sociological, political, and even juridical truths; and only midway through the CVR's work did they consider as part of their mandate the problem of legal truth and the need to gather evidence to prosecute perpetrators of human rights violations attributed to both the guerrillas and the security forces.[20]

A third reconfiguration in the adoption of the notion of right to truth facilitated by the legal work dealing with past violence was the subtle displacement of the question of clandestine mass graves from one focused on the problem of the disappeared to one focused on reburial of unrecognized victims of political violence. Early in its work, the CVR interpreted its mandate to include the question of clandestine mass graves in former war-torn areas as falling within the scope of that mandate, and consequently asked the Fiscalía to stop the procedures of exhumation it was conducting at the time. The CVR considered that, before continuing with this work, both institutions needed to reach an agreement about their mandate, responsibilities, and jurisdiction, as well as conditions in which this kind of work should be conducted. The CVR was certain that, as the legal institution entrusted by the law to deal with crime, the Fiscalía had jurisdiction and authority over the problem. However, the CVR contended that the Fiscalía was conducting exhumations without the expertise these kinds of cases demanded and that, as a consequence, crucial evidence of atrocities might already have been lost in the procedures. Soon, a tense relationship over the question of clandestine mass graves developed between the two institutions.[21]

After a series of exchanges and conversations, both institutions arrived at a working relationship that would lead them first to establish some verbal agreements to work together and then to sign *convenios* (signed agreements) of cooperation instituting the rules and procedures that would govern their conjoint work on forensic exhumations of clandestine mass graves.[22] In short, on the one hand, as the legal authority, the Fiscalía would conduct the legal and forensic procedures in their totality; that is, it would *formally* decide in which cases to intervene, appoint the personnel authorized to participate, recover evidence for prosecution, officially return the recovered bodies to their relatives, and provide the corresponding legal certifications. On the other hand, the CVR would suggest the names of independent forensic experts who, by means of their appointment by the Fiscalía, could be integrated into the official forensic teams. However, in a sign of political flexibility, the Fiscalía agreed *informally* to let the CVR decide in which cases it should intervene.

With this arrangement, both institutions vowed to ensure that their conjoint work on clandestine mass graves conformed to cutting edge international standards.

Because it gave the CVR ample maneuvering room, the agreement that allowed the CVR to decide in which cases to intervene turned out to be crucial for the CVR's own project of truth finding and truth telling. The selection of cases shows that during the CVR's tenure, rather than focusing primarily on the need to ascertain the whereabouts of the disappeared, forensic exhumation of clandestine mass graves ended up by focusing *primarily* on the need to articulate a moral discourse addressing the problem of unrecognized death among disenfranchised Quechua-speaking victims of violence. The CVR certainly continued to be concerned with collecting evidence of human rights violations through these forensic procedures; however, it shifted the emphasis of its work toward the problem of reburial with the purpose of bringing those forgotten deaths before the national gaze in order to confront mainstream Peruvian society with the truth of its obliviousness, neglect, and injustice. As we will see in what follows, not only did the CVR's politics of reburial resituate the problem of clandestine mass graves from one pertaining fundamentally to *unknown* death to one pertaining fundamentally to *unacknowledged* death, but it also failed to escape a nationalistic discourse that distinguishes between those who defended the nation and those who attacked it.

Reburial in Times of Truth

During the two-year period of the CVR's existence, the Fiscalía and the CVR conducted three conjoint forensic exhumations of mass graves followed by ceremonies of reburial. The first of these interventions took place in late January 2002, in Chuschi, Ayacucho—the Andean village where the Maoist Shining Path launched its armed struggle in May 1980. A modern multidisciplinary task group comprising commissioners, prosecutors, forensic experts from both the Instituto de Medicina Legal (Legal Medicine Institute, IML for its acronym in Spanish) and Equipo Peruano de Antropología Forense (Peruvian Team of Forensic Anthropology, EPAF for its acronym in Spanish) in representation of the CVR, officials of the Ombudsman's Office, and representatives of the Peruvian human rights community arrived in the village to conduct this highly symbolic act of (postconflict) state. By starting a major project of official recovery of the bodies of victims of political violence in the very place where the

Shining Path had launched its armed struggle two decades earlier, the group aimed to (re)proclaim the civilizational mission of the state. The intention was to declare the postconflict state's commitment to breaking with the violence and arbitrariness of the past and to performing its charge to redeem the suffering of survivors and relatives through the rational means of both the law and forensic sciences as well as through moral discourses of recognition.

The human remains to be exhumed in Chuschi belonged to eight Quechua-speaking peasants from the Andean community of Quispillacta who were detained and killed by the Peruvian army on May 15, 1983.[23] The victims were taken from their homes at gunpoint by an army squad, supposedly to be brought to the nearest military base for interrogation. However, they were summarily executed on the way in an isolated area of a neighboring community. The executioners threw two bodies over a cliff and left the others in the open. Villagers who had surreptitiously witnessed the killing buried the bodies hurriedly in the same place where the military had left them. The relatives soon found the remains of their slaughtered loved ones, but out of fear did not attempt to move the bodies to their village cemetery.[24] Because the relatives knew where the remains of their families were buried, the work of forensic exhumation and identification of the victims was straightforward and could be completed on a single occasion. The exhumation itself took a couple of days and the laboratory work, carried out in a mobile morgue set up in the school of the village of Quispillacta, took two more days.

Once the forensic and legal work of identifying the victims concluded, the prosecutor, representing the Fiscalía, presided over the official ceremony of returning the bodies to their relatives for proper burial. The eight coffins, each labeled with the victim's name, were lined up in the small courtyard of the village primary school. For each victim, the legal authority then called one close relative, first asking for that person's photo ID to prove his or her relationship to the victim, asked each to sign the log, and took each one's fingerprints to leave a record of the legal act; finally, the legal authority subsequently delivered the corresponding death certificate by means of which death was officially pronounced by the state. In each case, the prosecutor offered his condolences to the bereaved relatives on behalf of the Fiscalía. The victims' bodies, however, were not immediately released to their relatives for private burial. They first had to go through the official reburial ceremony, which in essence was a Catholic funeral mass celebrated in the village church, and which, unlike the legal ceremony, was open to the participation of the community at large.[25]

Two of the three Catholic priests who were CVR commissioners concele-brated the funeral ceremony.[26] The eight coffins were accommodated in the central nave of the small church. As the Spanish-speaking priests did not speak Quechua, the CVR's regional chief served as translator throughout the religious ceremony. At a certain point, as the priests asked them to share their thoughts with the audience, some relatives thanked the "doctores" [doctors] for having helped them to finally recover the remains of their relatives for proper burial. One of them said it was as if her son had eventually come back home after a very long trip. Right before the release of the coffins, the priest-commissioners asked the relatives not to open them. "They are closed for the good of you all," said one of the priests as a closing statement of the cere-mony.[27] Following the end of the mass, members of the forensic and legal teams, CVR personnel, representatives of the Peruvian human rights commu-nity, and some local authorities carried the caskets on their shoulders back to the school courtyard, where the bodies were finally released to their relatives for private burial. While this first CVR-sponsored ceremony of reburial be-came a local political event, it went unnoticed by national elites.

The second conjoint forensic exhumation and reburial took place in the Andean district of Totos, Ayacucho, in late August 2002. For these exhuma-tions, at the CVR's initiative, the Fiscalía appointed a team of three interna-tional experts to supervise the forensic procedures, as well as to train national experts in anthropological and archaeological techniques. Following the ex-humation and reburial in Chuschi, the first forensic task group disbanded in mid-2002, due to a series of political and technical disagreements. EPAF's forensic anthropologists resigned from their position as the CVR's experts. The details of this disagreement are beyond the scope of this chapter. Suffice it to say that, in the face of this contingency, the CVR reorganized its forensic work and, in mid-June 2002, along with the Fiscalía, the Ombudsman's Office, and the human rights community, constituted a joint platform of institutional cooperation for the investigation of clandestine mass graves in Peru. This plat-form would serve to coordinate the forensic work aimed at "contributing to finding the truth, *restituting dignity* to victims and their families and promot-ing access to justice."[28] While the Fiscalía would continue directing the corre-sponding legal and forensic procedures, the CVR would suggest the names of independent experts to be appointed by the legal authorities and integrated into the official forensic teams. With this arrangement, the joint platform vowed to ensure that these investigations conformed to the most advanced international standards.[29]

In the intervention in Totos, the Fiscalía and the CVR planned to recover the bodies of nineteen Quechua-speaking peasants who were detained and summarily executed by military patrols stationed in the military garrison of Totos.[30] The victims were executed on two separate occasions between April and May 1983. On one of these occasions, following a nine-day period of detention at the garrison, a military patrol summarily executed four villagers from Totos in a nearby area known as Ccarpaccasa and buried their bodies in shallow clandestine mass graves. The relatives soon found these graves and marked them. Some months later, the wives of two of the four victims transferred the remains of their slaughtered husbands to the village cemetery.[31] On the second occasion, in a series of week-long raids in the region, military patrols detained fifteen villagers from the area of Quispillacta and transported them by helicopter to the Totos garrison. After interrogating and torturing the detainees, the military took them to an isolated area known as Sancaypata, where they eventually executed them.[32] In contrast to the previous cases, because the killing and clandestine burial took place at a great distance from their village, the relatives had more difficulty in discovering where their slaughtered loved ones were buried. As these clandestine tombs were not marked, Sancaypata bore more resemblance to a typical case of forced disappearance than one of unacknowledged death.

The exhumation and identification of the four victims killed and buried in Ccarpaccasa was relatively quick and uncomplicated. The forensic team recovered three bodies in the area and one in the village cemetery. In contrast, much to the disappointment of the relatives, in the case of those killed in Sancaypata the forensic team could find parts and dispersed bones of only seven of the fifteen bodies they expected to recover. They concluded that the clandestine mass graves had apparently been broken into and that, most probably because of erosion or the action of scavenging animals, the human remains in these graves had been dispersed beyond recovery.[33] The subsequent identification of one of the victims in Sancaypata demonstrated that this was the site of killing and burial, but it also offered proof that the missing human remains would most probably never be found again. While the forensic experts determined that several other clandestine graves existed in the area, they decided not to open them because they did not belong to the case and thus there was no proper information and documentation about them.[34]

The exhumed human remains in both cases were taken to Ayacucho, the provincial capital, for further laboratory analysis on IML premises. After a week of work, the forensic experts determined that all the victims had been shot at close range, thus demonstrating that they had been summarily executed. They also managed to identify five bodies conclusively, following the usual procedures of biological profiling, recognition of clothing, and personal effects of the victims. However, only the families of the four victims buried in Ccarpaccasa accepted the outcomes of the forensic work. The relatives of the fifth identified victim, buried in Sancaypata, demanded DNA tests before accepting the conclusions of the forensic experts. On their side, the Quechua-speaking relatives of those whose bodies could not be found or identified demanded that the legal authorities continue the search for their missing loved ones, resisting the experts' suggestion that they should perhaps begin to accept that their remains would never be found again.[35]

In this case, the rites of reburial started with an official ceremony of return of the identified bodies to their relatives, held in the headquarters of the Fiscalía in Ayacucho city, on September 6, 2002. The district attorney presided over the legal procedure, representing the legal institutions. On the CVR side, showing how important the question of reburial was becoming for the commission, four of its members came from Lima to participate in the ceremony. The Ombudsman's Office and Peruvian human rights community were also represented. All these representatives of both public institutions and modern organizations addressed the Quechua-speaking relatives with words of consolation, and hoped for peace and unity among Peruvians to prevent the repetition of such painful events in the future. After prayers and religious songs, following the legal and political act, the attendants processed the coffins through the streets of Ayacucho toward the main square. The crowd stopped at the doors of the cathedral for the final legal and funereal ceremonies. Here, the legal authorities delivered the corresponding death certificates to the relatives, and local human rights organizations set up a candlelight vigil in a final public memorial to the victims. Finally, after a night of vigil in one of the rooms of a public charity institution in Ayacucho city, the relatives could eventually take the remains of their slaughtered loved ones back to Totos for private reburial.[36]

The third conjoint exhumation took place in the Andean district of Lucanamarca, Ayacucho, in early November 2002. In contrast to the cases of Chuschi and Totos, the forensic procedure this time focused on atrocities committed by the Shining Path. In what has since been defined as one of the worst attacks of the Maoist guerrilla group against Quechua-speaking peasant communities, on April 3, 1983, armed cadres of the Shining Path gathered forces from neighboring communities where they had support to carry out a punitive strike against those communities of Lucanamarca that had rebelled against the Maoists' rule. Not only had the villagers of these communities killed local guerrilla leaders, but they had also allied with the Peruvian military to fight back against the Shining Path. The guerilla forces closed in on the area of Lucanamarca and in their raid stabbed most of their victims, eighteen of whom were children under ten. By the end of the attack, the Shining Path had killed sixty-nine Quechua-speaking peasants.[37]

In several respects, the case of Lucanamarca constitutes a turning point in the CVR's project of forensic exhumations and postconflict reburial. To begin with, as in Chuschi and Totos, the relatives knew the exact whereabouts of their slaughtered loved ones' remains because they had managed to bury them themselves after the Shining Path's attack. Not only did they bury their remains, but they also arranged the burial sites, by putting tombstones on them, for instance, and had been commemorating their dead on a regular basis ever since through the available funeral rituals. In other words, these were anything but unmarked tombs or cases of unknown death. Secondly, the major perpetrators of the massacre, among them the Shining Path's top leader, had already been sentenced to life imprisonment for masterminding the carnage. The need to collect legal evidence for prosecution seemed therefore not to be a major driving force behind the exhumation. It could nonetheless be argued that, since the legal foundations on which the Peruvian military courts sentenced Guzman and his followers had been challenged, new legal evidence for their retrial was necessary anyway.[38] Moreover, at that time, the CVR was facing a powerful media campaign by some of the coastal elites who accused it of being soft on terrorism and biased against the Peruvian military. As a result, the CVR felt the need to respond to this campaign by demonstrating its impartiality, objectivity, and, perhaps more importantly, its absolute commitment to democracy and condemnation of terrorism. The reburial of the victims of Lucanamarca was to serve this purpose. However, this argument reduces to mere political calculation what was, in fact, a broader and much more complex ethical, political, and cultural initiative in postconflict Peru.

Given that the relatives knew the whereabouts of their slaughtered loved ones from the very moment of the massacre, the exhumation happened uneventfully for the most part and in a relatively short time, ending before schedule. The IML's forensic experts, under the direction of the international experts hired by the CVR, had recovered sixty-two bodies by the end of the exhumation. It was at this point that striking contrasts with the cases of Chuschi and Totos—which as we saw involved Quechua-speaking peasants killed by the Peruvian military—started to unfold. First of all, the CVR and the Fiscalía decided to transport the exhumed remains to Lima, the capital city of Peru. The brief explanation the CVR offered to the apprehensive relatives was that, given the large number of victims, the laboratory work needed to identify the victims and determine the cause of death had to be completed in the IML's headquarters in Lima. To assuage their concerns, the CVR invited four family representatives to participate as observers in the forensic procedures in Lima. While there seemed to be no real technical problem in realizing such laboratory work in Lucanamarca itself or Ayacucho, the regional capital, the argument about the large number of victims was compelling enough to justify transportation of the remains to Peru's capital city.

The contrast between Lucanamarca and the two previous cases is even more pronounced in regard to reburial. Both the CVR and the government performed a series of political and religious acts by means of which sections of Peru's Spanish-speaking coastal elites eventually offered their official recognition to the victims of the Shining Path almost two decades after the massacre, while reiterating their permanent and absolute condemnation of the guerrilla's brutal practices of terrorism. These ceremonies started on December 20, 2002, with a funeral mass offered at La Recoleta, one of Lima's most symbolically important Catholic churches. In what the CVR called a "ceremony of dignification,"[39] the sixty-two coffins were lined up in the church nave in the presence of the few direct relatives of the victims able to travel from Lucanamarca to Lima for the occasion. In contrast, a large crowd of politicians, CVR commissioners and staff, forensic experts, members of the Peruvian human rights community, representatives of NGOs, Lima-based associations of migrants from Lucanamarca, and nuns and priests, among others, gathered to offer their respects and recognition to the victims. Once the funeral mass ended, in a display of public mourning, CVR commissioners and staff carried the coffins on their shoulders in a small procession around the Plaza Francia, one of the most symbolically significant squares in downtown Lima. The coffins were eventually transported to the trucks that would carry them back to Lucanamarca.

Most significantly, on the only occasion on which a Peruvian president has taken part in a ceremony of reburial, the then president Alejandro Toledo traveled to Lucanamarca a couple of weeks later to inaugurate the special mausoleum his government had built in the village cemetery to house the victims of the massacre. At the meeting following the exhumation, when the CVR announced it was transporting the remains to Lima, the victims' relatives, who had formed an association called "Heroes del 3 de Abril" (Heroes of April 3), had handed the CVR a petition addressed to President Toledo calling for the construction of the mausoleum. On this occasion, one of these relatives had voiced the idea that, as people who had stood against the Shining Path, their loved ones should not be buried on plain ground like any other person, but in a special mausoleum to acknowledge their contribution to the community and the nation.[40] Thus, while the CVR interceded with the government for its construction, the special mausoleum was a specific demand of the surviving relatives who considered it a way of honoring the heroic stance taken by their slaughtered loved ones against the Shining Path.

In the end, this event even exceeded expectations. Following another Catholic funeral mass in the main village square, President Toledo asked the dead and the relatives for forgiveness on behalf of the Peruvian nation, not for something the forces of the state had done, but for not having been able to protect them against the evil forces of terrorism. Then, echoing the heroic language that the Peruvian elites had put into circulation early in the internal conflict, when Quechua-speaking peasant communities first started to resist the Shining Path, Toledo declared that the entire country would never forget the heroism of those "brave Peruvians" who offered up their lives in defense of democracy against the totalitarianism of the Shining Path. The mausoleum, he said, was just a small demonstration of the justice the victims deserved— justice, he went on to say, that demanded on the one hand, that the perpetrators of the massacre never be released from jail, and, on the other hand, that the central government take action to help survivors and the community in health, education, production, and security so as to develop their capabilities for the market economy. Toledo then concluded by elaborating on how his government conceived the notion of temporality in any engagement with past atrocities, asserting that the moment had come to move on toward reconciliation—which by no means meant the guilty should escape justice with impunity—and to look to the future with optimism—which by no means meant forgetting the violence of the past.[41]

The final reburial ceremony took place the next day, on January 10, 2003, following one last Catholic funeral mass. The ceremony was attended by two CVR commissioners and civil servants representing agencies of the central government. On this occasion, one of the commissioners addressed the relatives on behalf of the entire CVR. In striking contrast to President Toledo the day before, this commissioner did not praise the victims as heroes or present their deaths as a sacrifice in defense of democracy and the nation. Conversely, he spoke of the events as a tragedy. Moreover, he said, tragedies like that of Lucanamarca had also occurred in many other communities in rural Peru; and what the CVR wanted to accomplish with forensic exhumations like this was to confront mainstream Peruvian society at large with the truth of these tragedies, so as to overcome Peruvians' indifference to the suffering of their fellow nationals. He also said that the CVR hoped that, with this ceremony, a tragic chapter in the life of the community would come to a close. One of the main purposes of the exhumation, he added, was to recognize a fundamental human right; namely, the right to a proper burial: "What we have done with this exhumation here is to fulfill a fundamental duty of any human person toward their fellow humans; that is, to recognize the most fundamental human right, which is the right to life and which is the right to have at least a 'cristiana y decente sepultura' [decent Christian burial] when that life is tragically lost."[42] He ended his speech by asking the villagers to continue their work to transform Peruvian society through their local democratic organizations and institutions.

As this speech suggests, the CVR attempted to avoid a nationalistic and patriotic discourse to emphasize instead a discourse of victimhood. The recent past of violence should not be read through the lens of heroism, but through that of tragedy. If there was any lesson to be learned, it was the lesson of failure, the failure of mainstream Peruvian society to see what was happening to fellow nationals in rural areas. If any redress could be offered to these unseen and forgotten victims, now that the truth had been revealed, it should at least be the recognition of dignity that comes with proper burial. As a basic human right, such proper burial should be offered to every single victim of the tragic episode of political violence that had ravaged rural Peru. And yet, as we have seen, the rhetoric of redress and reconciliation appealing to moral sentiments of compassion and assumed to be a common human response to the experience of tragic death could not, in practice, escape the discourse of nationalism and heroism that always preestablishes a hierarchy of victimhood between those who defend the nation and those who attack it, by appealing to the figure of the "internal enemy." Suffice it to say here that the question about the whereabouts of the remains of those alleged members of the Shining Path killed by the villagers in 1983 was never raised at any point during the entire exhumation and reburial procedure in Lucanamarca.

Concluding Comments

In August 2003, following the end of the CVR's work, the Fiscalía appointed a team of experts who specialized in forensic exhumation of clandestine mass graves and recovery of remains of victims of political violence in former war-torn areas in rural Peru.[43] Under the name Equipo Forense Especializado (Specialized Forensic Team, EFE for its acronym in Spanish), this multidisciplinary team has, with few exceptions, been in exclusive charge of conducting the legal and forensic procedures ever since. And yet while exhumations have continued to take place in response both to the requirement to gather legal evidence for prosecution and the need to return the victims' bodies to their relatives for proper burial, political acts of reburial similar to those organized by the CVR during its tenure have been reduced to zero. As the political climate changed, no senior national authority, politician, intellectual, or religious figure has attended these events again. The official return of victims' bodies to their relatives has become a bureaucratic affair conducted in the premises of the provincial branches of the Fiscalía and reburial has become almost exclusively a local or, at most in a few cases, a regional affair.[44]

The CVR was unable to persuade the Peruvian Spanish-speaking coastal elites to embrace a policy of recognition and compassion toward their Quechua-speaking fellow nationals. More tellingly, some discursive practices legitimizing racially and ethnically targeted violence in the name of national security, which the CVR sought to eradicate from the political realm, have returned. For instance, in August 2009, the surviving relatives of the more than 120 Quechua-speaking peasants massacred by the Peruvian army in the Andean village of Putis, Ayacucho, in December 1984 were eventually able to give proper burial to the remains of their slaughtered loved ones in a special cemetery built for the occasion in the village.[45] The reburial was the culmination of a two-day funeral ceremony and procession that started in the city of Ayacucho and ended in the now semideserted village. On this occasion, former Peruvian minister of defense Rafael Rey asserted that the military institutions did not acknowledge any crime in Putis. "We are much more worried about what is happening there *now*, the deaths that are taking place now, than a burial of *things* that happened in the past," he declared.[46] With the idea of "now," this high-ranking official referred to the sporadic attacks carried out by some remaining groups of the Shining Path. Not surprisingly, his statement underscored the racial and ethnic saturation of the category of "terrorism" (Theidon 2006), to the extent that, for him, Quechua-speaking peasants' remains are "things." More tellingly, this statement also made evident how, in the view of the coastal Spanish-speaking ruling elites, the domains of national security and the rule of law do not belong to the same temporal (and racial and ethnic) sphere.

On the other hand, continuing demands from survivors and relatives for the exhumation and recovery of the remains of their missing loved ones indicate the crucial importance that human remains and proper burial have for any process of dealing with past violence, and how a response to the dead might provide grounds for reconciliation. However, as this chapter has shown, state-sponsored reburial of victims of violence can also be a discursive site for the (re)emergence of discourses of heroism and nationalism that deepen the divide between perceived defenders and attackers of the nation. As a public institution responding to previously constituted national audiences and navigating within previously constituted national grammars and languages, the CVR could not escape such a political divide. We need to ask, then, to what extent a form of reburial and response to the dead can provide a road to reconciliation that will not only unmake those racial, ethnic, class, and cultural cleavages that make some Peruvians more "killable" than others but also those lethal political divides that thrive on modern notions of the "internal enemy." The notion of "cristiana sepultura" (Christian burial) offers a line of critical inquiry for it belongs to a colonial genealogy of state sovereignty and occupation of space as well as to a historically and culturally situated grid of intelligibility through which modern Peruvians have sought to define what it is to be human.

Notes

1. "Fiscalía identificó los restos de más de mil víctimas de la violencia terrorista," Ministerio Público, Imagen Institucional, Lima, November 2012, http://www.mpfn.gob .pe/home/prensadetalle?id=9805, accessed on June 24, 2013. The term *dar cristiana sepultura* (to give somebody a Christian burial) is the Peruvian Spanish expression for "proper burial."

2. On the notion of finished and unfinished pasts, see Rojas-Perez (2010, 2013).

3. "Conclusiones Generales," CVR (2004:433.)

4. Salomon Lerner's speech presenting the CVR's final report in Lima on August 28, 2003. For an English version of the speech, see Lerner 2003; translation slightly modified.

5. The CVR found that over 40 percent of the sixty-nine thousand victims were

Quechua-speaking peasants from the highland department of Ayacucho. Of these, 79 percent lived in rural areas. The CVR situated these disturbing figures in the context of a national population in which only 16 percent speak Quechua or some other native language and only 29 percent live in rural areas. To emphasize how devastating this violence was, the CVR projected the number of fatalities on a national scale in the following terms: "If the ratio of victims to population reported to the CVR with respect to Ayacucho were similar countrywide, the violence would have caused 1,200,000 deaths and disappearances. Of that number, 340,000 would have occurred in the city of Lima" (CVR 2004:434).

6. On "killability," see Agamben (1998).

7. The Fiscalía de la Nación–Ministerio Público is the Attorney General's Office in Peru. In this chapter, I make use of the noun *Fiscalía* to refer to this legal institution.

8. Directiva No. 011–2001-MP-FN, issued on September 8, 2001. http://www.derechos.org/nizkor/peru/libros/fosas/cap4.html, accessed on October 6, 2014.

9. The justification of the directive asserts the following: "During the last months, the media has been denouncing the existence of clandestine graves containing human remains, which would be related to violations of human rights committed in the context of the social violence that ravaged the country in the 1980s and 1990s. In response to these accusations, the Fiscalía has been conducting the corresponding investigations through its provincial branches [fiscalías provinciales]. However, the Fiscalía has realized the need to establish uniform criteria of investigation [of these clandestine graves] so as to adjust them to the corresponding international standards [instrumentos] on this topic" (Directiva 011-2001-MP-FN) (my translation.)

10. In mid-July 1999, the Fujimori regime unilaterally withdrew from the Inter-American Court's jurisdiction following a ruling in which the court ordered a new trial for a terrorism suspect and demanded that the Peruvian state adjust its antiterrorist legislation to internationally accepted standards of due process. *Castillo Petruzzi et al. v. Peru*, judgment of May 30, 1999. This was the last episode of a two-decade period of troubled relations between the Peruvian state and the international system of human rights protection.

11. This ruling inaugurated a postamnesty era in Latin America in two crucial respects: first, amnesties are no longer available as legal mechanisms to address past state atrocities. Second, following the ruling, other national courts in Latin America reopened cases of state crimes that had been closed by amnesty laws in the 1980s. For more on this, see Burt (2009); Gonzales Cueva (2006); and Roht-Arriaza (2005).

12. Some perpetrators were subsequently prosecuted and even convicted, including Fujimori himself, who was sentenced in April 2009 on charges of crimes against humanity during his tenure. For more on the Fujimori trial, see Burt (2009); Youngers and Burt (2009).

13. Inter-American Court of Human Rights, Case of Barrios Altos v. Peru, judgment of March 14, 2001 (merits), p. 11, http://www.corteidh.or.cr/docs/casos/articulos/seriec_75_ing.pdf, accessed on April 24, 2013; emphasis added.

14. Not only does the right to truth emphasize the distinction between legal truth or evidence for trial and the truth of atrocity, but it also expresses the increasing reception in legal languages and institutions of the notion of trauma and the corresponding emphasis on narrative modes of truth telling as a means of healing traumatized bodies and souls. On the evolution and expansion of notions of trauma and narrative modes of healing in contemporary international politics, see Fassin and Rechtman (2009).

15. Cristina Olazabal, interview, Ayacucho, Peru, February 1, 2006. Olazabal is a dedicated, courageous, and sensitive prosecutor who, at the time of my fieldwork in Ayacucho, was in charge of investigating major cases of human rights crimes committed during the counterinsurgency campaign in the region. During her tenure, powerful political actors she indicted for human rights violations retaliated with legal persecution, harassment, and death threats. See also Rojas-Perez (2010, 2013).

16. For more on this new discursive regime, see Rojas-Perez (2010, 2013).

17. The Peruvian Truth Commission emerged out of negotiations not between the outgoing and incoming regimes but between a caretaker regime and Peru's strong human rights community. See Youngers (2003); Gonzales Cueva (2004, 2006).

18. Decreto Supremo No. 065-2001-PCM, emphasis added. While confirming the appointment of the commission, former president Alejandro Toledo (2001-2006) added the notion "reconciliation" to its name. Since then, the commission has been known as the "Comisión de la Verdad y Reconciliación" (Truth and Reconciliation Commission). Toledo also increased the commission's members from seven to twelve. Decreto Supremo No. 101-2001-PCM, CVR, http://www.cverdad.org.pe/ingles/lacomision/cnormas/, accessed on June 30, 2013.

19. Decreto Supremo No. 065-2001-PCM, emphasis added.

20. For an insider's detailed analysis of the CVR's mandate and its implications for the work of the CVR regarding the problem of prosecution of human rights violations, see Gonzales Cueva (2004, 2006).

21. It must be noted that the question of clandestine mass graves was just one component in a broader context of tension, distrust, and disagreement that marked the relation between the CVR and the Fiscalía throughout the two-year period of the former's existence. For more on this fraught relationship that prevented a more productive cooperation between both institutions, see Gonzales Cueva (2006).

22. See, for instance, "Joint Declaration by the Attorney General's Office, the Ombudsman's Office, the Truth and Reconciliation Commission and the Human Rights National Coordination Entity," CVR, http://www.cverdad.org.pe/ingles/apublicas/exhumaciones/declaracion.php, accessed on June 30, 2013.

23. According to the CVR, the victims' names are Narciso Achallma Capcha, Antonio Carhuapoma Conde, Valentín Núñez Flores, Julián Núñez Mendoza, Pedro Núñez Pacotaype, Hilario Núñez Quispe, and Máximo Vilca Ccallocunto. http://www.cverdad.org.pe/ingles/apublicas/exhumaciones/exhum_chuschi.php, accessed on May 10, 2013.

24. Anthropologist Kimberly Theidon suggests that the war in rural Ayacucho was experienced as a "cultural revolution," that is, as "an attack against cultural practices and

the very meaning of what it is to live as a human being in these villages." Central to these practices and meanings is the question of burial of the dead. In Theidon's words, "Many lament how they were forced to leave their dead loved ones wherever they had fallen, returning—if they could—only to 'bury them hurriedly like animals'" (2006:438). What Theidon's account misses is the fact that Quechua-speaking peasants are all too familiar with the legal procedures that prevent them from manipulating the bodies of the dead until the intervention of the law. Thus, survivors feared not only the forces of terror and violence but also the law itself. For more on law and death in the Andes, see Poole (2004).

25. See DVD produced by the CVR in 2002, *Chuschi-Restos en Ataúdes* (at the Centro de Información para la Memoria Colectiva y los Derechos Humanos [Defensoria del Pueblo]).

26. Bishop José Antunez de Mayolo and Father Gaston Garatea. Bishop Luis Bambaren was also appointed as commissioner—although he accepted the mission only as an observer.

27. *Chuschi-Restos en Ataúdes.*

28. "Plataforma Conjunta de Trabajo en la Investigación de Fosas Comunes," CVR, http://www.cverdad.org.pe/ingles/apublicas/exhumaciones/declaracion.php, accessed on June 30, 2013, emphasis added.

29. Ibid.

30. In the early 1980s, the Peruvian military set up a counterinsurgency garrison on the premises of the elementary school in Totos, which soon became infamous for its record of gross human rights violations. In this forensic intervention, the CVR aimed to gather evidence for prosecuting those who committed these atrocities. In late 2002, the CVR submitted a full legal report on the case to the Fiscalía for purposes of indictment. See Gonzales Cueva (2006).

31. "Exhumations in Totos," CVR, http://www.cverdad.org.pe/ingles/apublicas/exhumaciones/exhum_totos.php, accessed on June 30, 2014.

32. Ibid.

33. Ibid.

34. See DVD produced by the CVR in 2002, *Reunión Peritos Forenses-Familiares de Víctimas* (at the Centro de Información para la Memoria Colectiva y los Derechos Humanos [Defensoria del Pueblo]).

35. The names of the identified victims buried in Ccarpaccasa are Roberto López León, Julio Godoy Villena, Primitivo Tucno Medina, and Marcelino Zamora Vivanco. "Exhumations in Totos."

36. Ibid.

37. Abimael Guzman, the top leader of the Shining Path, himself acknowledged that the attack was decided by the party's central committee and that perhaps it went beyond what was planned. However, he eventually justified the massacre as a "necessary" strike to teach these communities not to rebel against the rule of the party. For Guzman's writings, see Borja (1989).

38. In 1993, a military court sentenced Guzman and most of the Shining Path's

central committee members to life imprisonment. One of the evidential grounds for Guzman's conviction was the massacre of Lucanamarca. In that the entire legal procedure leading to this conviction lacked basic guarantees of due process, the legitimacy of this sentence has been tainted ever since. At the time of the exhumation in Lucanamarca, the Peruvian Constitutional Court was revising the Fujimori regime's antiterrorist legislation so as to adapt it to accepted standards of human rights. In 2005, the Peruvian civilian courts retried Guzman and his followers. They sentenced Guzman to life imprisonment in 2007.

39. "Exhumations in Lucanamarca," CVR, http://www.cverdad.org.pe/ingles/apublicas/exhumaciones/exhum_lucanamarca.php, accessed on June 30, 2013.

40. A discussion of these subaltern constructions of heroism and nationalism is beyond the scope of this chapter. For more on this topic, see, for instance, Del Pino (1996); Degregori (1996); Coronel (1996).

41. See DVD produced by the CVR in 2003 on Toledo's remarks, *Videos Caso Lucanamarca* [clip 020203010501], (at the Centro de Información para la Memoria Colectiva y los Derechos Humanos [Defensoria del Pueblo]).

42. "Es un deber elemental de toda persona humana lo que hemos hecho con la exhumación de los cuerpos y con esta intervención forense; es el derecho más elemental, que es el derecho a la vida, es el derecho a que si se perdió la vida, tener por lo menos una cristiana y decente sepultura." Remarks of former CVR commissioner Carlos Ivan Degregori, in a DVD produced by the CVR in 2003, *Videos Caso Lucanamarca* [clip 020203010604], (at the Centro de Información para la Memoria Colectiva y los Derechos Humanos [Defensoria del Pueblo]), my translation.

43. For a history of these beginnings, see Equipo Forense Especializado, http://www.mpfn.gob.pe/iml/efe.php, accessed on December 12, 2012.

44. In July 2006, former president Alan García was elected for the second time. He himself has been accused of human rights violations during his first term in office; during his second administration, not only did investigations into human rights abuses slow down but an increasing hostility resurfaced against human rights discourse. Several attempts were made to reenact forms of amnesty for the military involved in human rights violations.

45. In one of the few cases in which a non-state-sponsored team could conduct forensic procedures of exhumation since the creation of the EFE, the EPAF exhumed the remains of victims in three different interventions starting in May 2008. Of the ninety-two bodies that the EPAF eventually recovered—of which at least 40 percent belonged to children and 41 percent to women—only twenty-eight had been formally identified by the end of the forensic work. http://justiciaparaputis.org/?page_id=143, accessed on April 28, 2010. The forensic exhumation was part of an ongoing criminal investigation that started as soon as a major Peruvian newspaper revealed the existence of the mass graves in late 2001. Subsequently, in its final report the CVR labeled the case as one of the worst massacres carried out by the Peruvian army against civilians during the counterinsurgency campaign of the 1980s and 1990s.

46. "Nos preocupa mucho más lo que está sucediendo ahora; las muertes que hay ahora, que las que un entierro de cosas que sucedieron en el pasado." In "Rey Brinda Polémicas Declaraciones sobre Putis," *El Comercio*, September 28, 2009, emphasis added, my translation.

Bibliography

Agamben, Giorgio. 1998. *Homo Sacer: Sovereign Power and Bare Life*. Trans. Daniel Heller-Roazen. Stanford, CA: Stanford University Press.

Borja, Luis Arce, ed. 1989. *Guerra popular en el Perú: El pensamiento Gonzalo*. Brussels: Luis Arce Borja.

Burt, Jo Marie. 2009. Guilty as Charged: The Trial of Former Peruvian President Alberto Fujimori. *International Journal of Transitional Justice* 3: 384–405.

Coronel, Jose. 1996. Violencia política y respuestas campesinas en Huanta. In *Las rondas campesinas y la derrota de Sendero Luminoso*, ed. Carlos Ivan Degregori et al., 29–116, Lima, Peru: Instituto de Estudios Peruanos.

CVR (Comisión de la Verdad y Reconciliación). 2004. *Hatun Willakuy: Versión Abreviada de la Comisión de la Verdad y Reconciliación Perú*. Lima, Peru: Comisión de Entrega de la Comisión de la Verdad y Reconciliación.

Degregori, Carlos Iván, et al. 1996. *Las rondas campesinas y la derrota de Sendero Luminoso*. Lima, Peru: Instituto de Estudios Peruanos.

Del Pino, Ponciano. 1996. Tiempos de guerra y de dioses: Ronderos, evangelicos y Senderistas en el Valle del Rio Apurimac. In *Las rondas campesinas y la derrota de Sendero Luminoso*, ed. Carlos Ivan Degregori et al. 117–188. Lima, Peru: Instituto de Estudios Peruanos.

Fassin, Didier and Robert Rechtman. 2009. *The Empire of Trauma: An Inquiry into the Condition of Victimhood*. Princeton, NJ: Princeton University Press.

Gonzales Cueva, Eduardo. 2004. The Contribution of the Peruvian Truth and Reconciliation Commission to Prosecutions. *Criminal Law Forum* 15: 55–66.

———. 2006. The Peruvian Truth and Reconciliation Commission and the Challenge of Impunity. In *Transitional Justice in the Twenty-First Century, Beyond Truth Versus Justice*, ed. Naomi Roht-Arriaza and Javier Mariezcurrena, 70–93. Cambridge: Cambridge University Press.

Lerner, Salomon. 2003. Peruvian Commission on Truth and Reconciliation: Speech of the Presentation of the Final Report, *ReVista* (Fall 2003). http://www.drclas.harvard.edu/publications/revistaonline/fall-2003/peruvian-commission-truth-andreconciliation (accessed on September 20, 2012).

Naqvi, Yasmin. 2006. The Right to the Truth in International Law: Fact or Fiction? *International Review of the Red Cross* 88 (862): 245–273.

Poole, Deborah, ed. 2004. *Unruly Order: Violence, Power, and Cultural Identity in the High Provinces of Southern Peru*. Boulder, CO: Westview.

Roht-Arriaza, Naomi. 2005. *The Pinochet Effect: Transnational Justice in the Age of Human Rights*. Philadelphia: University of Pennsylvania Press.

Rojas-Perez, Isaias. 2010. Fragments of Soul: Law, Transitional Justice and Mourning in Post War Peru. PhD diss., Johns Hopkins University.

————. 2013. Unfinished Pasts: Law, Transitional Justice and Mourning in Post War Peru. *Humanity* 4 (1): 149–170.

Theidon, Kimberly. 2006. Justice in Transition: The Micropolitics of Reconciliation in Postwar Peru. *Journal of Conflict Resolution* 50 (3): 433–457.

Youngers, Coletta. 2003. *Violencia Política y Sociedad Civil en el Perú: Historia de la Coordinadora Nacional de Derechos Humanos*. Lima, Peru: Instituto de Estudios Peruanos.

Youngers, Coletta and Jo Marie Burt. 2009. *Human Rights Tribunals in Latin America*. Washington, DC: George Mason University, Washington Office for Latin America, Instituto de Defensa Legal.

Chapter 8

Death on Display

Bones and Bodies in Cambodia and Rwanda

Elena Lesley

During the fifteen-day Pchum Ben holiday each fall, Cambodians make food offerings to the spirits of the dead in order to help them accumulate merit and peacefully transition through the cycle of life and death, including reincarnation. As the spirits, especially those who died "unnatural deaths," wander the earth, their living relatives travel throughout the country, bringing sticky rice cakes, curries, and other popular dishes to monks, who serve as intermediaries between living and dead. Although these offerings generally take place at pagodas, some Cambodians have begun to include sites of tremendous symbolic suffering, such as the Choeung Ek "killing fields" outside of Phnom Penh, as part of their Pchum Ben journey. Choeung Ek consists of around one hundred exhumed mass graves, many still displaying fragments of bone and cloth embedded in the ground. A tall memorial glass-walled *stupa* on the site houses the exhumed skulls and bones. For some Cambodians, this display conflicts with local Buddhist beliefs that stipulate remains must be cremated in order for the cycle of reincarnation to begin; in particular, the spirits of those who died "bad" deaths may remain trapped where they died or where their uncremated remains reside (Hughes 2006:106). During the 2012 Pchum Ben period, Chenda, a fifty-three-year-old woman, told me she believed she had discovered the final resting place of her missing aunt through spiritual means and came to Choeung Ek to make offerings so her aunt might eventually be able to transition to her next life: "I have been looking for my aunt for years. This year she came to me in a dream and told me she was here [at Choeung Ek]. I came here for the first time two days ago and my skin got tight and I could smell death.¹ Then I saw my aunt walking away from me; her hair was short and she was wearing black. I made an offering of bread and a bun and burned incense. This morning I came back at 4 A.M. with my nephew and threw rice and chanted the *dharma*;² some of the spirits are shy so you have to throw rice in the dark. Now I have come back with more packages of food." While Chenda performed her personal rituals near the tower filled with skulls, an official ceremony was taking place in another corner of the killing fields site. Villagers from the area brought offerings to the various monks assembled and local officials made speeches in honor of the estimated 1.7 million Cambodians who died during the period of Democratic Kampuchea (DK), from 1975 to 1979. The most important official in attendance, a district governor with the ruling Cambodian People's Party (CPP), told those assembled:

> Today we do dedication and offerings on behalf of the CPP from all levels and the CPP team leader from Phnom Penh to work together to honor those who sacrificed their lives. Some died individually, some as families. Some relatives are far away and may not know where their relatives died. So all of us today will dedicate on behalf of the CPP to all those who died during the Khmer Rouge. . . . I will remind you that almost every family lost people during the Khmer Rouge. Even those who we don't know where they were brought, we want to dedicate to them. People want to collect the bones but there was killing all over. There are many holes and we don't know which holes have which people's bones.

Ending his speech, he reminded the audience to "give gratitude to the three leaders of the CPP" for helping drive the Khmer Rouge from power and to "remind young people to register to vote" in the upcoming elections. While the CPP official seized on the opportunity to speak at the symbolically resonant Choeung Ek in order to remind those in attendance that they owe an obligation (in the form of votes) to the regime that ostensibly saved them from the Khmer Rouge, various individuals visiting the site had come for personal or spiritual reasons.

This juxtaposition shows the multiplicity of meanings and uses that can be derived from human remains; or as Katherine Verdery notes in her study of the politicization of dead bodies in postsocialist countries, "different people can evoke corpses as symbols, thinking those corpses mean the same thing to all present, whereas in fact they may mean different things to each. . . . What gives a dead body its symbolic effectiveness in politics is precisely its ambiguity, its capacity to evoke a variety of understandings" (1999:29). Memorial practices can intersect with mass graves and sites of exhumation, creating memoryscapes (see the Introduction to this volume). The remains displayed may serve as a flash point for evidentiary, political, or ritual tensions: "The site of memory becomes a source of political contestation about who owns the human remains and how their violent death should be remembered" (see Introduction).

In this chapter, I focus on two memorial sites in which human remains are prominently displayed—Choeung Ek in Cambodia and the Murambi Genocide Memorial Center in Rwanda, where 848 corpses from the 1994 genocide have been chemically preserved. This piece revisits foregoing arguments about the role of memorial sites in state-building practices, and how that role is complicated in efforts to commemorate mass atrocity (Williams 2007:20). In highlighting Choeung Ek and Murambi, I seek to evaluate through comparison the ways the goals of the state are represented structurally at each memorial and how the aims and narratives of the state are received, rejected, and recast by citizens of the polity. Before larger themes are pursued, however, it is important to note some key characteristics of the memorials under scrutiny and the contexts in which they were built. At first, it may appear the sites have little in common: one houses bodies, the other bones; Choeung Ek makes implicit appeals to Cambodian Buddhist aesthetics and symbologies, while Murambi is moving toward trying to accommodate Christian sensibilities. Moreover, the atrocities commemorated at both sites took place in vastly different contexts. Choeung Ek was part of a vast network of killing sites throughout Cambodia during the period of DK where perceived enemies of the Marxist Khmer Rouge regime were sent to be purged; the majority of the killing was Cambodian on Cambodian. Meanwhile, Murambi was one of numerous sites where, during a period of one hundred days in 1994, Hutu extremist *génocidaires* slaughtered members of the Tutsi minority and Hutu moderates.[3]

Nonetheless, the *similarities* between the sites as state structures are worthy of evaluation. Both are arguably being used to bolster the legitimacy of the regimes currently in power; drawing on transnational human rights discourses that stress the importance of remains for judicial purposes (see Introduction), they purport to provide physical evidence of the atrocities that have significantly altered their societies; and yet due to a continued tension relating to how human remains should be treated, both have made efforts to soften, sanitize, and "museumize" their displays for public consumption. As Susan Sontag writes, referring to struggles over explicit news footage, "What can be shown, what should not be shown—few issues arouse more public clamor" (2003:69). While societies often choose to distance themselves from the sufferings of those with whom they might be more intimate, this was not initially the case in Cambodia or Rwanda. Locals were obliged to confront the remains of those who may have been friends or family at sites created largely for foreign consumption. While the current displays would still be considered inappropriate by the standards of many societies, the governments of both countries have made some concessions to international and local concerns that remains were treated disrespectfully.

The fact that human remains have played such a crucial role in mapping out both memorialization strategies in Rwanda and Cambodia indicates the importance of corporeality not only in the two countries but, perhaps, to humanity as a powerful emblem of mortality and identification as humans. "More to the point is their ineluctable self-referentiality as symbols: because all people have bodies, any manipulation of a corpse directly enables one's identification with it through one's own body, thereby tapping into one's reservoirs of feeling," notes Verdery (1999:33). Both Cambodia and Rwanda have seized on this symbolism in an overt appeal to survivors and future generations, international actors, and those members of various opposing social or political factions they may wish to intimidate. As this chapter further demonstrates, both states are using bodies (or the remains of bodies) to establish their legitimacy. Yet in both contexts, local beliefs, attitudes toward spirits, political affiliation, and ethnic or social self-identification all seemingly disrupt or complicate the homogeneity of the site's role as communicated by the state.

Based upon fieldwork conducted in Rwanda and Cambodia, I make three claims: (1) given similarities in the ways mass graves have been instrumentalized through memorialization, human remains serve as a powerful tool of legitimization for postgenocide regimes, particularly those that wish to portray themselves as liberating forces; (2) while sites may serve as vehicles for communal mourning, the mass psychological impact of human remains can exacerbate political and social divisions; (3) the purported need to preserve evidence of atrocity both challenges and, in some cases, modifies the local spiritual beliefs and customs of citizen visitors. Ultimately, memorial sites pose a complex intervention in the eyes of the visiting public: they solicit a conformity of memory, yet are beholden to the inevitable variation of individual experience.

The ethnographic data I rely on to structure my argument was gathered during three months in Rwanda (from June to late August 2012) and two and a half months in Cambodia (late August to mid-November 2012). It should be noted that my work in Cambodia builds on two and a half years during which I lived in the country (2004–2005 and 2008–2009) working as a journalist and writing frequently about Khmer Rouge–related issues. I focused on two sites in each country—the Kigali Memorial Center and Murambi Genocide Memorial in Rwanda and the Tuol Sleng Museum of Genocide Crimes and Choeung Ek in Cambodia. My methodology consisted primarily of semistructured and unstructured interviews with Rwandans and Cambodians who worked with memorial sites in various capacities, as well as with local visitors to the sites. In addition, when possible, I engaged in participant observation with different individuals who worked at the sites, trying to get a sense of their daily lives both inside and outside the memorial environment. During my time in Rwanda, I conducted interviews (and sometimes multiple interviews) with thirty-one informants, including staff members at the National Commission for the Fight Against Genocide (CNLG), the government body that oversees all memorial sites; those who actually worked at memorial sites, from top-level administration to maintenance staff; Rwandans who worked for outside organizations that had some interaction with the memorial sites; and Rwandans of both Hutu and Tutsi heritage who visited the sites for various purposes. In Cambodia, I interviewed fifty-two people (some multiple times). My informants included staffers at Tuol Sleng and Choeung Ek, from administrators to former prisoners to cleaners; Cambodians from other organizations who worked with the memorial sites in some capacity; and Cambodian visitors to the sites, most of whom came through "Study Tour" groups organized by the Extraordinary Chambers in the Courts of Cambodia (ECCC), the UN-backed tribunal set up to try former Khmer Rouge leaders.

National Biographies—Collective
Memory, Collective Amnesia

Of course, memory is never fixed, or ever wholly individual. The ways that people recall the past and organize experience into meaningful and relevant stories are informed by a number of sources, including national and group narratives, popular representations, and mythologies. Maurice Halbwachs pioneered the concept of collective memory, and described how people use reference points determined by society—and external historical frameworks—to evoke and interpret their own, individual memories. Pierre Nora probed how cultural memory of historical events is ossified in national memorial sites (*les lieux de mémoire*), wherein "moments are plucked out of the flow of history, then returned to it—no longer quite alive but not yet entirely dead, like shells left on the shore when the sea of living memory has receded" (1997:7).

In her study of Tuol Sleng, the torture and detention center that served as something of a companion to Choeung Ek—prisoners were detained there before being transferred to the killing fields for extermination and disposal—Judy Ledgerwood (1997:82) invokes Benedict Anderson's conception of "national biographies": "Because there is no Originator, the nation's biography cannot be written evangelically, 'down time,' through a long procreative chain of begettings. The only alternative is to fashion it 'up time.' . . . This fashioning, however, is marked by deaths, which, in a curious inversion of conventional genealogy, start from an originary present. World War II begets World War I; out of Sedan comes Austerlitz; the ancestor of the Warsaw Uprising is the state of Israel" (Anderson 2006:205). Part of the project of creating a cohesive narrative of national unity involves a process of both remembering and forgetting historical tragedies. The divisive element, the component that may have set the nation on a completely different biographical path, must be forgotten. Yet citizens are obliged to constantly remember the "series of antique slaughters which are now inscribed as 'family history'" (Anderson 2006:201). In other words, such tragedies must be remembered in *a certain way*. Sontag writes that "what is called collective memory is not a remembering but a stipulating: that *this* is important, and this is the story about how it happened, with the pictures that lock the story in our minds" (2003:86).

War monuments have helped serve this purpose as they celebrate a country's mythologized triumphs, casting violent deaths as heroic sacrifices for the state. The task of creating a unifying and widely accepted national biography, however, becomes fraught in efforts to commemorate mass internal violence.

Trying to memorialize such events presents a number of challenges as citizen deaths cannot "easily be interpreted and represented as heroic, sacrificial, or somehow benefiting the greater good of society or the nation" (Williams 2007:20). Moreover, some events may be too fresh in the minds of the citizenry, too real rather than mythical, to be comfortably viewed as "reassuring fratricide" (Anderson 2006:201). Nonetheless, Paul Williams writes that there has been a massive proliferation of memorial museums, institutions created to commemorate mass suffering, over the past twenty-five years that "inevitably sees them play an increasingly important role in the shaping of public historical consciousness" (2007:157). While Choeung Ek and Murambi were originally more memorial site than museum, they have both been moving toward increased "museumification."

Development of the Choeung Ek "Killing Fields"

The mass graves at Choeung Ek were exhumed in 1980, around a year after Vietnamese forces drove the Khmer Rouge from power.[4] Of 129 such graves in the former Chinese cemetery, 89 were excavated at the time, and Vietnamese forensic specialists used chemicals to preserve the bones before they were placed in a wooden memorial pavilion (Hughes 2006:97). At the same time, the Vietnamese-backed People's Republic of Kampuchea (PRK) regime had started the process of turning the affiliated S-21 detention center into the Tuol Sleng Museum of Genocide Crimes. Although Tuol Sleng did not officially open as a museum to the public until July 1980, the PRK government began giving tours of the facility to delegations of foreigners before that time (Ledgerwood 1997:88). Ledgerwood quotes from a 1980 report from the Ministry of Culture, Information and Propaganda that says the Tuol Sleng museum "was used to show the international guests the cruel torture committed by the traitors to the Khmer people. . . . [T]he center was not open to the public, but for the international guests and participants [sic] only" (1997:88). While Tuol Sleng and Choeung Ek were eventually opened to the public, there is a good deal of evidence to suggest they were originally created for the purpose of justifying Vietnam's invasion of Cambodia to an international audience (Ledgerwood 1997:89; Hughes 2006:99–100). The initial motive for the invasion was defensive, considering that the Khmer Rouge continued to wage incursions into Vietnamese territory, but once confronted with the carnage left behind by the regime, the Vietnamese sought to justify their military action in humanitarian terms: "Evidence of trauma and its international exposure was integral to the political economy of post-1979 Cambodia. This was an economy fueled by actual and speculated international legal, humanitarian and economic aid" (Hughes 2006:100).

Appeals to international sympathy were particularly critical in the Cold War political context. Despite the crimes of DK, the United States, United Kingdom, People's Republic of China, and countries in the Association of Southeast Asian Nations all continued to support the ousted Pol Pot loyalists, who fought a guerilla war from the area of Cambodia near the Thai border. Moreover, the post-1979 repackaged Khmer Rouge coalition force retained Cambodia's representative seat at the United Nations. Struggling to win international recognition and legitimacy, the PRK government evoked symbols of atrocity highly salient to foreigners. They compared Pol Pot to Hitler and referred to the crimes of DK as "genocide," even though the majority of the killing, which was Khmer on Khmer, did not fit with the legal definition of genocide as outlined in the UN Convention on the Prevention and Punishment of the Crime of Genocide.[5] Cambodians living in PRK-controlled areas learned to refer to crimes of the DK period as *"bralay pouchsah,"* or to "kill within one's own family line."[6]

Given the complicated nature of killing during the Khmer Rouge period, the Vietnamese effort to create memorials to the dead encountered a number of challenges. In ousting a fellow communist regime, the PRK state sought to create a narrative explaining that the revolution in Cambodia had been hijacked by a criminal element—the "genocidal Pol Pot–Ieng Sary Clique"— beholden to a deviant strain of Maoism. This clique had misled other, true revolutionaries, such as the Khmer Rouge defectors now serving within the PRK regime (Hinton 2008:68). Unlike in Vietnam, however, the majority of those killed in Cambodia had not been fighting an external enemy. Rachel Hughes describes this contradiction in the interpretation of bones at Choeung Ek and Tuol Sleng:

Topographically, by maintaining a mass of human remains in the physical memorials, deaths considered valueless under Pol Pot[7] are reclaimed as artifacts to be "known" by the nation. What is "remembered" via the Memorial's display is a fundamental political principle of the Khmer Rouge: that all life in Pol Pot's Democratic Kampuchea was considered by the Khmer Rouge authorities as potentially traitorous to the regime and thus as life abandoned by the law. Recalling

Agamben, such life is that designated *as distinct from and external to political life*, as "bare life." It is impossible to restore value to such life lost, even in somber, costly memorialization, because the victims of a genocide cannot be understood as having been sacrificed. (2006:99)

This harkens back to Williams's argument about the differences between memorializing war dead and those who have been the victims of mass atrocities. Those targeted during a genocide have been dehumanized by their perpetrators to the extent that, like Agamben's *Homo Sacer*, they can be killed but not sacrificed (Agamben 1998: 12). Moreover, their deaths served no productive purpose in the eyes of the state, as might those of Vietnamese who died fighting the American enemy. Despite the complications of civilian massacres and Vietnamese who fought for the South,[8] "the end of the fighting in Vietnam signaled a clear victory to be claimed and cherished"; meanwhile, in Cambodia "the vast majority of those who died unnaturally did so largely at the hands of other Khmer, not against some external imperialist enemy" (Holt 2012:10). Moreover, "in Cambodia, in 1979, the major external aggressors, who styled themselves as liberators of a sort, were the Vietnamese whose presence, the longer it was sustained after the initial period, was not necessarily warmly welcomed" (Holt 2012:11).

Nonetheless, while the Vietnamese, particularly at first, may have been concerned with exposing the crimes of the Khmer Rouge internationally, they also sought to justify their presence in the country domestically. Documentation of local visitation to Tuol Sleng and Choeung Ek during the 1980s is somewhat scarce, but Cambodians I interviewed who had worked at the sites during that time or lived in the Phnom Penh area described coordinated efforts to bring people to the memorials. (This is apart from the flood of Cambodians who came individually to Tuol Sleng after it opened to look for information about missing relatives.) Several Cambodians I interviewed recalled being taken to the memorials with school groups during the PRK period. Dara, age fifty-two, said he had gone with a group to Choeung Ek in 1980, while the exhumations were under way: "There were skeletons and flies and it smelled bad. I could not eat or sleep after going there. The people looked like meat, killed and fresh, like meat at the market with flies and worms. Not all the bodies had been exhumed yet. The teacher scolded us for trying to stay away because of the smell and she told us, 'this is how the Khmer Rouge killed people.' Up until then I didn't know how people had been killed." Others recalled learning as children a popular Khmer-language song that had been written about S-21, "Tuol Sleng, Big Prison." Still, due to the dire living conditions in post-1979 Cambodia, the ongoing civil war, and the difficulty of travel, few Cambodians from outside the Phnom Penh area would have had the chance to visit these central and prominent memorials. However, smaller local memorials, generally containing human remains, were also constructed throughout the country during the PRK period and those who lived in the surrounding areas would gather at them for various occasions, including the May 20 "Day of Anger" holiday instituted by the PRK (Hughes 2006:111–112).

Plans for the famous monument filled with skulls at Choeung Ek were not enacted until 1988 under the guidance of Mai Lam, the Vietnamese general who had overseen the curation of the Tuol Sleng Museum. Lim Ourk, a local Cambodian architect, was employed to create a memorial stupa that would house the remains of those killed at Choeung Ek. Although such stupa generally hold the cremated remains of the dead, especially notable figures, the structure created at Cheoung Ek kept the bones intact and, through glass walls, allowed for their continued display. According to Mai Lam, the preservation of the skulls remained "very important for the Cambodian people—it's the proof" (Ledgerwood 1997:89). Hughes argues that Choeung Ek, though crafted in the model of a Cambodian Buddhist stupa, "is an inescapably modern monument. Although it draws on a number of traditional religious architectural forms, these forms are transformed under a thoroughly late-twentieth century dilemma: how to memorialize a genocide" (2006:103).

Nonetheless, the stupa at Choeung Ek was constructed during a time when Buddhist practice once again began to flourish in Cambodia,[9] and to various extents Cambodians have made room for such hybridity in their spiritual understandings and practices. The site has also continued to evolve, particularly as it has received increased visitation (both foreign and local) since the outreach activities prompted by the creation of the ECCC in 2003 began and as it is seen as an increasingly viable source of revenue. However, the CPP, the eventual successor to the PRK regime, has had a fluctuating relationship with DK memorial efforts over time, deemphasizing and also highlighting the crimes of the regime during periods when it is politically expedient. Partly, this is due to the affiliation of Prime Minister Hun Sen with the regime, and partly it has been the result of efforts to neutralize guerrilla forces in the 1990s and integrate former Khmer Rouge back into Cambodian society. Hun Sen, who served in the Khmer Rouge, is in the seemingly contradictory position of "trying to take credit for having liberated Cambodia from the Khmer

Rouge while also having been Khmer Rouge," a UN official told me during an interview. Although biographical details of Hun Sen's history are somewhat uncertain, according to the popular narrative in Cambodia, he defected from the Khmer Rouge in 1977 and joined other rebels mobilizing in Vietnam. He then fought with the Vietnamese and other defectors to drive the Khmer Rouge from power, ascending to the position of foreign minister and eventually prime minister within the PRK regime. Despite the United Nations intervention in 1992–1993 and transition of Cambodia to a purported multiparty democracy, he has remained in power since that time.

Some critics charge that he began advocating for an international court to try the leaders of Democratic Kampuchea in order to intimidate the Khmer Rouge military element still active in the country. Once they were demobilized, he reportedly retreated from this position and said in 1998 that Cambodians should "dig a hole and bury the past" (Human Rights Watch 2011). But domestic and international pressure pushed forward the creation of a court, and after years of protracted negotiations, an agreement was reached between the government and United Nations in 2003. The court did not try its first case until several years later and it has been dogged by allegations of political interference, particularly that Hun Sen has purposefully limited the scope of prosecutions to five "scapegoat" defendants (Giry 2012).

Meanwhile, in 2005, the Cambodian government entered into a partnership with the JC Royal Company to manage the Choeung Ek site and since that time it has been altered in a number of ways. Informational placards erected by the PRK regime in 1988 have been replaced with newer signs that place less emphasis on the Cold War imperative to fight imperialism; a small building contains new, museum-style exhibits about the history of DK and prosecutions under way at the ECCC; and, within the last year, an extensive multilingual audio tour was created by an Australian company that smoothly leads visitors through the site. Domestically, the site is managed by the Phnom Penh Municipality, while the Ministry of Culture is responsible for Tuol Sleng. Unlike the highly centralized oversight of memorials in Rwanda—as of 2008 they all fall under the auspices of CNLG—control of Cambodia's major memorial sites appears more dispersed. This could be because broadcasting a narrative of Khmer Rouge atrocities has now become less of a political priority in Cambodia. Nonetheless, recent improvements suggest not only that the sites are potential financial assets but also that their exhibits can be useful vehicles for conveying the narrative of history being crafted by the UN tribunal.

Development of Murambi

The Murambi Genocide Memorial has also been creating a more standard-ized, museum-like experience for its visitors, although it is arguably in an earlier stage of the process than Choeung Ek. This is not surprising, given that only eighteen years have elapsed since the genocide in Rwanda, as opposed to thirty-four since the Khmer Rouge were driven from power. Murambi, a tech-nical school that was nearing completion of its construction at the time of the genocide, sits in a breathtaking location, at the top of a hill surrounded, as is common in the Rwandan landscape, by other steep, lush hills. It is also highly visible and feels very exposed—it would be difficult to escape down the hill unnoticed by those in the surrounding area. In other words, it is an ideal lo-cation for the isolation and extermination of a group.

As was the case throughout the country, Tutsi and Hutu sympathizers fled to certain locations, especially churches, because they believed they would be safe there. The several survivors I interviewed at Murambi told me that they had been instructed to go to the technical school by local officials, who said they would be protected. Rather, concentrating them all in one location made easier the job of the génocidaires. The running water system that served the building was cut off and food was scarce; those crammed into the technical school became gradually weaker. Although those in the school managed to fight off several advances by *interahamwe*, or Hutu militia, they were eventu-ally overcome and slaughtered en masse. United Nations Assistance Mission for Rwanda troops stationed at Murambi from August to October 1994 buried the bodies scattered through the site. As Jennie Burnet writes (and as I found through my own interviews), some survivors interpret the UN troops' actions as an attempt to cover up the crimes of the génocidaires (2009:97).

After the Rwandan Patriotic Front (RPF) invasion ended the genocide—or "liberated the country," in the government's terminology—the recovering state had to confront a landscape strewn with bodies, both buried and exposed. According to Clarisse, a Tutsi who moved back to Rwanda after 1994, "Geno-cide has been a catastrophe symbolically. Death must be as peaceful as possible. In the genocide, bodies were dumped in disrespectful places and violated. There is a national traumatization. There's a collective desire to make peace with the dead. Bodies were everywhere in the early years. When I first came back, I bought a house and there were bodies around the property. I had to hire people to take them away. I couldn't think about who they were or I would go crazy." Efforts throughout the country were made to collect and respectfully bury the bodies—many had been dumped in latrines, crude mass graves, or rivers or simply left where they were killed. Often ordinary people and survivors contributed to this process. Peter, a genocide survivor who now works for CNLG, volunteered as a teenager: "I was motivated to do it; I have always been able to control my emotions. Many people were traumatized and didn't want to participate. I was around fifteen or sixteen at that time. People showed me how to wash and care for the bodies. I wanted to help the community and I was also searching for my relatives; I thought I might be able to find them." Peter said that because even those who had been buried were dumped disrespectfully into mass graves, when such graves were found, the bodies would be exhumed. They were then washed, placed in body bags, and reburied.

The exhumations at Murambi proceeded somewhat unusually. Before the 1996 commemoration ceremony, which takes place each year during the period of the genocide (from April to July), twenty-seven thousand bodies were exhumed from the area of the technical school (Vidal 2004:584). The majority of the bodies were then reinterred during the 1996 ceremony, while over eighteen hundred were mummified using lye and placed on wooden racks (Burnet 2009:98). Staffers at Murambi told me that, according to the post-1994 Rwandan constitution, areas where mass killing occurred must be transformed into memorial sites; they said survivors, as well as local and national government officials, all participated in the exhumations at Murambi. Rachel Ibreck writes that survivors' associations were involved in the creation of the memorial at Murambi, as was also the case at Bisesero and Nyamata. Yet she also notes that "the extent to which survivors were directly involved varied; they have worked in partnership with, been regulated by, or been dependent upon the state or international agencies" (2010:335). Meanwhile, Burnet writes: "when I asked the staff on the site, as well as people living in the surrounding area, I received various conflicting stories as to when, why and by whom the bodies had been prepared in this way. Whether or not the regime had made an explicit decision to mummify the bodies, they mobilized the bodies as part of the mythico-history of the genocide. The bodies regularly appeared on the nightly national television news as a feature in the official diplomatic visits of international dignitaries" (2009:98).

I also witnessed the visits of numerous foreign delegations to various memorial sites—both in person and on national television—during my time in Rwanda and was struck by the ways in which the RPF government has used this potent symbolic capital internationally. Various arguments have been put forth as to the government's motives in highlighting gruesome memorial sites:

they are trying to counter genocide deniers; they are trying to shame the international community for its failure to intervene during the genocide; they are trying to silence critics. Yet while the sites have played a key role internationally, they also receive significant numbers of Rwandan visitors. Unlike foreigners, who come individually or in small delegations throughout the year, Rwandans visit primarily in large, organized groups during the three-month official commemoration period, said staff members I interviewed at Murambi and the Kigali Memorial Center. Some Rwandans I interviewed said they felt an obligation to participate in such visits, even if they didn't necessarily want to. This was particularly true of those who had been to Murambi, given the fact that it is the only memorial site to display corpses in such raw and horrific poses.

Since 1996, there has been a great deal of controversy surrounding the display of human remains at Murambi. However, the government now appears to be taking steps to ease this tension. While over eight hundred corpses remain exposed in the small classrooms behind the main building at Murambi, twenty-five of the best-preserved bodies have been selected for a joint project with a team from Cranfield University in the United Kingdom. They will be treated by forensic experts and then placed in airtight glass coffins within the museum exhibit portion of the site. Thus, they will be given something of a burial, in accordance with Rwandan custom, while also remaining on display. It is unclear at this point what will happen to the other mummified bodies at Murambi. Staffers I talked to at CNLG, Murambi, and the Kigali Memorial Center seemed to fall into two categories: some hoped that all the bodies could be properly preserved and displayed in glass by the U.K. team, but doubted whether the resources would be available to do so; others thought the bodies had deteriorated to the point that they should just be buried.

At the same time, the opening of an extensive museum exhibit in May 2011 at the site's main building helps mediate and narrativize the experience for visitors. The exhibit was created in cooperation with the Aegis Trust, the British-based organization responsible for the development and management of the Kigali Memorial Center, and the informational displays in both locations are quite similar. They each tell a story of a peaceful precolonial Rwanda divided by racialized social categories during German and then Belgian rule. Years of cyclical violence followed independence, finally resulting in the genocide of Tutsi within the country as Rwandans (predominantly Tutsi living in exile) organized under the RPF staged a military return to their homeland. Both exhibits emphasize that the international community turned a blind eye to the violence and it was ultimately the heroic RPF that stopped the genocide and liberated the country. Staffers I interviewed at Murambi said they welcomed the opening of the exhibit because it helped prepare visitors psychologically and emotionally for the shock of seeing the mummified bodies in the classrooms.

State Narratives, Blame, and Social Divisions

While both Choeung Ek and Murambi help bolster the legitimacy of the PRK/ CPP and RPF, respectively, portraying the powers that be as national liberators, they assign blame in somewhat different ways. Memorials in Cambodia try to hold culpable a small criminal element at the top of the Khmer Rouge hierarchy. Under the PRK, this meant emphasis on the "genocidal Pol Pot– Ieng Sary Clique"; today, it translates into highlighting the five defendants being held at the Khmer Rouge tribunal. Meanwhile, memorials in Rwanda assign blame much more broadly to the country's Hutu population. Burnet notes a shift in the early years of genocide commemoration: "Beginning with the ceremony on 7 April 1996, in Murambi commune in southern Rwanda, the symbolic use of the dead took a dramatic departure from the first annual ceremony in which Hutu and Tutsi victims were buried side by side. Rather than honoring both Hutu and Tutsi victims of the genocide, the 1996 ceremony shifted its emphasis to distinguishing between genocide 'victims' (understood as Tutsi) and 'perpetrators' (understood as Hutu)" (2009:97). Tutsi were the primary targets of the genocide, but the roles of Hutu varied. Some were perpetrators; some were killed, often along with their Tutsi family members; some were bystanders; and some sheltered Tutsi (Thomson 2011:377). Thus, a frequent criticism lodged by Hutu I interviewed against the current government was that they believed, through the government's memorial campaign, the word *Hutu* had become synonymous with *génocidaire*.

The limitation and expansion of culpability also ties in with legal efforts in both countries. It took years of negotiation and pressure from the international community before the Cambodian government, led by Prime Minister Hun Sen, would agree to the creation of the ECCC. Numerous activists and human rights groups have criticized the narrow scope of prosecutions, contending that crimes against humanity were perpetrated throughout all levels of DK; they say to fix blame on only five former leaders creates an inaccurate historical narrative of the period. Yet Hun Sen is in a delicate position. In

order to put an end to Khmer Rouge guerilla attacks in the late 1990s, he offered amnesty to former Khmers Rouge and even gave many comfortable
positions in the current government. Thus, a certain feeling of betrayal is already present in former Khmer Rouge strongholds like Pailin, in the country's
northwest, where some residents believe it was unfair for the government to
proceed with any trial whatsoever. Moreover, critics of the CPP often charge
that Hun Sen is thwarting the expansion of prosecutions because going further down the chain of command would implicate those holding important
positions in the current government.

Meanwhile, Rwanda has taken a completely different approach to judicial
accountability. Realizing that the International Criminal Tribunal for Rwanda
in Tanzania would only try top leaders, the local *Gacaca* court system was
implemented throughout the country to address the problem of lower-level
perpetrators. Based on a traditional model of Rwandan community justice,
the courts tried nearly two million people between their creation in 2001 and
closure in June 2012. Their legacy has been somewhat controversial. Supporters claim they have allowed for a widespread level of accountability that would
have been impossible through a traditional court system; critics say they en-
dangered the lives of Tutsi witnesses in some locations (Ibreck 2010:339) and
have led to increased social marginalization of Hutu (Thomson 2011:378). In
contrast to the case in Cambodia, President Paul Kagame and numerous RPF
leaders came to Rwanda from positions of exile, so they do not have to worry
to the same extent about being potentially tainted through affiliation with the
previous regime.

Unlike the "reassuring fratricide" described by Anderson, projects of collective national memorialization in Cambodia and Rwanda can actually highlight social cleavages. And the use of human remains, due to their tremendous
psychological and emotional weight, only raises the stakes. Sontag describes
how "for a long time, some people believed that if the horror could be made
vivid enough, most people would finally take in the outrageousness, the in-
sanity of war" (2003:14). In some ways, the efforts to display gruesome remains seem to fall in line with this impulse—the shock value may attempt to
arouse universal sympathy and revulsion. But as Sontag explains, this is not
necessarily the case. Political and social contexts will affect how people view
the remains, or whom they believe the remains belong to. Residents of former
Khmer Rouge strongholds I met in Cambodia who had visited Choeung Ek
often responded quite differently to the site than those from other areas. They
were more likely to think the bones should be buried or cremated[10] or to

doubt the physical evidence itself. Ratana, age fifty-six, a former Khmer Rouge nurse, traveled to Choeung Ek from Pailin with a tour organized by the tribunal and said she did not believe that the Khmer Rouge had committed the crimes they were accused of at the memorial: "The leaders wanted us to be happy and to live a good life. If there was any killing it was only near the end [of Democratic Kampuchea] because Vietnamese spies were trying to undermine the regime. Many people died during the fighting between the Khmer Rouge and Lon Nol and there were many bodies. We don't know whose bodies those are. And the clothes at Choeung Ek don't look like the same material of the Khmer Rouge clothes." Interestingly, Ratana's twenty-year-old son contradicted his mother, saying he did believe the evidence he had seen at Choeung Ek. It is not unusual, however, even for members of younger generations to doubt the story displayed at memorials. Unable to grasp why Cambodians would kill fellow Cambodians, they may revert to "mythical explanations," particularly that the Vietnamese were responsible for the carnage at sites like Tuol Sleng and Choeung Ek (Impunity Watch 2012:23).

Memorials such as Murambi and other commemoration efforts in Rwanda may also exacerbate social divisions. While the current government has sought to create a message of unification, the overwhelming emphasis on the Tutsiness of genocide victims appears to contradict this effort. Within Rwanda, the events of 1994 are known as the "genocide against the Tutsi" and no other potential descriptions—"civil war," "massacre," "Rwandan genocide"—are officially acceptable. There is some mention made of moderate Hutu victims and also Hutu rescuers at Murambi, but these appear almost as perfunctory afterthoughts, dwarfed by the ever-present focus on Tutsi as genocide victims. Although the RPF's national unity policy discourages any mention of "Hutu" or "Tutsi" in public, Rwandans have developed "a new language for discussing ethnicity," largely using the events of 1994 as a referent; this new constellation of terms has polarized "discussions of the genocide by leaving no room for Hutu victims and by globalizing blame on Hutu, regardless of whether they participated in the genocide" (Burnet 2009:89).

Rwandans I interviewed of Hutu background told me they felt "ashamed" to be Hutu and that "after the genocide, people thought all Hutu were demons." One Hutu teacher told me of her visit to Murambi: "Everyone put on a mask of sadness. No one dared to ask questions because they could be misinterpreted and that would cause problems." A Rwandan man, half Hutu and half Tutsi, said he visited Murambi with his church choir and prepared himself psychologically during the entire bus ride so he would be able to control his emotions. When he actually saw the bodies with his fellow choir members, and heard their words of anger toward the Hutu, he said he remained upset for two weeks after the trip. In some cases, these divisions and feelings of alienation have also led Rwandans to question the authenticity of the remains on display. How do we know these are Tutsi and not Hutu? they ask. How do we know these are people killed during the genocide and not during the war? While states like Cambodia and Rwanda may claim the need for physical evidence to prove the crimes of the past, this logic seems somewhat flawed. As Sara Guyer writes, "for those who defend them, memorials composed of unburied bones offer the clearest physical evidence of the genocide. But this clarity is obscured as soon as one recognizes that any body can make bones (and some of the bones collected at these sites may belong to people murdered after the genocide as part of the retaliation campaigns)" (2009:156).

Nonetheless, officials in Cambodia and Rwanda continue to stress the need for physical evidence. And it seems clear that, even while some may deny the authenticity of the remains, for others the emotional horror resulting from such displays is proof enough of their utility. One Tutsi survivor told me: "At Murambi, you see life and death right there. It still smells like death. The smell has permeated everything—walls, floors—and you can still smell it when you leave. Murambi tears you down. You would have to be inhuman for it not to. It is the most powerful memorial—you don't need any explanation or a degree to know what it is." In other words, supporters of the display believe the emotional weight of Murambi sends a clear message—to survivors, perpetrators, foreigners, and future generations.

Spiritual Implications and Complications

This drive to display human remains not only potentially exacerbates social divisions, but also creates tensions with preexisting funerary rituals and spiritual beliefs. In both Cambodia and Rwanda, there is particular concern for those who die bad, or "unnatural," deaths and that their spirits may continue to linger on earth, causing misfortune for the living. According to Hughes, "for this reason, Choeung Ek is considered by many Cambodians to be a dangerous place and they refuse to visit the memorial. To have the uncremated remains *on display* is considered by some to be a great offense, and tantamount to a second violence being done to the victims" (2006:106). Once again, the responses I received from Cambodians related to this conundrum were varied. Many visitors said they did indeed believe there were spirits at Choeung Ek, but that they would not harm them, especially because they came to visit in a large group during the daylight hours. Yet one woman, Thida, told me that as soon as she entered the site, she heard voices calling her name and she decided to return to the tour bus while others continued with their visit. She said another woman in her group became so distraught and sick that she had to be carried from Choeung Ek back to the bus. The same woman died around a year later, which Thida suspected might have been connected to her experience at the site.

Staff members reported hauntings at Choeung Ek, but seemed to agree that they had become less frequent over time—and that the site had become less frightening in general—given its continued development (museumification) and the large number of visitors it was receiving. Rith said he had several spiritual encounters around the time the stupa was built in 1988. He and two guards had sought shelter under the stupa at night due to a rainstorm: "We heard the sound of flip-flops on the mud, around twenty or thirty people, but we looked all around when the rain stopped and no one was there. So we made an offering and burned incense; we told the spirits we were here to protect the site, not to cause trouble." Another staff member told me: "In the past, the spirits used to come out at night, but now there aren't as many as before because we have prayed for them and made offerings for many years."

The presence of unburied bodies in Rwandan memorials also creates spiritual concerns. Burnet contends that "by tradition, Rwandans are horrified of cadavers" (2009:98), and Guyer writes that "unlike other parts of Africa, in Rwanda, there is no tradition of displaying bones or fetishizing corpses" (2009:159). Rwandans I interviewed stressed the need for a divide between the worlds of the living and dead and said that in precolonial times bodies were either left in the forest or buried and that people did not return to visit them (as in the Western Christian practice of visiting graves). Rather, they constructed small spirit huts near their houses where they made offerings. Under colonial Catholicism, Rwandans were urged to bury their dead and to put them in cemeteries. Of course, some elements of precolonial religion remained and numerous Rwandans told me that, until the genocide, it had been unusual for people to visit graves and cemeteries. Henriette, age thirty-three, explained, "in our culture, we used to fear places where people are buried. Rwandans prefer to go to memorials in groups because of their spiritual power. Cemeteries are places for evil things. People are afraid to pass by them at night." Although the fear of corpses predated colonial times, Catholicism also has a history of ascribing great spiritual power to human remains. Antonius Robben writes that starting in medieval times, followers believed that they could be healed by the relics of saints; in nineteenth-century Argentina, the remains of enemy combatants were mutilated so as to weaken their power over the living (2004:139).

In Rwanda, those who died tragically, particularly girls who were never able to have children or get married, need special attention to transition to the afterlife peacefully. Today, many Rwandans believe this means they need a proper burial. Although it is not politically correct to discuss indigenous beliefs and spirits in Rwanda, I did hear several stories of hauntings at Murambi. Janvier, who works at the site, used to guard the classrooms with the bodies at night: "Sometimes the spirits would talk and light fires. People in the villages around here ask how I can stay here with the spirits—they think they are angry because of the way they were killed. At night, they say they hear people singing and babies crying. At first I was scared, but now I am used to this place." Since the genocide, there has been a surge in popularity of non-Catholic denominations of Christianity (such as Pentecostals, Jehovah's Witnesses, and Seventh Day Adventists), and some Rwandans I interviewed said that, because of their belief in religion, they did not think spirits of the dead continued to haunt the earth—and even if they did, their Christianity would protect them against any potential harm.

In both countries, I also found that people were able to accommodate memorials into their preexisting spiritual beliefs to some extent given the historically disruptive nature of genocide and what they perceived as a need for evidentiary proof. Partly, this is the result of the inability to identify most of the human remains on display in memorials—neither Cambodia nor Rwanda has the resources to undertake a large-scale DNA identification process. And even if they did, because whole families were often murdered, there may be no remaining relatives to claim the bones or bodies. Thus, while many Cambodians may prefer cremation as a means of easing the passage of spirits through the cycle of life, death, and rebirth, they also acknowledge that only families can cremate the remains of their deceased. Several people I interviewed told me that they believed other funerary rituals would not be sufficient to appease the spirits of the dead, but most said they believed continued offerings and merit accumulation would allow them to transition.

In the Peruvian context, Isaias Rojas-Perez has described how, despite the emphasis on bodily integrity and a "proper burial" for victims "disappeared" during the government's counterinsurgency campaign of the 1980s and 1990s, their relatives have developed rituals to sanctify the sites of mass exhumations. It is important to note a key difference in the Peruvian case: there has not been a major regime change since the counterinsurgency campaigns and thus the current government is not using past atrocities and human remains to bolster its own legitimacy. Rather, Rojas-Perez writes that the push for exhumations and "proper burials" by families of victims becomes a mode through which they "contest the injustice of the present by reconfiguring the past" (2010:75). At the same time, it is often impossible to retrieve the bodies of the disappeared—only fragments remain—and because of this the exhumation areas become sites of collective mourning.

To some extent, one can observe this phenomenon at memorial sites in Rwanda and Cambodia. The violence in both countries produced landscapes in which anonymous bodies and remains were strewn throughout, sometimes concealed and other times not, while the specter of the absent bodies of loved ones lingered in the memories of those left behind. In Peru, Rojas-Perez observed how the mothers of the disappeared present at exhumations began to perform rituals at the sites and call for the construction of a memorial: "Both justice to the dead and mourning without the body are dependent upon bringing the desaparecidos back to a social existence through a sacralization of the site of torture and killing and ritualized forms of social—and political—acknowledgement of their death. By sacralizing the site of exhumation, the mothers and relatives seek to situate the existence of their missing loved ones within socio-spatial and temporal coordinates in which their place in the world is acknowledged" (2010:318–319). He goes on to write that, through this process, relatives seek to restore relations between the living and dead. While they may not be able to locate the body of any particular missing individual, sacralizing the site housing the remains of others who suffered in a similar manner and met the same fate provides powerful collective symbolic acknowledgment. While independently performing mourning rituals at the major memorial sites I studied may not be widespread in Cambodia and Rwanda (particularly among former members of perpetrator groups), it does indeed take place, particularly among survivors. I interviewed a significant number of those who lost loved ones in both countries who said they often wondered whether their relatives may be among the remains at sites like Choeung Ek, Murambi, and the Kigali Memorial Center. Like the mothers in Peru, they continued to perform rituals and mourn at such sites, which have become potent symbols of collective suffering, in order to restore balance between the worlds of living and dead and to help make the tragic deaths socially intelligible.

Botum, age seventy-five, who testified at the ECCC about the arrest and execution of her husband, has regularly come to Cambodia's two largest memorials since 1990 to make offerings. Although she does not know the specific details of his fate, his picture hangs at Tuol Sleng among those of inmates to be purged, suggesting he was most likely killed at Choeung Ek. She said she first organized a large offering ceremony for him at Choeung Ek in 1990, inviting family members and a monk who had been an acquaintance of her late husband. At the end of the tribunal's first case, she organized another large offering at Tuol Sleng: "I called out my husband's name and told him I had fulfilled my duty to him at the court," she said. In her spare time, she also goes to Choeung Ek alone to pray. "Those were good and innocent people who died there and they have received many offerings, so I don't think their spirits stay there anymore," she said.

In fact, several people whose relatives had died at Tuol Sleng and Choeung Ek said they already knew their loved ones had been reborn. Chan, whose wife was killed at Choeung Ek, said, "I don't know where exactly her bones are but it is ok because she has been reincarnated. She is the young niece of my new wife. Even though she is only a child, she is always cursing my wife and accusing her of stealing her husband." Phatry, whose father disappeared during DK, said all the members of his home village in Kampong Chhnang Province believe the spirit of his father lives in a man who was born in 1980. "When he was a child he said, 'I was Mr. Sen' [the name of Phatry's father], and he told the story about his life and wanted to know where his wife and son Phatry were. He even pointed out the man in the village who people think killed my father. He shot him with a slingshot and said 'you killed me!'" Such stories of post–Khmer Rouge reincarnation are not unusual and, many Cambodians told me, if you want children to forget their previous lives, you can feed them eggs, which are symbolic of fertility and rebirth.

Despite the acceptance that spirits may be reincarnated without cremation, Cambodians still acknowledged that if they could find and identify the bones of their relatives, they would nonetheless want to retrieve and cremate them. Rwandans expressed similar sentiments. While they might accept the display of bodies and bones to some extent, they repeatedly told me that if they knew where their relatives were, they would want to take and bury the remains. According to Ibreck's research, "reburial is generally described as therapeutic—in the words of a female survivor: 'If you bury someone it's like a medicine you have taken' (employee of the Kigali memorial museum, 2006). The desire for reburials is connected to a profound need to restore the dignity of the victims: 'The killers did everything they could to make sure their victims didn't die in dignity'" (2010:338).

Multiple mass exhumations for the purpose of burial have also occurred throughout the country, most recently due to a 2008 law that prohibits the independent burial of genocide victims. Even though mass reburials took place in Rwanda in the years immediately following the genocide, people were interred in the general areas where they were killed because of a lack of resources. In a somewhat controversial decision, the RPF has declared that the bodies of genocide victims should eventually all be moved to official memorial sites in order to ensure preservation of genocide proof (Jessee 2012). In addition, the government has ambitious development plans and leaving small-scale mass graves strewn throughout the country is simply impractical, CNLG staff members told me. Survivor reaction to the government position has been divided. Some survivors told me they approved of the policy because they believed their loved ones would be protected and honored. Others said they took offense at what they saw as unnecessary relocation of bodies—"before the genocide, exhumations would have been unthinkable," one told me—and said they would prefer to bury and remember their relatives outside official state dictates.

Still, some Rwandans I interviewed (mostly survivors) described how they have come to incorporate official memorial efforts into their own spiritual and commemorative practices. Despite the lack of tradition of visiting graves in Rwandan culture, many told me they went to memorials regularly to pay their respects, lay flowers, and say prayers. They said visiting the sites brought them a sense of peace and made them feel they were close to their loved ones. Eugenie, who lost multiple family members during the genocide, explained, "normally it's not part of our culture to take flowers and visit graves, but genocide is a special case. People go even when it's not the time for mourning. Genocide is exceptional." She has visited the Kigali Memorial Center several times and said that during the next commemoration period she would like to keep vigil at the site overnight.

As statements such as Eugenie's show, there is no social or religious template for confronting the horrific legacy of genocide and the remnants of those left behind. Cambodian Buddhism does not make provisions for the ritual treatment of millions of mostly unidentified bones—neither does indigenous Rwandan religion or Christianity. States may try to harness these relics to legitimize their power and craft a historical narrative that emphasizes their role in purported national liberation, but they cannot control the ways in which their efforts are received. This is particularly true in societies where memory of the crimes committed is still raw, where time and psychological distance have not yet created a story of "reassuring fratricide." Citizens may accommodate official narratives into their own understanding of history, and they may reject them. They may find postgenocide memorial efforts distasteful and spiritually offensive, or they may incorporate new rituals and understandings within their religious practice. Human remains, due to their symbolic power, become a flash point for social, political, and spiritual cleavages. Yet they are just one element of the larger, messy struggle to manage memory and rebuild a coherent national narrative in societies where the most fundamental bonds between people have been shredded. As Jean de Dieu, a Tutsi survivor, explained, "This is a traumatized country. Foreigners say there's too much focus on genocide here, and maybe there is. But people don't know anything else. We reached the bottom of human cruelty. The way people see the community after that kind of event will not be ordinary. Genocide is in our memories."

Notes

1. Cambodians I interviewed described "tight skin" and "smell of death" as indicators that the spirits of one's relatives are nearby.

2. Although Pchum Ben offerings to spirits are generally made through monks, people believe it is also possible to feed some kinds of spirits directly; this usually must be done very early in the morning before the sun rises.

3. A great deal of debate exists concerning the categories of Tutsi and Hutu and what exactly they represent. In precolonial Rwanda, societal divisions included Tutsi (who were predominantly pastoralists), Hutu (predominantly agriculturalists), and Twa (indigenous forest dwellers). Although Twa still exist in Rwanda, their political presence has been relatively marginal. The nature of these categories is somewhat unclear due to the dearth of written material in precolonial Rwanda, but they appear to have been social or occupational designations with some degree of flexibility. In *Sacrifice as Terror, the Rwandan Genocide of 1994*, Christopher Taylor writes that Hutu who achieved social prominence could become Tutsi, and Tutsi who descended in social status could become Hutu (1999:66). Under the colonial regime, these categories became fixed and racialized. Europeans determined that the minority Tutsi were a foreign and superior race that had migrated to Rwanda and conquered the Hutu. They thus devised a system of indirect rule through a Tutsi elite. After Rwanda gained independence in 1962, Hutu took control of the country and Tutsi were marginalized, persecuted, and often driven into exile. Yet under the Second Republic, starting in 1973, the government began to describe Tutsi as an indigenous ethnic group. Nonetheless, because the majority of those living in exile

were not allowed to return to the country, they formed the Rwandan Patriotic Front (RPF) with fellow refugees in Uganda and began a military campaign in 1990. This fueled the growth of the "Hutu Power" movement within the country, which resuscitated racialized colonial tropes of the Tutsi as an alien race (Mamdani 2001:189–190). Since the RPF victory in the campaign, the state has favored a narrative stressing that Tutsi, Hutu, and Twa lived peacefully together before colonial intervention and that the designations were social categories based on class and wealth in the form of cows. However, as Taylor notes, despite these efforts, many Rwandans have nonetheless internalized these differences as racial or ethnic categories, and this continues to affect social relations in the country (1999:56).

4. Although some of the longtime staffers I interviewed at Choeung Ek claim that they were aware of the presence of mass graves before that time, it is difficult to corroborate their stories. Rith said he returned to his home village, which was around two hundred meters from Choeung Ek, several days after the Vietnamese invasion: "I came to the old Chinese graveyard [Choeung Ek] to dig for cassava and while I was digging I started to notice a bad smell and hear the sound of flies. I followed the smell and ten meters away there was a pile of bodies. I was so scared I left all my cassava there and ran home." Rith added that while he told other people in the village about what he had seen he didn't tell authorities because he didn't know who was responsible for the killings. "I thought it could be people killed by the Khmer Rouge, but I also thought it could be people killed by Vietnam. It was a very uncertain time and I didn't know who might be a Khmer Rouge spy."

5. The 1948 UN Convention on the Prevention and Punishment of the Crime of Genocide, which came into being after World War II, defines genocide as "any of the following acts committed with intent to destroy, in whole or in part, a national, ethnical, racial or religious group as such." While DK disproportionately targeted minority groups that would be included in the convention, such as the Cham Muslims or Vietnamese living in Cambodia, the majority of killing was Khmer on Khmer. Although other groups based on characteristics such as political affiliation and social class were discussed in negotiations over the UN Genocide Convention, they were ultimately not included in the law. This omission has caused a great deal of controversy over time: "By the end of the 1940s, it was clear that political groups were often targeted for annihilation. Moreover, the appellations applied to 'communists,' or by communists to 'kulaks' or 'class enemies'—when imposed by a totalitarian state—seemed every bit as difficult to shake as ethnic identifications, if the Nazi and Stalinist onslaughts were anything to go by" (Jones 2010:11). Scholars have often adopted broader definitions of genocide that include the targeting of collectivities based on characteristics such as class or political affiliation, and the crimes of DK are commonly referred to as "genocide."

6. Today, however, Cambodians use a number of different terms to describe the period of Democratic Kampuchea. They may use "*bralay pouchsah*," "the Pol Pot time," the "period of three years, eight months, and twenty days," or the "*kosang*" (establishment) period. Such diversity of terminology is currently unacceptable in Rwanda.

7. A familiar expression during Democratic Kampuchea was "to keep you is no benefit, to destroy you is no loss."

8. See Heonik Kwon's *After the Massacre: Commemoration and Consolation in Ha My and My Lai* (2006) for more information regarding the difficulty the Vietnamese state encountered in confronting noncombatant war death.

9. Holt (2012) applies Kwon's analysis of a return to ancestral rituals in Vietnam to Cambodia in the late 1980s. Kwon notes, "The demise of the centrally-planned socialist economy resulted in the revival of ancestral rituals as a way of strengthening the moral basis of the family—a principal unit in the new economic environment" (2006:3).

10. "They should be cremated—it's miserable to look at," one former Khmer Rouge soldier from Pailin told me. "They should be buried so people who are alive can be calm and relaxed."

Bibliography

Agamben, Giorgio. 1998. *Homo Sacer: Sovereign Power and Bare Life*. Trans. Daniel Heller-Roazen. Stanford: Stanford University Press.

Anderson, Benedict. 2006. *Imagined Communities*. New York: Verso.

Burnet, Jennie. 2009. Whose Genocide? Whose Truth? In *Genocide: Truth, Memory and Representation*, ed. Alexander Laban Hinton and Kevin Lewis O'Neill, 80–110. Durham: Duke University Press.

Giry, Stephanie. 2012. *Necessary Scapegoats? The Making of the Khmer Rouge Tribunal* (blog). *New York Review of Books*. http://www.nybooks.com/blogs/nyrblog/2012/jul/23/necessary-scapegoats-khmer-rouge-tribunal/ (accessed on January 12, 2013).

Guyer, Sara. 2009. Rwanda's Bones. *Boundary* 36(2): 155–175.

Hinton, Alex L. 2008. Truth, Representation and the Politics of Memory After Genocide. In *People of Virtue: Reconfiguring Religion, Power and Moral Order in Cambodia Today*, ed. David Chandler and Alexandra Kent, 62–81. Copenhagen: Nordic Institute of Asian Studies.

Holt, John Clifford. 2012. Caring for the Dead Ritually in Cambodia. *Southeast Asian Studies* 1(1): 3–75./

Hughes, Rachel. 2006. Fielding Genocide: Post-1979 Cambodia and the Geopolitics of Memory. PhD diss., University of Melbourne.

Human Rights Watch. 2011. Khmer Rouge Trial Is Justice Delayed. News release, June 24. http://www.hrw.org/news/2011/06/24/cambodia-khmer-rouge-trial-justice-delayed (accessed on January 5, 2013).

Ibreck, Rachel. 2010. The Politics of Mourning: Survivor Contributions to Memorials in Post-Genocide Rwanda. *Memory Studies* 3(4): 330–343.

Impunity Watch. 2012. *Perspective Series Conference, Breaking the Silence: International Memory Initiatives Exchange Forum.*

Jessee, Erin. 2012. Promoting Reconciliation Through Exhuming and Identifying Victims in the 1994 Rwandan Genocide. *Africa Portal: A Project of the Africa Initiative.* http://www.africaportal.org/articles/2012/07/20/promoting-reconciliation-through-exhuming-and-identifying-victims-1994-rwandan-g#chapter5 (accessed on January 2, 2013).

Jones, Adam. 2010. *Genocide: A Comprehensive Introduction.* 2nd ed. New York: Routledge.

Kwon, Heonik. 2006. *After the Massacre: Commemoration and Consolation in Ha My and My Lai.* Berkeley: University of California Press.

Ledgerwood, Judy. 1997. The Cambodian Tuol Sleng Museum of Genocidal Crimes: National Narrative. *Museum Anthropology* 21(1): 82–98.

Mamdani, Mahmood. 2001. *When Victims Become Killers: Colonialism, Nativism and the Genocide in Rwanda.* Princeton: Princeton University Press.

Nora, Pierre. 1997. General Introduction: Between Memory and History. In *Realms of Memory,* ed. Pierre Nora, 1–21. New York: Columbia University Press.

Robben, Antonius C. G. M. 2004. State Terror in the Netherworld: Disappearance and Reburial in Argentina. In *Death, Mourning and Burial: A Cross-Cultural Reader,* ed. Antonius C. G. M. Robben, 134–149. Oxford: Blackwell.

Rojas-Perez, Isaias. 2010. Fragments of Soul: Law, Transitional Justice and Mourning in Postwar Peru. PhD diss., Johns Hopkins University.

Sontag, Susan. 2003. *Regarding the Pain of Others.* New York: Picador.

Taylor, Christopher. 1999. *Sacrifice as Terror: The Rwandan Genocide of 1994.* Oxford: Berg.

Thomson, Susan. 2011. The Darker Side of Transitional Justice: The Power Dynamics Behind Rwanda's Gacaca Courts. *Africa: The Journal of the International African Institute* 81(3): 373–390.

Verdery, Katherine. 1999. *The Political Lives of Dead Bodies: Reburial and Post-Socialist Change.* New York: Columbia University Press.

Vidal, Claudine. 2004. La Commémoration du génocide au Rwanda: Violence symbolique, mémorisation forcée et histoire officielle. *Cahiers d'Etudes Africaines* 44(175): 575–592.

Williams, Paul. 2007. *Memorial Museums: The Global Rush to Commemorate Atrocities.* New York: Berg.

Epilogue

Zoë Crossland

In a poetic and somewhat elegiac memoir, *The Stone Fields* (2004), Courtney Angela Brkic writes about her experiences working as a forensic anthropologist in Bosnia and Herzegovina in 1996. Drawing on her own family's history in the region she imagines the pain of displacement and persecution reverberating over generations. She evokes her grandmother's struggles before and during the Second World War, and juxtaposes this painful history with her own experiences of present-day Croatia and Bosnia-Herzegovina. Her narrative expresses the tension between the needs and desires of relatives and the efforts of the state (or of transnational legal institutions) to control and order exhumation and reburial. Embodying this tension herself, her effort to reconcile the work she is carrying out with her own family history almost undoes her, and she unravels in the face of the suffering of those she encounters. The work of those who exhume is often positioned in the mass media and popular press as, paradoxically, politicized and yet objectively scientific, emotionally fraught and yet detached and dispassionate. Much depends on the perspective of the journalist or publication that reports on the work, but this shifting between different goals and affects can take place even within the same text, and it is clearly a tension that also exists within the work of exhumation itself.

Brkic writes of the different way in which she experienced the excavations and morgue analysis from that of her colleagues. As with Clea Koff's memoir recording her time working as a forensic anthropologist in the former Yugoslavia and Rwanda (2004), Brkic's youth and gender seem to have allowed her to sidestep the detached and somewhat masculinized affect that often seems to characterize much writing on forensic anthropology. She notes that she quickly fell in to the role of "little sister" (2004:30). But she describes another difference, a sense of connection with the dead that grew out of her own family background in the region: "For most of the others, there was no personal dimension to the work, and there were no Bosnian or Croatian team members. . . . Bosnia was just one stop along the way, and I remained quiet while listening to them describe projects in other countries" (29). This then is not a simple account of an archaeologist's adventures abroad, although it certainly shares some of the tropes of travel narratives. Where the text differs is in its composition as a memoir of belonging and alienation, of being "with and apart." Here we have another kind of anthropology of exhumation that explores the work from the perspective of someone both inside and outside the world that is being unearthed. Brkic's text draws on her family history to imagine the pain of displacement and persecution reverberating over generations and her account points to the complex and shifting constellations of relationships around the dead, as well as the complex ways in which the living are "with and apart" from those who are exhumed. The chapters in this volume explore similar ambivalences and ambiguities, not simply in the various tensions between different actors but in the ways in which the process of exhumation is fraught with contradictions even for those who advocate for it.

As Brkic found, exhumation returns the dead to the community of the living, and in so doing it also brings back history, and allows narratives that have been suppressed to emerge into a wider discursive arena. Brkic's memoir makes use of the often-unrecognized metaphorical link between the exhumation of the dead and the bringing to light of a painful history. This provides her with a way to think through the complexities of absence and the return to presence of individuals through the return of human remains. As well as the absences of those who were disappeared we also see the absence of responsibility and punishment: the absence of acknowledgment of past violence, the absence of historical memory, and the hopes that in exhuming the dead these absences can, if not be occupied, at least be mediated, made sense of, or challenged. This is a material working through of metaphor, where the return to presence of those who are missing is also thought to fill other lacks, and to address questions of impunity.

As the chapters in this volume have explored this terrain, they have shown the heterogeneity of exhumation, revealing its different possibilities and the various ways in which such work attempts to fill the painful voids left by the dead and the missing. In shifting between the absences of the missing and those of historical memory the work of exhumation is situated in a space that is simultaneously intensely personal and inherently public. Taken together the chapters collected here suggest that many of the tensions of forensic work seem to emerge from the effort to balance its involvement in histories of individual suffering, persecution, and tragedy on the one hand and attempts to compose national or collective historical narratives—or indeed anthropological narratives—on the other. How to keep not only bodies but people in view? How also to remember the broader implications of every individual death? In this volume we see some of the ways in which different communities and interest groups have attempted to negotiate this treacherous landscape.

The notion of history as something that lies hidden and buried seems to have emerged alongside the development of an antiquarian interest in the past. By the end of the nineteenth century it was in common use, for example coming readily to hand for Sigmund Freud in his description of the excavation of the repressed unconscious (Kuspit 1989; Thomas 2004; Ucko 2001). But there is also a longer genealogy that can be traced in the history of postmortem interactions with the dead of western Europe. Bodies have been exhumed for the needs of criminal investigation for centuries. Roy Hunnisett (1961:9–12) observes that the work of the English medieval coroner's office was mostly concerned with inquests on dead bodies. For a charge of murder to be brought, the coroner had to view the body, whether entire or not. If buried, it would be exhumed and could be brought to the courtroom; the visible presence of the dead was essential to the inquiry. The history that the coroner's court composed therefore needed the dead body to begin being told, regardless of the feelings of those involved. It was only once the murder and death had been narrated that funerary ritual could be properly carried out.

Similarly, forensic and humanitarian exhumation is located both as part of a tradition of judicial inquiry and as a necessary step in the completion of funerary ritual. This becomes particularly clear in the absence of viable prosecutions based on the evidence of the dead, where the focus of excavation and recovery is to return remains to family members. Writing of how she experienced forensic work in the former Yugoslavia, Brkic senses "the dark, unknown transition into death" of the murdered family members of the women she encountered there. She reflects that almost a year later, "there we were, the first to touch the bodies of their men when they emerged on the other end into the light of day" (2004:19). The assertively scientific and medico-legal work of forensic inquiry perhaps masks the ways in which these exhumations also become a form of ritualized mortuary practice, an important stage in the process of shifting the dead between different categories. How this is conceptualized differs from context to context, but in most cases only a restricted group of specialists are allowed to engage with the dead, and only in rigorously controlled conditions. Brkic writes of crossing "an invisible border" in the work that she carried out (34), separated from the mundane world of the rest of the living. Acknowledging the transitional and somewhat liminal space-time of forensic work, official accounts and mass media reports often frame the work of exhumation in terms of the preservation of memory or of the regenerative possibilities provided by the reincorporation of the dead back into society. This is a process that Isaias Rojas-Perez explores in his contribution to the volume, in which he describes how, "perhaps more clearly than any other, the figure of the *desaparecido* inhabits the temporality of the finished and unfinished past of the postconflict state." If history can be brought to light with exhumation, equally it can be laid to rest, perhaps prematurely, by reburial of the dead, whether this takes place as part of state ceremonial or in the context of the family. In this sense the rituals of reburial can be about forgetting as much as about memory. Rojas-Perez notes the apparent lack of interest by Peruvian officials in the recent funeral ceremonies for people who were disappeared and murdered by the state. The former Peruvian minister of defense made clear the connection of burial with the historical erasure of certain people and past events : "We are much more worried about what is happening there *now*. . . than a burial of *things* that happened in the past."

A number of the chapters demonstrate the reiterated attempts by different governments to translate past violence into agreed-upon accounts that impose one collective frame of remembrance. As narratives are composed at the level of the state or of the international community, so the dead can be enrolled into stories that do violence to their memory and to the experiences of relatives and survivors, as Elena Lesley describes for the display of uncremated remains in Cambodia. Similarly, the role of religious authorities can be contested, as outlined by Francisco Ferrándiz for Spain and Heonik Kwon for South Korea, another locale where viewpoints on the past are disputed, often with tensions between local knowledge and national narratives. Excavations take place in order to prosecute legal cases, to provide bodies for relatives, to allow grieving, to disseminate knowledge of past atrocities. Despite the oft-stated claims of political authorities, transitional or otherwise, the goals of exhumation are not stable or unified; equally they do not always align. The individualizing work of forensic practice provides a good example of the complexities. One of the key foci of forensic excavation and analysis is to establish the number of the dead and to identify individuals, defining distinct persons from within the collective assemblage of the grave. The loss of the anatomical echo of the dead can do great violence to their remembered personhood, and to efforts to re-constitute them for family members, but it is not always a priority, or indeed possible, to locate individuals for reburial, as Lesley shows in her chapter. Turning to the case of the former Yugoslavia, Sarah Wagner carefully delin-eates the breaches between the goal of identification of the Srebrenica dead through DNA, the return of a person's remains, whole or in part, and the re-ligious recognition of what constitutes a person. Wagner observes that foren-sic anthropologists seek "to rebuild individuals, trying to address loss of life and identity, alongside loss of physical, corporeal integrity." This raises a num-ber of issues, including which parts of the dead need to be recovered for the person to be understood to be retrieved, as noted by Kwon. Also, how and when to notify relatives when remains are identified, an issue that is also sa-lient for the repatriation of the war dead, as Wagner explores. How is person-hood understood in relation to the dead body in different contexts, and how might this change the assumptions around the elements necessary to identi-fication? Wagner shows how anthropologists negotiate these different goals, and act as go-betweens, mediating between different actors. The interplay of different goals and needs in the work of exhumation is complicated and there is no simple path through it.

Luis Fondebrider's chapter provides another perspective on forensic prac-tice. He locates exhumation as just one part of a broader sequence of work, also showing how the boundaries that are often erected between different forms of anthropological practice are indistinct and easily traversed in the context of human rights work. This also seems an important issue to explore given the push within the forensic anthropological community to standardize methods. The move toward standardization grows from an effort to increase transparency and accountability. But whose methods get standardized? Does this leave room for dealing with specific historical circumstances and diver-gent beliefs and practices around the dead? Ideal practice in one context may be far from ideal in another. Fondebrider's chapter reveals how techniques and expectations developed in the context of North American and western European criminal investigations have had to be adjusted when moving into other worldwide contexts. At the moment much of the flow of knowledge and resources is from the United States and western Europe to other parts of the world, despite the great depth of experience of forensic specialists working in Latin America, and Fondebrider makes a strong case for cultivating more productive exchanges. His contribution gestures toward the lacunae that forensic anthropologists from Argentina and elsewhere in Latin America might find in the training provided in the United States and Europe. In exploring the complexities of international forensic interventions, Fondebrider's essay demonstrates the importance of locating scientific exhumation within broader historical and social practices around the dead.

Fondebrider writes of the difficulties of working closely with families, while also carrying out excavations for national or transnational prosecution or accountability. Similarly, Wagner explores "the dynamic interplay between scientific knowledge and social meaning," the "extraordinary successes . . . and ethical dilemmas raised by evolving forensic practice." What becomes clear is the improvised and provisional nature of work with human remains in a forensic or humanitarian context. The chapters collected here point to how in translating forensic practice from one context to another, new challenges arise and new forms of practice must be extemporized. Elena Lesley notes the lack of any "social or religious template for confronting the horrific legacy of genocide." As do the other authors, she notes how states may try to co-opt the dead in legitimizing acts that purport to establish an agreed-upon historical narrative, but she observes, "they cannot control the ways in which their efforts are received."

In offering the contrasting case of Greece, Katerina Stefatos and Iosif Kovras outline how the country has resisted exhumations for fear of the past actions the work could reveal and the political controversies it could prompt. This is to highlight the conditions of possibility that allow exhumation to be undertaken in the first place. Stefatos and Kovras note that the excavations carried out at different moments at Lesvos from the 1950s to 2009 were always "informal, local, and depoliticized." They suggest that the exhumations "have the potential to bridge the gap between . . . the individual right of the relatives to know the truth and the societal perception that silence is the best way to move forward." Breaking the earth provides nonconfrontational ways to break silence, a choice that is political and depoliticized in the same moment. This can be compared with the contested exhumations that took place in Argentina in the 1980s and 1990s (Crossland 2000; Gordon 1997; Robben 2000). In this case one group of the mothers of the disappeared refused to acknowledge the dead, recognizing precisely that the exhumations could be understood as apolitical and conciliatory. Instead they argued that it was not the dead who should speak about the past, but rather those responsible for the atrocities (Crossland 2002; Schirmer 1993). Things have changed in Argentina since then, particularly as prosecutions have been carried out on the basis of abducted and illegally adopted children of disappeared people, and a younger generation has become involved in the struggle against impunity (Robben 2005; Taylor 2003). In his contribution to the volume Antonius Robben traces the ways in which exhumations in Argentina and Chile have resisted the meanings given to mass graves by the military and "substituted for them the countermeanings of bereaved relatives . . . without ever succeeding completely." His chapter shows how the political narratives that emerge from the evidence of the dead are shaped in part by the regimes of disappearance, death, and bodily disposal through which gravesites come into being. As corpses are brought to light, so the clandestine actions of those responsible are revealed, while also directing the material-discursive worlds of possibility that come forth. As these papers demonstrate, the dynamics of changing attitudes and styles of exhumation over time and in different regions are important to consider. Equally important are the various ways in which the material configurations of mass graves and other spaces of terror enter into discourse and work upon historical memory.

Governmentality and the Translation of the Dead

In the context of international human rights investigations the work of exhumation is often framed as part of a tradition of medico-legal inquiry. Yet the enduring legal concern with the visible presence of the murdered body parallels another long history of founding political and religious legitimacy on the bones of the dead. Both traditions speak to the intimate relationship between governance and the dead, and also show the very real need for particular and specific bodies in the creation of narratives about the past. The early medieval ritual of the *translatio*, the movement of the relics of the saints from tomb to the altar of a church, was essential to the consecration of a church, making the saint present in a way that was not restricted to bones alone. Patrick Geary (1978) has explored how relics could be stolen as the first act of establishing a new church; by controlling the body of the saint a visible statement was made that asserted his or her acquiescence. The incorruptible bodies of the saints offer a resonant resource for political imaginaries, drawn upon most notably in the embalmed corpses of the architects of the former Soviet Union, as traced by Katherine Verdery (1999). In exploring the politics of the dead body Verdery acknowledges the power of the corpse as a material symbol, but also recognizes the complicated nature of this materiality. She notes that although relics seem to gain their efficacy from the claim that they make to being a part of a saint or other valued historical figure, these claims cannot be easily tracked and validated. Indeed, relics have had the habit of multiplying. This, she argues, suggests that it is not the physical link with the dead that matters, but rather the perception of one (1999:28). Ferrándiz's chapter in this volume shows that this is the case even when the dead are not present; the very act of turning the earth and of searching for the traces of the past is enough to bring memories to the surface. How then to think about this material-symbolic efficacy and to acknowledge that there is some sense in which the presence of the dead can rupture particular readings, deny or reveal some discourses?

There can be a great deal of dissonance between the feelings and stories of families and the accounts sponsored by the state, however constituted. In the case of South Korea, confrontations between families and local authorities over the memory of those civilians massacred during the civil war have coalesced around burial sites, and Heonik Kwon outlines how after the coup of May 1961 one of the first acts of the military authority was to arrest "representatives of the bereaved families' associations . . . accusing them of having committed an 'extraordinary anti-state activity,'" and sentencing one of them to death. Kwon remarks that the dead were also punished, with memorial stones destroyed, the tombs desecrated, and remains removed. As Giorgio Agamben has explored, it is precisely in the state's ability to exercise this sway over life and death with impunity that its power over ordinary human relationships is felt and known (1998, 2005). The grandiose memory projects of Francisco Franco's state, in-cluding the exhumation and reburial of the (predominantly Nationalist) dead in the Valle de los Caídos, was a similar claiming of the dead for the Nationalist project of Franco's government and an assertion of the ability of the state to write history. Why are the dead so necessary to this kind of narrative? The need of the state or other political authority to control the disposition and placement of human remains points to a vulnerability, an acknowledgement that the dead can create a site of challenge for narratives that claim to present a complete historical account. Yet, while there is certainly a power to the revelation of what was hidden, and the presence of the dead seems to demand a response, at the same time these fluid and shifting contexts cannot be reduced to any kind of uniform pattern. The ways that the dead are drawn into different historical circumstances are complex and unpredictable.

The physical search for the dead seems in many cases to allow survivors and others to think about the unthinkable, to construct a narrative that begins to make sense of what took place in the past. Where this narrative comes into conflict with other perspectives, the focus falls naturally onto the human remains that underwrite it. Lesley observes how "projects of collective national memorialization . . . can actually highlight social cleavages," noting that in Cambodia residents of former Khmer Rouge strongholds "were more likely to think the bones should be buried or cremated or to doubt the physical evidence itself." One way to think about these challenges is to consider the different orders of evidence that are in play in any set of circumstances, with evidence here conceptualized as a complex set of relations as much as a material trace (Crossland 2013). Evidence is always of and for something, and is thus an unfolding relationship between at least three elements: the material sign, that which it offers evidence of, and the purpose toward which such evidence is marshaled. In the case of exhumation the remains of the dead act as an unstable and yet tangibly corporeal sign at the center of these relations. As the dead come back into the world of the living, so the events of the past are brought into relation with the desires and goals of different actors. These 'goals' may be inchoate: a search for a feeling of recognition and an attempt at closure, as much as any more developed narrative. If the remains of the dead lie at the center of the relation between past and present, they also act as powerful signs at the center of different interests and claims, providing a point of intersection within a range of often-contested relationships. To destroy or to mobilize the remains of the dead is to act on the material sign that forms the fulcrum holding together different evidential claims. It is to try to reconfigure the evidential relation itself, a way of rewriting history, and of restricting the possible purposes to which such evidence may be put.

Despite the apparently straightforward and empirical claims made through forensic exhumation, clearly this is not unambiguous labor. It can seem to be doing very different things depending on one's location within the process. To understand how work around the dead is linked materially and metaphorically to work around memory and justice, it is important to take account of how different understandings emerge as bodies move from context to context, hidden, exhumed, and reburied by relatives or the state. Human remains may act as material evidence, central to investigations into the past and aspirations toward the future, but this evidence is never stable. If evidence is always a relational entity, then its composition must shift as the dead themselves move between new contexts. The translations that take place around the dead are not simply attempts to control language, but are also practical, affective, and nondiscursive.

Here again the older notion of translation, used in the context of medieval relics, is useful, evoking a sense of movement, as the remains of the saints were exhumed and transferred to new places. To translate is to bear across, to shift from one context to another, and this is certainly what happens when the dead are exposed and brought back into the midst of the living. The *translatio* was a dynamic and material notion of translation, in which the repositioning of the dead provided opportunities for new meanings to emerge. When we take account of present-day translations around the dead, their tangible presence and physical movement between contexts is as important as the way in which they are positioned within language. Bruno Latour has written about translation as the displacement of action into another place, or time, or actor (e.g., Latour 1999). This notion of translation locates the agency of the dead not in the tangible presence of the dead body but in the dense and knotted relationships within which the dead are caught up. It is the variable ways in which they are situated within these relationships that give rise to such different responses, as the essays in this volume show so elegantly. However, a full account must also be made of the material impact of human remains on discourse, of the ways in which the dead can shape or influence the narratives that are told about them.

The Tangible Signs of the Dead

In the context of Spain, Francisco Ferrándiz's chapter traces how the dead are brought back to presence, and the violent preoccupations of the first half of the twentieth century reemerge into changed political circumstances. Ferrándiz explores the preservation of memories in relation to the topography of the dead, showing how the remembered site of the grave can be preserved and act as a muted reminder of past events but also as a site that maintains the terror of the past. He observes that the stories told around the gravesite and during the labor of excavation are a vital dimension of the process and of efforts to remember and honor the dead. The ability to narrate the past, to translate remembered events into a form of communal and individual commemoration is thus closely tied to the tangible materiality of the grave, and to its power to reveal past violence and to forcefully insert this spectacle into the present.

There are diverse ways in which the work of exhumation conjures particular imaginaries that in turn direct speech and structure knowledge claims. Sarah Wagner's chapter illustrates how anxieties over the partitioning and fragmentation of bodies not only create challenges for mourning and ritual processes but also serve to illustrate the partial and fragmentary nature of accounts about the past. Here the disaggregated and comingled bodies become a metaphor for the fragmented, confused, and incomplete knowledge of what took place, but they also operate metonymically, providing one part of a larger and ungraspable whole. Lesley notes the affective force and ability to shock of the memorials in Cambodia and Rwanda. This is evidence that is not designed for prosecution, but rather to evoke a complex array of feelings, including horror, fright, grief, determination, and others. The monumental collections of bodies operate to evoke an affect as a starting point for telling a story about the past. They present a tangible image that, as in the former Yugoslavia, operates as a kind of iconic sign of the scale of the violence of the past, as well as a clear index of the pain that was suffered by so many. Over the course of the varied accounts compiled in this volume we've seen various forms of witnessing and testimony about the past, the challenges to these evidential practices, the strategies through which they play out, as well as problems around their appropriation and translation. Questions of authenticity and of the legitimacy of different forms of testimony become important here, and as Fondebrider indicates, there are a variety of forms of testimony that are important in these struggles against impunity, including the evidence of the bureaucracy of the state—which like the evidence of the dead is also often destroyed, partial, and hidden.

The comparative orientation of the volume speaks forcefully to the need for interdisciplinary dialogue, and for better understanding of the particular histories and beliefs that are caught up in this work. The powerful comparative cases developed by the authors reveal the commonalities of experience and shared problems faced by relatives, survivors, forensic specialists, and others. They also illustrate the particular and often divergent ways in which the work unfolds in any specific case. Coming back to Brkic's memoir of being "with and apart," of painful histories excavated and brought to light, it is clear that exhumation is always already a form of history. The dead bring the past into relation with the present, and they provide the material hinge on which historical narrative is fixed. It is here that the evidential relationship is at its clearest, but this is not to say that the search made by families is any less evidential. Relatives may struggle against the impetus to subsume the dead into state narratives, and against the alienation of the dead from family memory. Such a refusal of state narrative can be asserted through funerary ritual as Rojas-Perez explores, or through the more radical act of refusing to recognize remains. The former works to reframe the dead within family and community memory, counterpoising feeling to narrative in the search for evidence of personal identity. The latter disassembles historical narrative altogether by refusing the central sign that pins together its claims.

All of the different modes of intervention and the heterogeneous forms of work that are carried out around the dead constitute ways of being "with and apart"—of reconfiguring evidential relations as much as personal relationships, of entering into some modes of discourse and abjuring others. The chapters collected here attest to the diversity of the work that we term *exhumation*, demonstrating the complexity of forensic and humanitarian engagements with the dead. They direct our attention to the agency of past actors in the narratives that are composed around them, whether this is manifest in the reverberating traces of past atrocities, made present in the remains of murdered relatives, or sensed in the presence of ancestral or ghostly entities. In dealing with the violence of mass graves, the contributions in this book powerfully demonstrate the difficulties posed by exhumation and reburial, the evocative power of the dead body, and its varied role in commemorating the past and offering narratives for the future.

Bibliography

Agamben, Giorgio. 1998. *Homo Sacer: Sovereign Power and Bare Life*. Stanford, CA: Stanford University Press.

———. 2005. *State of Exception*. Chicago: University of Chicago Press.

Brkic, Courtney Angela. 2004. *The Stone Fields: An Epitaph for the Living*. New York: Farrar, Straus & Giroux.

Crossland, Zoë. 2000. Buried Lives: Forensic Archaeology and the Disappeared in Argentina. *Archaeological Dialogues* 7(2):146–159.

———. 2002 Violent Spaces: Conflict over the Reappearance of Argentina's Disappeared. In *Matériel Culture: The Archaeology of Twentieth Century Conflict*, ed. John Schofield, William Gray Johnson, and Colleen M. Beck, 115–131. One World Archaeology. London: Routledge.

———. 2013. Evidential Regimes of Forensic Archaeology. *Annual Review of Anthropology* 42:121–137.

Geary, Patrick J. 1978. *Furta Sacra: Thefts of Relics in the Central Middle Ages*. Princeton, NJ: Princeton University Press.

Gordon, Avery. 1997. *Ghostly Matters: Haunting and the Sociological Imagination*. Minneapolis: University of Minnesota Press.

Hunnisett, Roy F. 1961. *The Medieval Coroner*. Cambridge: Cambridge University Press.

Koff, Clea. 2004. *The Bone Woman: A Forensic Anthropologist's Search for Truth in the Mass Graves of Rwanda, Bosnia, Croatia, and Kosovo*. New York: Random House.

Kuspit, Donald. 1989. A Mighty Metaphor: The Analogy of Archaeology and Psychoanalysis. In *Sigmund Freud and Art: His Personal Collection of Antiquities*, ed. Lynn Gamwell and Robert Wells, 133–151. London: Freud Museum.

Latour, Bruno. 1999. *Pandora's Hope: Essays on the Reality of Science Studies*. Cambridge, MA: Harvard University Press.

Robben, Antonius C. G. M. 2000. State Terror in the Netherworld: Disappearance and Reburial in Argentina. In *Death Squad: The Anthropology of State Terror*, ed. Jeffrey A. Sluka, 91–113. Philadelphia: University of Pennsylvania Press.

———. 2005. *Political Violence and Trauma in Argentina*. Philadelphia: University of Pennsylvania Press.

Schirmer, Jennifer. 1993. "Those Who Die for Life Cannor Be Called Dead." In *Surviving Beyond Fear*, ed. Marjorie Agosin, 31–57. Fredonia, NY: White Pine Press.

Taylor, Diana. 2003. *The Archive and the Repertoire: Performing Cultural Memory in the Americas*. Durham, NC: Duke University Press.

Thomas, Julian. 2004. *Archaeology and Modernity*. New York: Routledge.

Ucko, Peter J. 2001. Unprovenanced Material Culture and Freud's Collection of Antiquities. *Journal of Material Culture* 63:269–322.

Verdery, Katherine. 1999. *The Political Lives of Dead Bodies: Reburial and Postsocialist Change*. New York: Columbia University Press.

Contributors

Zoë Crossland is associate professor of anthropology at Columbia University. Her main theoretical interests lie in semiotic archaeology and archaeologies of death and the body. She works in historical archaeology and the archaeology of the recent past, focusing particularly on nodes of controversy where conflicting sets of beliefs and practices converge. This is expressed in two main research topics: the archaeology of encounter in Madagascar and the production of the excavated body in exhumations. Her most recent book is *Encounters with Ancestors in Highland Madagascar: Material Signs and Traces of the Dead* (Cambridge University Press, 2014).

Francisco Ferrándiz is tenured researcher at the Spanish National Research Council (CSIC). He has a Ph.D. in anthropology from the University of California, Berkeley, funded by a Fulbright Scholarship. Since 2002, he has conducted research on the politics of memory in contemporary Spain through the analysis of the exhumations of mass graves from the Civil War (1936–1939). On this topic, he has recently published *El pasado bajo tierra: Exhumaciones contemporáneas de la Guerra Civil* (Anthropos/Siglo XXI, 2014). He has also published his research in journals such as *American Ethnologist, Anthropology Today, Critique of Anthropology, Journal of Spanish Cultural Studies,* and *Ethnography.*

Luis Fondebrider is an Argentine forensic anthropologist and cofounder and current president of the Argentine Forensic Anthropology Team (EAAF). At the request of truth commissions, local and international courts, and other organizations, he has worked as expert witness or forensic adviser in Argentina, Chile, Brazil, Bolivia, Peru, Paraguay, Colombia, Venezuela, Guatemala, El Salvador, Haiti, Croatia, Bosnia, Kosovo, Romania, Iraq, the Philippines, Indonesia, Cyprus, Georgia, South Africa, Zimbabwe, Ethiopia, Morocco, Libya, Vietnam, Thailand,

Solomon Islands, Sri Lanka, Sudan, Kenya, and Namibia. He teaches forensic anthropology in the Faculty of Medicine of the University of Buenos Aires.

Iosif Kovras is a research fellow at the Institute for the Study of Conflict Transformation and Social Justice at Queen's University, Belfast. He has articles published or forthcoming in *Comparative Political Studies, Comparative Politics, West European Politics, Nations and Nationalism, Electoral Studies, Cooperation and Conflict, Ethnopolitics, Time and Society,* and *History and Anthropology.* His first book is *Truth Recovery and Transitional Justice: Deferring Human Rights Issues* (Routledge, 2014).

Heonik Kwon is senior research fellow at Trinity College, University of Cambridge, and previously taught anthropology at the London School of Economics. Among his recent works are *Ghosts of War in Vietnam* (2008) and *The Other Cold War* (2010). He is working on a book that deals with an intimate history of the Korean War.

Elena Lesley is a Ph.D. student in anthropology at Emory University. Her chapter emerged from master's thesis research in Cambodia and Rwanda funded by the Council of American Overseas Research Centers. Previously she lived in Cambodia for a combined two and half years as a Fulbright Fellow and Henry Luce Scholar writing about the Khmer Rouge tribunal. She holds a master's in global affairs from Rutgers University and a bachelor's in political science from Brown University.

Antonius C. G. M. Robben is professor of anthropology at Utrecht University, the Netherlands. He has been a research fellow at the Michigan Society of Fellows, the Harry Frank Guggenheim Foundation, and the David Rockefeller Center of Harvard University. His books include the ethnography *Political Violence and Trauma in Argentina* (University of Pennsylvania Press, 2005), which won the Textor Prize from the American Anthropological Association in 2006, and the edited volumes *Iraq at a Distance: What Anthropologists Can Teach Us About the War* (University of Pennsylvania Press, 2010) and *Ethnographic Fieldwork: An Anthropological Reader* (Wiley-Blackwell, 2012; coedited with Jeffrey Sluka).

Isaias Rojas-Perez is assistant professor of anthropology at Rutgers University-Newark. He specializes in anthropology of the state, legal anthropology, human rights studies, and Latin American studies with particular focus on the Andean region. His research interests include transitional justice, memory and mourning, forensic exhumation of mass graves, and postconflict prosecution of state atrocities. He has conducted ethnographic work among Quechua speaking survivors of state terror and relatives of the disappeared by the state during the counterinsurgency campaign of the 1980s in the Peruvian Andes. He is currently completing a book, "Fragments of Soul: Law, Transitional Justice and Mourning in Postwar Peru."

Katerina Stefatos holds a Ph.D. in politics from Goldsmiths College (University of London) and an M.Sc. in gender and the media from the London School of Economics. She has also studied politics and international relations in Greece and the United States. She is currently an adjunct assistant professor of anthropology at Lehman College, City University of New York, and the Hellenic Studies Program coordinator at Columbia University. She is currently coediting (with Victoria Sanford and Cecilia Salvi) a volume entitled *Gender Violence, Conflict and the State* (Rutgers, forthcoming). She has published her work in several edited volumes and in the Journal of Modern Greek Studies.

Francesc Torres is a multimedia artist. His work is represented in many international public and institutional collections and has been supported by the Rockefeller and the Bohen Foundations. He has been the recipient of many grants, including the National Endowment for the Arts Individual Artist's Fellowship, the New York Council for the Arts Fellowship, and the Massachusetts Council for the Arts and Humanities Fellowship. He also received twice the Visual Arts National Prize (Catalonia, Spain). He is the author of *Dark Is the Room Where We Sleep* (Actar, 2007), a photographic essay on Spanish exhumations.

Sarah Wagner is an associate professor of anthropology at George Washington University and author of *To Know Where He Lies: DNA Technology and the Search for Srebrenica's Missing* (University of California Press, 2008), and coauthor with Lara Nettelfield of *Srebrenica in the Aftermath of Genocide* (Cambridge University Press, 2014). She has published several book chapters and articles on the identification and commemoration of missing persons in Bosnia and Herzegovina and by the United States military, focusing on the intersection of forensic science, memory politics, and postconflict repair.

Richard Ashby Wilson is the Gladstein Distinguished Chair of Human Rights and professor of law and anthropology at the University of Connecticut Law School and founding director of the Human Rights Institute there. He studies international human rights, and in particular postconflict justice institutions such as truth and reconciliation commissions and international criminal tribunals. His research on truth commissions focused on how successor governments seek to write history and to forestall retributive justice. His most recent book, *Writing History in International Criminal Trials* (Cambridge University Press, 2011), was selected by *Choice* in 2012 as an "Outstanding Academic Title" in the law category. His next project is "Words of Conviction: Prosecuting International Speech."

Index

CPSIA information can be obtained
at www.ICGtesting.com
Printed in the USA
BVOW08s1913220317

479214BV00001B/1/P